VINTAGE

POWER WITH..

R. Balasubramaniam, also known as Balu, is a widely respected development activist, leadership trainer, thinker and author. The founder of Swami Vivekananda Youth Movement and Grassroots Research and Advocacy Movement, Balu embodies a rare blend of grassroots and macro perspectives along with policy, drawn from his multifaceted experience spanning nearly four decades.

A former Rhodes Professor at Cornell University, USA, he coaches and mentors senior leaders in the non-profit, corporate, government and educational sectors globally, and also conducts leadership workshops for them. He is currently serving as the member-HR at the Capacity Building Commission, Government of India. He has authored nine books in Kannada and English—three of them, *i, the Citizen, Voices from the Grassroots* and *Leadership Lessons for Daily Living*, are globally acclaimed. More information about him, his work and his books can be found at www.drrbalu.com.

ADVANCE PRAISE FOR THE BOOK

'Dr Balasubramaniam offers lessons in leadership through the lens of Indian culture, languages and history. Drawing on his decades of experience engaging with rural and tribal communities, he explores how indigenous knowledge and centuries-old wisdom can inform global leadership today and accelerate progress for some of the world's most under-resourced communities. He highlights examples of persistence amid adversity during the Covid-19 pandemic, and the policies and community partnerships created under the leadership of Prime Minister Modi'—Bill Gates, co-chair, the Bill & Melinda Gates Foundation

'As an investor or a voter, one looks for a leader who can bring transformational change, be it to the economy or social delivery. This book unravels the unconventional secret sauce behind PM Modi's success in this regard—rooted in experiential learning and the wisdom of Indian civilization. A must-read!'—Amit Chandra, chairperson, Bain Capital India, and co-founder, A.T.E. Chandra Foundation

'In 2013, a meeting with Shri Narendra Modi, then chief minister of Gujarat, completely reshaped my world view of technology. His strong focus on impact over tech prowess, emphasizing the importance of understanding tech from users' needs left an indelible mark. This principle has tremendous resonance in today's era of AI—where it's imperative to shift our focus from its technological prowess to its potential to effect positive change, to get AI right. As Prof. R. Balasubramaniam aptly states, leadership is an evolving journey—a sentiment exemplified by Mr Modi's visionary path. His lessons resonate deeply with those of us striving to transcend the pursuit of mere success and embrace the pursuit of significance'—Debjani Ghosh, president, the National Association of Software and Services (NASSCOM)

'India's rise as a Vishwa Guru brings with it the message of peace, people, planet and profits. Taking the nation in this direction is Narendra Modi's vision and destiny. Modi will be the most-studied global leader in the centuries to come, but what one needs is an "in-prism" understanding of his leadership from our civilizational world view. Dr Balu fills an important gap here. In helping us study Modi's journey through the Indic principles and multiple perches that make up public leadership, he helps us discover ourselves and our roots'—Ajay Piramal, chairman, Piramal Group

'A thought-provoking book that will undoubtedly change perspectives and perceptions on powerful leadership'—Anand Mahindra, chairman, Mahindra Group

'R. Balasubramaniam's *Power Within: The Leadership Legacy of Narendra Modi*, is a compelling exploration of leadership dynamics that has propelled India to greater heights. The Honourable Prime Minister Narendra Modi has been a huge advocate and proponent of celebrating the role of entrepreneurship and women in India's growth story.

'By seamlessly integrating Eastern wisdom with Western paradigms, this book offers a holistic and realistic perspective on leadership in today's global world, serving as a beacon of inspiration—whether you're a scholar, a policymaker, or an advocate for gender equality'—Falguni Nayar, founder and CEO, Nykaa

'Now, as India rises economically and geopolitically after centuries of challenges, the time has come to revive our ancient culture, wisdom and knowledge systems. Our culture is thriving, and we are finding our ancient voice once again, fused with the best of the youthful energy today. Prime Minister Modi is at the heart of all this, either leading this movement directly or playing the role of a catalyst so that others may contribute in their capacities. He is doing it step by step, patiently and methodically. Since that will make the change last. And that which lasts is dharmic. Read this book to understand how Prime Minister Modi is reviving our dharmic civilization, so that India re-emerges as a Vishwa Guru'—Amish Tripathi, bestselling author

'*Power Within* is a timely, well-researched and accessible book on effective public leadership that draws on valuable research, principles and perspectives from both the East and the West. Specifically, the book fills an important gap in the public leadership space by moving beyond the well-established paradigms of instrumental and transformational leadership to analyse Indian tradition and wisdom. Key leadership concepts are illustrated through illuminating vignettes of Prime Minister Modi's personal journey and public leadership. They offer new directions for our understanding of inclusive and effective public leadership paradigms'—Deepa Mani, deputy dean, executive education and digital learning, Indian School of Business

'In *Power Within: The Leadership Legacy of Narendra Modi*, Dr Balu encapsulates the essence of true leadership through the life and philosophy of Prime Minister Narendra Modi. Modi's journey, marked by unwavering resolve and integrity, exemplifies the seamless alignment of inner beliefs and external actions, reminiscent of the ancient sage-king Janaka's dual embodiment of spiritual depth and practical governance. He is not just a leader of a party or a republic but truly a leader of the people. For him, everything finally boils down to how he can effect an irreversible and transformative impact on the people known and unknown to him.

'With an ear to the ground, yet eyes set to the skies, Dr Balu brings a unique blend of work ethics that harmonizes a pragmatic problem-solving approach at the grassroots level with a very comprehensive vision at the very apex. His contributions are many, but a book on the leadership legacy of Sri Narendra Modi through the lens of his life's experiences would be one of the most important ones that would guide and inspire generations of leaders. It's easy to be biased when it comes to Mr Modi, for his charisma and aura can sweep you off your feet. Yet, Dr Balu's presentation of the man is careful and balanced, without being proud or prejudiced'—Sadguru Sri Madhusudan Sai, spiritual leader, global humanitarian and philanthropist

POWER WITHIN

The Leadership Legacy of
NARENDRA MODI

R. BALASUBRAMANIAM

VINTAGE

An imprint of Penguin Random House

VINTAGE

Vintage is an imprint of the Penguin Random House group of companies
whose addresses can be found at global.penguinrandomhouse.com

Published by Penguin Random House India Pvt. Ltd
4th Floor, Capital Tower 1, MG Road,
Gurugram 122 002, Haryana, India

First published in Vintage by Penguin Random House India 2024

Copyright © R. Balasubramaniam 2024

ISBN 9780143470533

Typeset in Sabon Lt Std by MAP Systems, Bengaluru, India

www.penguin.co.in

This book is dedicated to Bharat's timeless wisdom,
to which I bow my head reverentially.

Disclaimer regarding the websites mentioned in the Notes

~

Usage of Sanskrit words

The Sanskrit words used in the text employ their common and popular usage. A detailed diacritic version of how these words need to be pronounced as well as their meanings are included in the glossary, with explanations wherever needed.

~

Proceeds

All proceeds received from the sale of this book will be donated to PM CARES and to other charities working in the development sector.

Contents

IV. Expanding the Leadership Horizon

Epilogue: A Legacy of Transformation

Foreword

R. Balasubramaniam's engaging new book on Narendra Modi's leadership reminds me of a passage from the Upanishads that my dear friend Ajay Piramal often quotes:
You are what your deepest desire is.

As is your desire, so is your intention.
As is your intention, so is your will.
As is your will, so is your deed.
As is your deed, so is your destiny.

Modi's life is a fabulous illustration of this set of ideas.
From his earliest days, his deepest desire was to lead India and help it realize its immense potential as a nation.
That desire eventually translated into intention: Although Modi was initially reluctant to enter political life, at some point, he realized that volunteering could only go so far and that to fulfil his desire, he must commit himself to an intentional life in politics.
That intention led to a deep will to move India forward. Despite the nation's one-step-forward, two-steps-back history of progress that is often rationalized by the complex challenge of governing the largest, most pluralistic democracy in the world, Modi determined to relentlessly drive the country forward through his force of will.
Through his deeds—an ever-expanding portfolio of audacious national programmes—he's taking tangible steps to

expand every citizen's access to essential services like electricity, sanitation, health, education and economic opportunity.

Modi sees his destiny as leading India to reclaim its historical place among the world's great nations.

Balu brings a valuable background to this study of Modi as a leader. I have known Balu since his days at Harvard's Kennedy School of Government, which is now more than fifteen years ago. I have followed his career closely as he returned to India to continue pursuing his initiatives that give citizens more transparency into how their government works and more agency to advocate for themselves. Because of Balu's devotion to improving people's lives, he was invited to join the government, focusing on capacity-building, where he has continued his life's work of improving human capacity and well-being. Working in the government gives Balu a unique opportunity to observe Prime Minister Modi and his team. He gained first-hand access to the PM and those who work closely with him and developed a better understanding of the PM's leadership. Leaders like Modi inevitably have ardent admirers and vocal critics in today's globally polarized political scenario. Balu's vantage point allows him to observe the Prime Minister from close quarters and form a more comprehensive view that is generally not seen by either his admirers or critics.

Balu examines Modi's leadership through a unique East-meets-West lens in this book. He draws on Western leadership literature to analyse Modi wherever it is useful. What makes the book special are the powerful perspectives Balu gleaned from ancient Indian texts to illustrate how Modi is a great case study of an Indic view of leadership. This intriguing lens leads to a book filled with new insights.

Reading this book encouraged me to also examine Modi's leadership through the various theories I have studied and taught at Harvard Business School over the last four decades. A framework that felt especially resonant was one I introduced (with my co-author Bob Eccles) in a 1992 book *Beyond the Hype: Rediscovering the Essence of Management*. In that book, we identified three core elements of good leadership: rhetoric, action and identity.

Prime Minister Modi excels at rhetoric or persuasive communication. Aristotle wrote that great communicators utilize logos, pathos and ethos to simultaneously appeal to their listeners' logic, emotions and values. Modi does this instinctively, whether speaking to large audiences or smaller groups. He makes it a point to provide the reasoning behind his words. He has the remarkable ability to simplify complexity and make it more readily understandable by everyone. Even as he appeals to the listener's mind, Modi knows how to stir their hearts. He speaks with passion and evokes the same strong emotions in his audience. Most importantly, as Aristotle emphasized, Modi's strength of character shines when he speaks, leading people to trust him. When it comes to delivering large-scale public speeches, reaching people through his monthly radio talks, or connecting with them using social media, Modi will likely be remembered alongside leaders like Lincoln or Churchill—his rhetorical effectiveness is *that* good.

Taking bold action comes instinctively to Modi. Although Balu highlights numerous examples in this book, three have special significance for me. My father grew up in a village with no electricity. He devoted much of his career as an executive at Crompton Greaves, whose mission was to expand access to electricity. So, it was a profoundly meaningful moment for my entire family when Modi announced and achieved the ambitious goal of bringing electricity to every village in India. This is just one of many instances in which Modi has taken action to reach and improve the life of every Indian citizen. Another example of an action I admire comes from a parallel in American business history. What made America an economic juggernaut in the twentieth century was uniting its numerous states into one integrated national economy through laws that enabled interstate commerce and a transportation infrastructure that connected the entire country. By enacting the GST bill and investing heavily in the country's rail, road and telecommunication infrastructure, Modi has taken vital actions to enable India to benefit from the tremendous opportunities its large domestic market presents. As a final example, I want to highlight the new India digital stack that Prime Minister Modi has championed. From the universal Aadhaar card to free digital payments to the account aggregator, India can now boast a digital infrastructure that is second to none and will enable it to thrive in the rapidly expanding information economy.

Leaders like Modi understand their ultimate purpose is to make people proud of their identity. They know how good people feel when they experience themselves as winning when they feel confident their future will be better than their past, and when they can feel proud of the family, company or nation to which they belong. Modi has tapped into his country's citizens' pride in their historic heritage and aspirations to realize the potential they have long sensed and now feel ready to seize. It was masterful how he used its 75th year of Independence to remind the country of its glorious past, to exhort it to break free of its colonial vestiges, and to look forward with self-confidence and collective determination. By asking each Indian to find a personal way of flying the Indian flag, he encouraged them to embrace and celebrate their national identity fully. When I visit India now, I am struck by how ubiquitously I see its *Tiranga* flying—a tactile symbol of its strong sense of identity.

I was seven when I watched the Apollo 11 lunar landing on a grainy black and white TV in India. I had similar chills go up my spine watching the 2023 lunar landing of Chandrayaan-3, this time as it was being streamed live to my cellphone. Seeing the Indian rover touch down, the cheer that went up at mission control seemed to reverberate throughout the nation and, indeed, across the world. Moments like this, or when India hosted the G20 summit, are ways in which Modi is helping India visualize and realize its identity as a nation that can now occupy centre stage in the world. Modi has so many followers because he represents the change and identity they want to see in India.

Power Within: The Leadership Legacy of Narendra Modi is a wonderful book that enables us to understand this remarkable leader better. It helps us appreciate Modi's formidable and abundant strengths. Modi shows that you must lead first and foremost by playing to your strengths! Yet, this book is not about a perfect leader. The best leaders are constantly evolving. They (and their followers) remain open to their critics. They have the humility to listen and to learn. As Balu reveals, this drive to learn and get better is the hallmark of a truly great leader like Prime Minister Narendra Modi.

Boston, Massachusetts   **Nitin Nohria**
June 2024

Preface

In a world teeming with literature on leadership and its myriad forms, the inception of this work may prompt one to wonder, 'Yet another book on leadership?' This thought echoed in my mind as I embarked on a journey not just to explore the nuances of public leadership but to delve deep into the profound wisdom that the Indic civilization offers on this subject. It is a civilization that has, through millennia, articulated concepts of leadership that transcend the personal and touch upon the universal. This preface is a glimpse into the contemplations and preparations that guided the formation of this narrative, aiming to enrich not just the individual reader but the global discourse on leadership.

My fascination with how public leadership is forged and operates is what led me to Harvard Kennedy School. Trying to fathom a politician's thought process, how one arrives at decisions, how they convey the right emotion at the right juncture, how they navigate through the complexities—these facets intrigued me greatly. I grew convinced that policymaking encompasses more than just evidence, human development or political expediency; it is all this and much more. Most importantly, effective policymaking hinges on public leadership that exudes competence, passion, conviction and the right blend of intellect and emotion. In essence, it's about the leadership a policymaker exhibits. While this is easy to articulate, finding an individual who consistently embodied these qualities proved to be a challenge. After numerous courses, extensive reading and journeys around the world, I remained convinced that locating

a person with the right amalgamation of skills, the mindset to
transcend self and a dedicated intent to serve, all while resisting
the allure of power and position, was a rare find. Moreover,
I came to realize that the prevailing idea and definition
of leadership were largely influenced by Western research
spanning the last few centuries. Western thought focuses more
on the trait-oriented and behavioural approaches to leadership
with the emphasis on 'being a leader'. Whereas the principles
of self-realization and self-awareness derived from Indian
philosophy play a role in shaping the fundamentals of Indian
leadership thought and the emphasis is more on the 'exercise of
leadership'. The focus is more on the leadership actions rather
than the individual leader. While there is a growing body of
work by contemporary Western scholars to comprehend the
concepts of mindfulness, meditation and self-awareness, I felt
that a significant portion of the understanding of leadership
globally would remain incomplete without incorporating the
Indian perspective.

This led me to delve into the wisdom of the Indic
civilization—as conveyed through Puranas[1], *itihasa* (history),
cultural folklore, indigenous knowledge and scriptures—and
how it has influenced the global conception and manifestation
of leadership. The deeper I went, the more I realized that
finding concrete examples to illustrate the theory would be
challenging. Even more daunting was the prospect of expecting
one individual to encapsulate the diverse descriptions I was
discovering. I started to believe that no single person could
comprehensively embody the full spectrum of leadership
expression. It would require numerous examples to elucidate the
various facets of leadership across different eras and cultures.
This became the focus of my book, *Leadership Lessons for
Daily Living*[2], which I wrote a few years ago.

Feeling overwhelmed by the magnitude of the endeavour
I planned to undertake, I began to wonder whether finding
a person who could become the subject of the case study for

this book might even be possible. I sought a globally renowned figure, someone who had diligently cultivated their leadership capabilities and who embodied the Indian scriptural message of using *seva* (service) as *sadhana* (spiritual practice) for spiritual evolution. I shared these thoughts with my guide and mentor, Swami Sureshanandaji, a few years ago. Swamiji was a monk of the Ramakrishna order and someone I deeply admired for his *advaitic*[3] perspective on life. Advaita, or non-dualism, advocates an inclusive and unified approach to existence that Swamiji embodied through his daily living. Swami Sureshanandaji has had a significant impact on my leadership journey, and I remember him suggesting the name of Narendra Modi, the then chief minister of Gujarat, as the person whose life would closely align with the ideals of Enlightened Leadership that I had in mind.

The idea was exhilarating but seemed highly improbable. Here was an individual who had devoted his life to the concept of public service, living the life of an RSS *pracharak* (a full-time worker), serving as the chief minister of Gujarat for thirteen years, and currently holding the office of the Prime Minister (PM) of India. He is a living testimony to how a commoner can reach an exalted position through a life of hard work, dedication, a value-based existence and commitment to selfless public action amidst all the criticisms and obstacles he faced in this journey. How could I even fathom observing someone of such eminence, let alone gather insights into how his leadership expression manifested? Moreover, I understood I would have to navigate through enormous challenges within the formal system to undertake a task of this magnitude. These considerations made writing about him a daunting task. I had no insider perspective on his worldwide performance and my knowledge was limited to media interpretations, which often represent extreme opinions on both sides of the spectrum. The prevailing discourse was becoming increasingly polarized, with viewpoints entrenched in either 'for' or 'against'. Any attempt to write about him risked being dismissed as sycophantic. I never imagined I would have the opportunity to truly know him, observe him up close, or appreciate the immense effort he exerted in expressing his leadership. So, I let the idea drift away and then the Covid-19 pandemic struck.

The world observed the PM's leadership in response to Covid-19; how he worked to foster an adaptive culture, mobilizing citizens and connecting with them through his *Mann Ki Baat*[4] talks. His initiative rekindled my desire to study his leadership and attempt to capture it in a book. Yet, I remained tethered to the reality that undertaking such a task seemed highly improbable.

But fate had other plans. I was appointed as a member–human resources at the Capacity Building Commission (CBC)[5] by the Government of India in April 2021 under Mission Karmayogi.[6] As a CBC member, I had to report to the PM and his HR Council, affording me a closer view into the inner workings of the corridors of power and granting access to individuals who worked closely with the PM. Importantly, the role provided me with first-hand experience of the PM's visionary and humane character. Upon interacting with him on several occasions, I glimpsed into the strategic thinker, the impassioned nationalist, the expansive humanist, and the pragmatic political leader that he is.

The hard work that forms the foundation of one's achievements is often underestimated when glancing at their current state. The efforts, discipline and determination that go into building character and shaping a life are best understood through a deep exploration of the person, their responses to unfolding events, and conversations with those who are inspired or otherwise impacted by their work. Despite having access to only one phase of his leadership journey, I've attempted to draw connections to the immense effort he has invested over several decades.

My study of the Prime Minister and his leadership revealed a side rarely seen on television or his public appearances. His visible humility, determined optimism, sense of humour and inspirational persona motivated me to write this book. This book is not primarily about the person or his personality; it delves into the potential—each person's capacity—to recognize their inner strengths, engage in the necessary practices for self-evolution, and allow this evolution to manifest as a societal good. It is an exploration of leadership through the lens of Indic thought, a discipline in its practice, and an effort to contribute to a better world. It is as much an attempt to capture the leadership expressions of a constantly evolving person as it is about portraying a role model of leadership for each one of us to emulate.

In addition to showcasing examples of the phenomenal leadership of PM Modi, I hope the book serves as a wellspring of inspiration for politicians, policymakers, corporate and civil society leaders, academics, and the millions of young people who invest hope in their leaders. It seeks to convey that such leadership is not only attainable but is also essential. Expressing this leadership as a service to society is, perhaps, the most effective way to forge a better world.

June 2024   **R. Balasubramaniam**
New Delhi

Author's Note

In this book, I dig deep into the nuanced leadership style of Prime Minister Narendra Modi—an exploration that intertwines the rich traditions of Indic philosophy with Western leadership theories. While he seeks to be on a lifelong journey of learning and evolution, he stands out as the only contemporary public leader who is comprehensive in his leadership expression, making him a good example to study, analyse and write about.

I aim to engage a diverse audience, encompassing scholars, students, leadership practitioners and the wider public, providing varied perspectives on a global stage. While addressing such a wide audience comes with its challenges, I hope that there are valuable leadership insights for everyone.

My analysis is deeply rooted in my personal belief that spirituality entails individual growth, self-exploration and an interpretation of the universe and one's role within it. It reflects a journey towards understanding one's deeper self and the lessons that can be drawn from Indic scriptures in this pursuit. I acknowledge that these scriptures can be interpreted in many ways. While I have endeavoured to stay true to the several commentaries and translations of the texts referenced here, the perspective of viewing leadership through this prism is entirely my own. I accept full responsibility for any inaccuracies or oversights resulting from this approach.

To authentically convey the cultural richness of the topic, I have incorporated Sanskrit and other Indic terms into this narrative. To assist readers who may not be familiar with these terms, I have italicized them when using them for the first time in the book. Additionally, the book features a glossary with the words written in their diacritic English transliterations and includes explanations whenever necessary to enhance comprehension and accessibility of these terms.

In narrating Modi's story, I have chosen to use terms like 'Prime Minister', 'PM', 'Modi', 'PM Modi', 'Modiji' and 'Narendra Modi' interchangeably. India and Bharat are also used interchangeably throughout the book. This stylistic decision is intended to enhance the narrative's flow and readability.

The book follows Penguin Random House's global in-house style guide. It follows British spellings, with the exception of 'z' spellings which are an American convention.

A pivotal aspect of this book involves contributions from numerous individuals who offered invaluable insights. These interviews, conducted with oral consent, add depth and perspective to the narrative and a list of these persons is provided separately at the end of the book. Persons referred to in this book are addressed by their first and second names with no prefixes or suffixes as a gesture of uniformity and respect. Although countless people interact with the Prime Minister, this book includes experiences from those I had access to and could meet personally and some public domain quotes from those that I could not. While these limit the variety of experiences that one could bring in to explain different leadership expressions, I hope that the key ones have been captured in this book.

This book is structured into four distinct sections, each highlighting a specific aspect of leadership. The first section addresses the imperative of Enlightened Leadership in today's complex world, featuring a chapter dedicated to Narendra Modi's visionary leadership and his deliberate public-life goals. The second section delves into the personal dimension, focusing on Modi's renowned communication skills, his inherent qualities, and the influence of spiritual growth on his leadership style. The third section offers an in-depth look at how his leadership philosophy translates into impactful public actions, discussing his engagement with grassroots communities and his adaptability in leadership roles. The fourth section explores how Modi's leadership, rooted in civilizational values, is making a global impact. The book concludes with an epilogue that reflects on his enduring legacy and the unique leadership lessons he offers to the world, highlighting the aspects of his approach that could benefit leaders globally in creating a more positive future.

Anecdotes from the PM's life are interwoven into the narrative to highlight the leadership constructs that one can learn from, and they are not chronologically sequenced.

This book is also not a biographical attempt. Readers will notice a deliberate repetition of certain themes across chapters. This is a strategic choice, not a redundancy, designed to emphasize key concepts and facilitate a thorough and integrated understanding.

Leadership is a journey that continually evolves as a person strives to perfect it. In the case of a lifelong learner like Modi, the insights captured in this book might soon seem outdated, as his leadership saga continues to unfold and inspire future generations. However, I hope to have encapsulated the essence of his leadership journey as it stands today, offering a snapshot of a leader in continuous growth and evolution.

I

The Leadership Paradigm

उत्तिष्ठत जाग्रत प्राप्य वरान्निबोधत ।
क्षुरस्य धारा निशिता दुरत्यया दुर्गं पथस्तत्कवयो वदन्ति ॥

uttiṣṭhata jāgrata prāpya varānnibodhata |
kṣurasya dhārā niśitā duratyayā durgaṃ
pathastatkavayo vadanti ||

—Kathopanishad 1.3.14

Arise, awake, find out the great ones and learn of them; for sharp as a razor's edge, hard to traverse, difficult of going is that path, say the sages.

~

History is often lauded as the ultimate arbiter, with posterity serving as its devoted attendant. As we find ourselves at a pivotal juncture in history, the myriad challenges that confront the world—from multifaceted global crises to the growing polarization within societies—lay bare the inadequacies of authority-based leadership models in providing viable solutions. Today's leadership must not only draw lessons from history but also embody adaptability, pragmatism, cultural sensitivity and spiritual maturity. It must aspire to be enlightened.

What constitutes the embodiment of Enlightened Leadership? By examining Prime Minister Modi's leadership approach through the prism of ancient Indian civilizational wisdom, we explore how such a leadership model may offer solutions to the complex issues of a world that is Brittle, Anxious, Non-linear and Incomprehensible (BANI). The path to Enlightened Leadership is forged through reflective practice, deep engagement with the rich cultural and spiritual traditions of human societies, and the nurturing of profound connections with the communities that leaders aim to serve. These avenues are crucial for cultivating the attributes of Enlightened Leadership, potentially offering a beacon of hope and direction in navigating the tumultuous waters of our contemporary world.

~

Introduction: The Leadership We Need

Leadership requires courage and a deep, selfless commitment to service. Exercising leadership is a risky business and the leader walks a thin edge, exposing oneself to both praise and criticism, often at the same time. And when such leaders commit errors, either intentionally or inadvertently, the world they operate in is often unforgiving. It is even more challenging when one operates under constant public glare, in an environment where millions of people are affected by their decisions. Researchers have studied and written extensively about practising leadership in the public domain, assessing everything from how a person talks and dresses, to their personal tastes, private life and the company they keep— everything is always under scrutiny. Remaining unaffected and focused on one's work in such a situation demands an enormous commitment to both one's self and the public cause at hand. Consistent public performance coupled with the responsibility of delivering electoral successes all the time is challenging, and there are very few leaders in public positions who have succeeded in both respects.

The world over, people continue to look up to their political leaders, elected or otherwise, to provide them with answers to the major challenges humankind faces—our 'wicked problems'.[1] Today's wicked problems in areas of education, global warming, healthcare, geopolitics, human conflicts and human rights are complex and demand newer skills to tackle them. But as people acquire knowledge about relevant subjects, many find themselves inadequately prepared for taking on public leadership positions and overwhelmed by the diverse issues that a rapidly changing world presents.

Many of the issues we face are mostly influenced by—or, in some cases, stem from shortcomings in public leadership. For instance, the recent Covid-19 crisis has not only left the world crippled on several fronts but has also laid bare the inadequacies of public leadership in many countries. While theories of leadership may explain why many leaders fail, few resources provide leaders with a fundamental understanding of how to exercise their leadership in a mindful and empowered manner. The prevailing approach of examining leadership through the narrow lenses of competencies, traits, skill sets and toolkits only enables individuals to operate from their comfort zones and does not empower them to demonstrate the resilience and awareness required to accept themselves as they are, generate the humility to collaborate and operate with equanimity under stressful conditions.

Traditional thinking also associates leadership with authority. Leadership is then intuitively interpreted as having the *power* to lead people and organizations to bring about the change that one desires; and when people occupy these positions of authority, they begin to rely more and more on the power attached to the position. Over time, people overly concerned with power tend to start operating with the misplaced conviction that they are critical to the system around them and often take on roles and responsibilities beyond their capacity.

Leadership is not about power or authority, it is about understanding one's 'self'[2] and others around us—coming to terms with our inner potential and what we are capable of, and exploring how we can expand our capacities by mobilizing others. It is about having a vision and keeping the focus on the 'work at the center'[3] of translating this vision into reality. It is about being mindful of one's own capabilities, having an observer's appreciation of the context in which one is operating, having the ability to recalibrate one's actions and the ability to operate with social, emotional and intellectual freedom.

The need for value-driven leadership is further accentuated by the emergence of a polarized world where opinions are stated as facts, where fake is more real than the truth and where human values are spoken rather than lived. There are only a few exemplary individuals who can be honest with themselves, come to terms with their strengths and weaknesses, and not lose sight of their life's vision. Such people, with the courage to experiment and the wisdom to learn from challenging situations, can provide sustained leadership to their organizations and countries.

Leadership involves more than just exerting influence and power over others; it's about recognizing and harnessing one's own immense potential. We need leaders who can discern meaning from the dynamic culture surrounding them and pave a way forward, grounded in shared understanding. We need leaders who operate from an intellectual dimension while not allowing the surrounding noise to distract them; leaders who can communicate rather than confuse. Only through such leaders can the journey towards healing and mutual understanding truly commence.

The world is seeking individuals who can go beyond mere political leadership and can mobilize people and teams from different domains—religious, academic, civil society, sports, media, arts, industry and the common citizens to go beyond the conditions that authorities create and learn to form bonds of trust amongst each other. A leader needs to be like a protective parent who holds a child with love and care, provides guidance, and at the same time, corrects defects. The parent can enable and restrain simultaneously, keeping the best interests of the child in mind. We need leaders who are willing to cross-pollinate and embrace diverse perspectives, build new capacities and demonstrate a willingness to learn.

A leader should be someone who can be vulnerable and humble and embraces the desire for lifelong learning. Leaders who see the world through different perspectives while forging a common path ahead to achieve the vision are the ones who can truly transform society. Leadership expert Warren Bennis asserts that people who can hold on to two contradictory thoughts at the same time are the ones who can provide the much-needed leadership the world requires today.

Providing public leadership to solve complex problems requires operating with this kind of enlightened approach. It is about a new kind of value-based leadership that is collaborative and self-aware. More than ever, public leaders must integrate knowledge and talent from individuals, teams and organizations in the business, non-profit and government sectors, to advance the common societal good. This Enlightened Leadership should be driven by higher values and be at once adaptive, pragmatic and culturally well-informed. It should take organizations, countries and the world forward in times of increased interconnectedness and rapid change and serve as a means of personal self-transformation.

Embedded in the civilizational wisdom of Bharat, the concept of leadership is encapsulated by the word 'neta', used in Hindi and Sanskrit to denote a leader. Both Neta and *Netr* (meaning vision or eye) have similar etymological origins and neta embodies the essence of leadership or *netrtva*. A neta is one who can assess situations, envision solutions and guide people towards them.

The world needs pragmatic, compassionate and firm visionary leadership. We need leaders who are humble yet steadfast, vulnerable and consistent, simple and grounded. We need leaders who are willing to communicate, while at the same time staying open to intense listening; people who are willing to risk their reputation by being different and having the courage to trust the other. And when such people use their authority wisely, then change will begin to set in slowly. Only when we see such leadership emerging on all sides, will we see the gradual emergence of a relatively happy and stable equilibrium. Only by persevering with love, compassion and trust, will society move towards overcoming negative forces and become open to going beyond mere tolerance to universal acceptance. Leaders should not only learn but should also be willing to teach by example. This kind of leadership is important and needed urgently. With such an enlightened attitude, leaders can go beyond prevailing conflicts and negativism and lead the world to a better place.

The world is increasingly looking to India to help solve several problems—whether it is the fight against poverty, mitigating climate change, providing disaster response, reducing inequities, preventing conflicts or embracing diversity. Recent public interventions initiated in India are lessons not just for countries in the Global South but for the Global North as well. One such example is India's methods deployed for managing the Covid-19 pandemic and its after-effects despite the nation's population size and the reality of its federal structure. India's case is an example of how strong and determined leadership at the top can guide a country through such challenges.

Prime Minister Narendra Modi's brand of leadership sets a compelling precedent for heads of nations navigating a world characterized by perpetual shifts, from one crisis to the next. From combating poverty and driving economic growth to democratizing development and leveraging technology for citizen-centric services, his proactive approach exemplifies the kind of visionary and dynamic leadership required in today's fast-paced global landscape. Additionally, through astute diplomacy and a steadfast commitment to humanitarian global efforts, Prime Minister Modi extends his influence beyond national borders, fostering collaborative solutions to pressing international challenges.

In his book *On Becoming a Leader*, Warren Bennis underscores the essential elements that pave the way for success in both leaders and organizations: Ideas, Relationships and Adventure.[4]

Bennis argues that Ideas catalyse change, reinvention and the cultivation of intellectual capital. Relationships involve the art of assembling teams composed of exceptional individuals who collaborate harmoniously with a sense of empowerment and belongingness. Adventure is characterized by a penchant for risk-taking, a bias towards action, and the virtues of curiosity and courage.

Whether navigating the complexities of the digital revolution, implementing a cohesive tax regime in a federal State, undertaking space missions to the Moon and Mars, or exploring innovative realms such as green hydrogen and quantum computing, Prime Minister Modi consistently demonstrates the ability to foster a social architecture where Ideas, Relationships and Adventure not only thrive but also propel transformative initiatives. This is also evident in his social change endeavours, ranging from ensuring housing for all to championing total sanitation to ensuring financial inclusion for most of the country's population. With an unwavering dedication to addressing pressing issues and strategic utilization of resources, Prime Minister Modi offers a model of leadership that resonates not only in India but serves as a beacon of inspiration for leaders worldwide.

Drawing enormously from his over five decades of experience working with people at different levels, from being the chief minister (CM) of Gujarat for thirteen years to being the Prime Minister (PM) for the last ten years, he has consistently demonstrated how value-driven leadership, reflective capacities, predictive abilities, social connect, mindful existence and sensitivity to the needs of the common masses can shape a democratically elected government's public action. His ability to provide sustained presence and commitment to transitioning India into a developed country, his ensuring that the citizens' basic needs are taken care of, and his transforming the State into a facilitating partner for progress, all embody the advice that Bhishma gave Yudhishthira on *Rajadharma* in the Indian epic: Mahabharata.[5]

The Pandava king, Yudhishthira, asks the grand elder Bhishma to counsel him on Rajadharma. Bhishma clarifies that all the king's actions are for the welfare of the people and never for meeting the king's selfish ends. A well-known path in the *Bharatiya* tradition is the sustained desire to work in the service of others and go beyond self-gratification. The king is therefore advised to discard his personal likes and dislikes. Discussions on the nature of this path are found in the Shanti Parva, the twelfth of the eighteen Parvas of the Mahabharata. The essence of Bhishma's response to Yudhishthira outlines the role good governance plays in societal well-being. He says, 'Like the harness is to a horse or the goad is to an elephant, so is Rajadharma to the world. In ancient times, the rajarishis upheld that *dharma* without which the dark cloud of anarchy and confusion prevailed. It is said, as the footprints of all other animals are subsumed by the elephant's, so are all other dharmas subsumed within Rajadharma.'

Rajadharma emphasizes ethical governance and the welfare of the people above all else. The ten fundamental principles of Rajadharma are:
1. Righteousness and Integrity: The ruler must govern the kingdom with honesty, integrity and fairness. Decisions should be made based on dharma (righteousness) rather than personal gain.
2. Welfare of the Subjects: The primary duty of the ruler is the welfare of the subjects. This includes ensuring their security, health, prosperity and education.
3. Impartial Justice: The king is expected to administer justice without favouritism or prejudice. Justice should be based on the principles of dharma, ensuring that everyone is treated equally before the law.

4. Protection and Security: Protecting the subjects from internal disturbances and external aggressions is a key duty. This includes maintaining a strong defence, law and order, and safeguarding the kingdom's borders.
5. Economic Stability and Growth: The ruler should actively work towards the economic development of the kingdom, ensuring a stable and prosperous economy that benefits all sections of society.
6. Preservation of Culture and Religion: Upholding and promoting the kingdom's cultural and religious heritage is a part of Rajadharma. This includes supporting temples, educational institutions and cultural activities.
7. Consultation and Counsel: A wise ruler seeks the counsel of learned and experienced advisers before making significant decisions. This ensures that decisions are well-considered and based on a wide range of perspectives.
8. Environmental Stewardship: Ensuring the protection of the environment and natural resources for future generations is also an aspect of Rajadharma.
9. Ensuring Social Harmony: The king must work towards maintaining social harmony and peace among the different communities and social groups within the kingdom.
10. Personal Conduct: The personal conduct of the ruler is of utmost importance. The king must lead by example, showing restraint, moral fortitude and dedication to duty.

To be able to govern, the ruler must develop the qualities of a *rishi*, a seer-saint. Areas in particular which the sovereign must focus on during his rulership are *yogakshema* (bestowing what is desired by his public and securing that which has been acquired for their sakes), and *lokasangraha* (societal welfare). Living these values of Rajadharma requires great discipline, courage, compassion, sensitivity, focus on the work at hand and tenacity. It calls for humility, the ability to listen and respond to the needs of others, and a sense of empowered surrender to a higher guiding force. To be able to lead, one must learn first to follow. Surrender instils several values in us, two among which are *shraddha* (faith and devotion)—the seed of untiring effort, and *vairagya* (detachment)—the seed of equanimity.

Leadership literature, spanning business, politics and the military over the last five centuries, has undergone significant development, predominantly influenced by Western narratives thus far. In the realm of business, leadership is tied up with individuals in high-ranking managerial roles and the functions they fulfil. Its definition has evolved to encompass those at the pinnacle, charting a course for their companies, and rallying those alongside them to achieve a shared vision. In the military sphere, leadership has conventionally been viewed as a central authority that issues commands and exerts control. Simultaneously, military leadership also serves the crucial function of motivating individuals to make ultimate sacrifices for the nation or a greater cause when circumstances necessitate it. While comprehending the essence of military leadership and the reason behind its endurance is possible, this perspective may appear somewhat detached from the broader civilian world today.

Biologically, leadership has been depicted through the alpha figure who guides a flock or group, ensuring order and overseeing collective sustenance. In this context, the leader operates as the dominant nucleus around which the rest of the group instinctively congregates and defers. In the political arena, leadership has almost always been equated with the individual in authority, possessing substantial influence, occupying a prominent position, and being endowed with the capacity to lead a party or government with decisiveness and command.

It was Thomas Carlyle, a Scottish historian, who in the nineteenth century, came up with his explanation of 'great men' predisposed with having personality traits that propel them to become leaders and exercise leadership.[6] Later theorists argued

that it was not great men who made history but historical
circumstances that brought out their greatness and propounded
the situational[7] approach to leadership. Dwelling briefly on
the various theories of leadership, the contingency theory[8]
posits that the style of leadership would be contingent on the
prevailing situation, while the transactional theory[9] examines
the specific interactions between the leader and his followers and
the influence he gains over them. McGregor[10] saw leadership as
a process of leaders inspiring and empowering their followers
to attain greatness.

While these narratives and definitions have a bearing
on which leadership was understood and practised, they
are inadequate in capturing the core of public service that is
driven by the attitude of being a *sevak* (servant). Appreciating
leadership from the perspective of service and sacrifice needs
the context of a cultural foundation that is integral to the Indian
way of thinking and living. A good working definition, as
viewed from the Indic perspective, would be to see 'leadership'
as understanding the self, the others around us, and the selfless
actions that bind the self to the other.

Definition of leadership

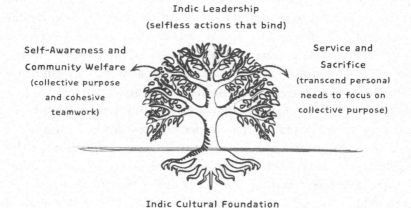

Indic Leadership
(selfless actions that bind)

Self-Awareness and
Community Welfare
(collective purpose
and cohesive
teamwork)

Service and
Sacrifice
(transcend personal
needs to focus on
collective purpose)

Indic Cultural Foundation

Understanding the self involves seeing ourselves as players of roles, our lifestyles and behaviours being shaped and driven by the various role-relationships that we have with others. This understanding also lets us appreciate that some roles are brief, others are embedded in the contexts, and some others are relatively long-term. It is rare for individuals who can measure up to this definition and understanding of leadership. It is these few, like Modi, who can transcend their personal selfish needs and stay focused on the larger collective purpose. These are the people who not only understand how to exercise leadership but also appreciate the real spirit and advantage of a cohesive team.

The West has always seen itself as the dominant leader of the world and has always been hesitant to concede this status to any public leader from the Global South. It is against this backdrop that one should see the emergence of Narendra Modi as a leader occupying the global platform not by the display of power, but by the expression of public leadership that is grounded and responsive, while at the same time, global and expansive.

Apart from closely examining the leadership style, this book also encapsulates the civilizational wisdom of Bharat through the lived experience of Prime Minister Modi over fifty years of his public life. It explores the journey of his discovering purpose after a quest that began during his formative years with an exploration across India. The narrative not only highlights his personal leadership qualities but also illuminates their tangible manifestation in the pursuit of public good. This book aims to capture his leadership journey, interpret it through the Indic lens, and provide a road map for sincere practitioners aspiring to a life of public service. Additionally, it captures poignant anecdotes that showcase the relentless hard work that has propelled him to his current position and underscores his ongoing quest for self-discovery in the service of others.

Several decades ago, Samuel Huntington in his famous essay, 'The Clash of Civilizations', wrote, 'In the politics of civilization, the peoples and governments of non-Western civilization no longer remain the objects of history as targets of Western colonization but join the West as movers and shapers of history.'[11] By his expression of leadership, Narendra Modi now occupies this unique position to shape—not just India's—but the global destiny. He has been able to use his charisma responsibly in helping craft a decolonized outlook while restoring the dignity and pride of being a citizen of Bharat. This book is as much about him being an exemplar as it is about giving the hope that a bright future awaits the world, provided more and more public leaders are able to emulate and demonstrate the leadership qualities elucidated here. It is as much about his efforts at inner spiritual growth as it is about this evolution being expressed as leadership to bring about societal betterment. This Enlightened Leadership that Modi embodies is possible and necessary to make this world a better place.

अमन्त्रमक्षरं नास्ति नास्ति मूलमनौषधम् ।
अयोग्यः पुरुषो नास्ति योजकस्तत्र दुर्लभः ॥

amantramakṣaraṣ nāsti nāsti mūlamanauṣadham |
ayogyaḥ puruṣo nāsti yojakastatra durlabhaḥ ||
—Mahasubhashita Sangraha 2423

There is no letter which doesn't have a charm, there is no root which doesn't have medicinal property. There is no person who is not able, but rare is the one who knows his/her proper application.

~

A vision possesses the same potential for growth as a seed does. It flourishes when nourished by the refreshing waters of experience. The early years of Narendra Modi's life depict a remarkable evolution from an eager young person, deeply inspired by Swami Vivekananda's principles of service and sacrifice, to a grounded leader harbouring a clear and compelling vision for both the nation and the globe. The quest for purpose and meaning constitutes a pivotal initial step in the journey towards effective leadership. It is through the nurturing of this purpose, enduring profound challenges, and emerging more resilient and focused, that one paves the way for the development of a vision. The ancient Indian practice of *Darshana*, which means 'to see' or 'to witness', plays a crucial role in this context. It enables an individual not only to understand the world in which they operate but, more significantly, to comprehend their true self. This concept underpins PM Modi's ambition to transform India into a developed country, highlighting the significance of authenticity, resilience and the collective endeavour towards a common vision for the betterment of society.

~

Charting a Bold Course:
Visionary Leadership in Action

Morbi is a small city in the state of Gujarat, best known for its ceramic industries. It rained heavily on 11 August 1979, leading to a breach in the Machchhu-II earthen dam in Morbi district. An estimated 10,000 people were killed, and many others lost enormous amounts of livestock and property. The district administration was unaware of the dam's collapse until about fifteen hours after it began and had initially presumed that the river was just overflowing. All the ingredients of administrative inefficiency were reflected in this disaster: a communication system on the verge of near collapse, depleted power reserves and a lack of organized administration. Considered one of the worst disasters in Gujarat's history, the event exposed the state's inefficiency and unpreparedness to face such calamities.

The Rashtriya Swayamsevak Sangh (RSS) then swung into action and helped in the rescue, rehabilitation and last rites. The RSS is one of the largest volunteer-based sociocultural organizations in the world today and was founded in 1925 in Nagpur, India, by Dr K.B. Hedgewar.[1] With a mission and vision of selfless service and character formation, the RSS has generally been a first responder to many of the natural and man-made disasters in India. Operating through a network of *shakhas* (branches) and *swayamsevaks* (volunteers), it has also been at the forefront of many social reform initiatives undertaken through its various groups such as Seva Bharti, an organization for service of the needy; Saraswati Shishu Vidya Mandir, an organization for affordable education for all; Bharatiya Mazdoor Sangh, a labour union; Vanavasi Kalyan Ashram, a nonprofit working for tribal welfare; and several more.

Narendra Modi, then a twenty-nine-year-old RSS pracharak, was one of the first members to reach the disaster area and was part of the rescue efforts. Modi recollected this incident in an interview for a Gujarati newspaper:

> People had turned their backs on the dead, but the Sangh stepped forward to remove the bodies. First, we removed all the dead bodies using gloves. There was such a foul smell from the corpses that even the police refused to pick up the corpses of people from their own fraternity, but the Sangh volunteers got the job done. There were some corpses that were so swollen that even six people couldn't lift them. In the absence of wood, over twenty-five corpses were cremated simultaneously by sprinkling diesel over them.[2]

The aftermath of the tragedy was stark, with terrible scenes of bodies buried under mud and grime, animal corpses hanging from power lines, and an unbearable stench that set within a few days of the tragedy. The only resources that the volunteers could command were their own inner resolves and hearts filled with compassion and empathy.

Inspired from a young age to dedicate his life to the cause of national service, Modi had grown on stories of courage, *viveka* (discernment) and *vairagya* (non-attachment or renunciation). One of his favourite stories was of King Shibi, who ruled over the ancient Kingdom of Shivi and was known for his wisdom, generosity, fairness and compassion. He was a popular monarch, who appears in both the Indian epics of the Mahabharata and the Ramayana. His popularity was the envy of even the Gods, and they decided to test his conviction in his values. One day, a dove came to King Shibi seeking his protection from a hawk that was chasing it. King Shibi promised to protect that dove and offered his own flesh to the hawk in exchange for the dove's safety. The hungry hawk agreed, but as it began to take pieces of flesh from the king, it soon became clear that no matter how much flesh was given, it would not be satisfied. Seeing that Shibi was willing to sacrifice his whole body and life to ensure that the hawk was satiated, the Gods appeared before him and praised him for his selflessness and generosity.

India's civilizational literature is replete with such stories elucidating the need for and importance of human values and concepts of service. Swami Vivekananda, one of India's greatest spiritual leaders and thinkers, had repeatedly stressed that the country's ideals were *tyaga* (sacrifice) and *seva* (service). His inspiring call to India's youth was to imbibe these values rooted in the country's ancient spiritual and cultural traditions. He appreciated that the period of one's youth is when one's energy is limitless, creativity is at its best, and the 'never say die' spirit is at its peak. He wanted this energy of the youth to be productively channelled for a societally beneficial cause.

Youth is also an impressionable period wherein we try to mould our lives to align them with our role models. This is the time when we are ready to take on any task, however onerous; the time when our ideals can drive and determine our actions, and the time when we believe that we can do anything under the sun. This is also the time when we are easily motivated by the environment and by what we see and value around us. Sixteen-year-old Narendra in 1966 was no different and was restless with an inner desire to make a difference in the world and to do something far bigger than himself or his personal needs. This restless quest led him to seek input from a variety of people and sources and to ultimately turn towards the powerful youth icon—Swami Vivekananda. Inspired by his life and message, Narendra decided to travel the country and gain for himself an understanding of what Bharat stood for, and how people lived their everyday lives in this *punyabhumi* (holy land).

Hindu scriptures elucidate the concept of darshana or witnessing. Darshana's purpose is to eventually discover what

binds humans to this materialistic world and how one can free
oneself from this bondage. But in practical terms, darshana is
also an external quest of acquainting oneself with the world,
through travel or pilgrimage, so that the mind is opened and
one's ego is brought under control. Coming from a very ordinary
background with very little financial support, travelling was
no easy decision for this young man. But he was in no mood
to let the challenges of mundane existence come in the way
of discovering himself. Over the next two years, he travelled
far and wide, getting to intimately know his *matrbhumi*
(motherland), traversing many states and meeting thousands of
people along the way. His journey took him to Ramakrishna
Mission[3]; an institution founded by Swami Vivekananda at
Belur in West Bengal, where he spent a lot of time interacting
with the monks and learning from them. Unfortunately for him,
he also discovered that he could not join them formally as a
novitiate as he was yet to acquire a bachelor's degree which
was a qualifying requirement. Disappointed, he continued
to travel, which took him to several hermitages and ashrams
across the country, including the Advaita Ashram[4] at Almora in
present-day Uttarakhand. Modi spent a lot of time wandering
and learning in the Himalayas before he finally returned to
Vadnagar[5], Gujarat, his hometown.

Upon his return, Modi deepened his engagements with the
RSS and regularly visited the Ramakrishna Ashram in Rajkot,
a city close to his hometown. This was also the centre where
Swami Vivekananda had physically visited and stayed, so this
became a place of pilgrimage for the young seeker. Swami
Atmasthanandaji—the head of the centre there—became his
mentor and guide, engaging with him regularly, encouraging
his spiritual quest and providing answers to the unending
existential questions that the young man posed.

When people his age were more likely to seek opportunities
that provided them with financial and professional securities,
young Narendra Damodardas Modi found nothing inspiring
in living a regular conformist life. He was obsessed with the

eternal quest of personal self-discovery and saw monastic life as the means to attain this self-knowledge. Modi met with Swami Atmasthanandaji to seek his blessings and formal approval to take up the life of a *sannyasi* (monk). But fate willed otherwise. The Swami (who later became the supreme head of the Ramakrishna Math and Mission) was a farsighted seer and knew that Narendra was destined for something else. Noticing Narendra's innate *svabhava* (natural tendencies) to serve others, Swami Atmasthanandaji realized that Narendra's potential was ripe to serve the highest of dharmas, that is, the Rajadharma, the duty of the ruler. He dissuaded Narendra from taking on a monastic life and instead advised him to seek avenues for serving his fellow countrymen.

As American writer Mark Twain famously said, 'The two most important days in your life are the day you are born and the day you find out why.' In Narendra's life too, once he was made aware of his true calling of being a sevak, embodying the spirit of national service through public life—he was a changed man. In the current era, while his contribution to public service has been a constant, his vision for the future of India and what it should stand for continues to expand.

Although disappointed that monastic life had evaded him, Narendra decided that he would make serving the nation and his countrymen his spiritual mission. Narendra knew that all human life had a higher purpose and that this could be achieved even while living within the limitations and boundaries of human existence. He gave himself a noble ideal to strive for and in this striving, he found answers to the material problems of the millions of suffering countrymen. He understood that his inner evolution had to find an external expression through the service of others. '*Atmano mokshartham, jagat hitaya cha*'[6], meaning 'actualizing oneself through the service of humanity', became his mantra. This vision that Modi set for himself turned out to be the foundation of his dedication, which he has used to serve India.

Narendra's first brush with seva occurred at the age of eight when he started attending the local shakha of the RSS in the evenings, after working as a server in his father's tea stall during the day, even while he was attending school in the morning hours. It was then that he first met Laxmanrao Inamdar.[7] Inamdar (popularly known as vakil saheb) inducted young Narendra as a *bal* swayamsevak and began to teach him about what it meant to be a volunteer. Recalling the influence of Inamdarji and the RSS on his life, Narendra Modi described it as the 'silent revolution of making men' in an organization built around 'renunciation, dedication and hard work'.[8]

Finding purpose and meaning in one's life is the most important foundational step to exercising leadership. Purpose gives meaning to life and shapes our choices and our leadership expression. Purpose is not merely about seeking something exclusively for oneself; it has to go beyond one's personal needs and reflect a larger societal good. It is about living our lives for others and going beyond the narrow constructs of our own small selves. Exercising leadership is a way of giving meaning to our lives by contributing to the lives of others. And such an opportunity to express leadership crosses our paths every day. What is required is the sensitivity to recognize purpose when it emerges and the courage to act on it as a labour of love.[9]

For many, certain crucible moments in their life help them discover their purpose. Leadership expert Warren Bennis defines 'crucible' as a transformative experience through which an individual comes to a new or an altered sense of identity. Difficult, and in some cases, career- or life-threatening events are called 'leadership crucibles'. They are trials and test points that force us into deep self-reflection, making us question who we are and what really matters to us. Characterized by a confluence of threatening intellectual, social, economic and/or political forces, crucibles test one's patience, belief systems and core values.[10]

As a young child, PM Modi experienced a poignant incident that would become a defining moment, shaping his purpose in leadership and influencing the trajectory of his life. Growing up in a close-knit community where neighbours were like extended family, any event in one household resonated throughout the entire neighbourhood.

One particular family faced considerable economic hardship, much like Modi's. This couple, who had been childless for years, were overjoyed when a child was finally born to them after a considerable period of longing. The entire community celebrated this long-awaited blessing. Tragically, the infant passed away just a week later, casting a pall of sorrow over everyone.

Narendra observed that the cow in this family's home, too, seemed to share their grief, refusing to eat and appearing equally despondent. Amid their collective sorrow, the cow also eventually succumbed, further deepening the family's pain. Unable to comprehend this phenomenon, he turned to his father for an explanation. It was then that his father revealed a profound truth: the cow had, in its own way, expressed solidarity with the grieving family. This revelation struck a chord with young Narendra. If an animal could feel and empathize with human suffering to such an extent, how much more deeply should he, as a human being, relate to the pain of others?

In that pivotal moment, he made a heartfelt commitment to stand in solidarity with those facing adversity, pledging to leverage his abilities to alleviate their suffering. His dedication to championing people-centric initiatives arises from the transformative impact of this experience and the profound insights it bestowed upon him.

While crafting a vision is an important step, sustaining it throughout one's life, ensuring that it continually evolves, driven by context and growth of one's abilities, is easier said than done. Sourcing energy from within and providing it to those who subscribe to this purpose, staying focused on the core goals—all this requires grinding labour, discipline, personal sacrifice and, most of all, faith in oneself and one's convictions. Leadership experts James M. Kouzes and Barry Z. Posner in their popular book, *The Leadership Challenge*[11], describe the importance of finding one's voice, clarifying values and expressing them. To become a credible leader, we need to comprehend fully the values, beliefs and assumptions that drive us. They describe the importance of genuineness in expressing oneself through these values and that words themselves aren't enough, no matter how noble they are. It is this unwavering commitment to building a resurgent India and his willingness to always stand up for this belief, even at enormous personal cost, that makes millions of people around the world admire Modi.

In Modi's own words, when he left home to join Swami Vivekananda's monastic order, he was 'undecided, unguided, and unclear'. He met many saints and ascetics, roamed around the Himalayas and many a time slept without a roof over his head. Yet through all of this, he never felt lonely, or less at home.

> I experienced revelations that help me till today. I realized that we are all tied down by our thoughts and limitations. When you surrender and stand in front of the vastness – you know that you are but a very small part of a large universe. When you understand that, any trace of arrogance you have in you melts and then life truly begins.[12]

Visionary leaders are not afraid to take risks and try new things. They are creative problem-solvers, and they constantly seek out new and better ways to do things. Being forward-thinking, optimistic and creative, they see opportunities and possibilities that others might miss. They use their perception to guide their decision-making and work tirelessly to turn their ideas into reality. To achieve this, one must have strong communication skills, the ability to build trust in the team, the capacity to manage change, and to navigate complex challenges. Such a person must also be able to think beyond immediate concerns and take a long-term view, focusing on the future and their decisions' impact on the generations to come. Rajiv Gauba, a senior career bureaucrat and the current cabinet secretary recalls how he sees these qualities play out in the weekly cabinet meetings that Prime Minister Modi presides over. The ability to strategically envision inspires Cabinet colleagues and bureaucrats alike, and the incessant drive to innovate newer ways of thinking are lessons that stand out for him after every interaction with the Prime Minister.

Jitendra Singh has been the minister of state in Prime Minister Modi's Cabinet since 2014, and he oversees several ministries, including the Ministry of Personnel and the Department of Science. Being attached to the Prime Minister's Office, he has a ringside view of how the Prime Minister operates. He recalls how he has never heard Modiji say anything out of context, and how the PM is always measured in his talk and knows when, how to and how much to speak: 'Watching him perform is one continuous lesson on staying in the present while not losing sight of the future.' Singh recalls how the PM once told him that he is working all the time in the interests of the nation or thinking about how best to do this work.

Even as early as December 2019, Modi cautioned his Cabinet colleagues of the impending consequences if the Covid-19 pandemic reached India. It is not just Modi's ability to strategize, be prepared and do the work required but also his ability to mobilize his team and galvanize the entire nation that Singh finds exemplary. From discovering the potential of those around him to seeking learning opportunities constantly, from raising one's own benchmark to being one's own competitor, Singh says that there are several lessons to learn from observing Prime Minister Modi. He sums it all up by calling Modi one of the greatest visionaries and authentic leaders that India has seen in public life.

Throughout his tenure, Modi has sought to build unanimous consensus for the party's legislation such as Goods and Services Tax (GST)[13], as opposed to forcing it through Parliament with a brute majority. In his 2014 Independence Day speech, he said: 'We are not for moving forward on the basis of majority. We are not interested to move forward by [the] virtue of majority. We want to move ahead on the basis of strong consensus, on the basis of *sangachhadhwam*'.[14] This profound concept of consensus with which Modi wants to take India forward appears as a well-known mantra in the Rig Veda[15]: '*Sangachhdhwam sam vadadhvam sam vo manamsi janatam*' meaning, 'May we come together, speak together, may we think and resolve together and be in accord.'

The attributes of an authentic leader have been characterized as the demonstration of passion for one's purpose, practising values consistently, irrespective of the demands to compromise, leading with heart and head in tandem, establishing long-term meaningful relationships and having the self-discipline to achieve results.[16] These attributes are aligned with Modi's lived philosophy. His journey from a humble background of selling tea on the platform of a railway station, to becoming a full-time pracharak, then becoming the chief minister of Gujarat and finally, the Prime Minister of India, has provided him with the context as well as the channel to make an impact in the world. Leadership is hard work and requires a constant commitment to self-improvement. One needs the ability to reflect on their experiences continually and the courage to develop self-awareness from these experiences. Acting on this awareness, even while staying authentic and rooted in one's own value system, is a difficult task and requires enormous adherence to an intention. Balancing the achievement of this purpose while being guided by core inner values and keeping one's own physical and emotional needs in check requires a deep understanding of oneself, of others, and the actions that continuously bind us with those around us.

Translating ideas into reality is not the work of just one person. A vision as expansive as that of building a nation economically, politically, socially, culturally and ensuring inclusive, sustainable development needs the active participation of a large number of people. Apart from building the convening power, a leader is required to be honest, competent and inspiring.[17] Gaining electoral legitimacy requires strategizing and an in-depth understanding of how representative democracy works. While electoral victories can be easily seen and credited to Modi today, one needs to keep in mind several roles he has played in the past. Decades of hard work that he put into communicating a larger symbolic vision of rebuilding the nation, getting people to shake away their collective slumber and break free from the colonial burden of the past is not easily achievable. The role of Prime Minister is just another role Modi sees himself in, and he considers it an opportunity to operationalize the vision of service that has been with him from his early days.

Any vision has to come from within but also needs to align with the context and situational realities prevailing in the ecosystem in which one operates. To get millions of people of all kinds to resonate with this and to inspire them to work towards fulfilling it requires a grounded understanding of the existing realities. Being a pracharak, constantly travelling around the country, living out of a *jhola* (small cloth sling bag), being at the mercy of his hosts for food and lodging, provided Modi with the contextual relevance and the cultural appropriateness for the actions that he subsequently undertook. Be it his commitment to *Antyodaya*[18], the environment, Swachh Bharat Mission[19], or developing an indigenous Covid vaccine; be it his deep empathy for the marginalized or the push for infrastructure, all initiatives gather their philosophical underpinnings from the varied experiences Modi has had as the 'common man' before taking up high office. When it is a nation like India that is to be inspired, to be made to believe in itself after it was made to feel inferior and slavish for decades because of repeated colonizations, it is no easy task. Throughout his term, Modi has stressed the need for mental decoloniality[20], which is now included as one of the *Panch Pran*[21] for India Vision 2047.[22]

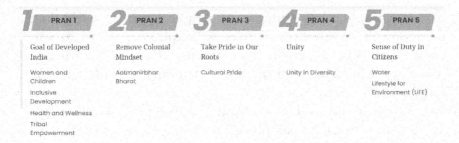

1 PRAN 1	**2** PRAN 2	**3** PRAN 3	**4** PRAN 4	**5** PRAN 5
Goal of Developed India	Remove Colonial Mindset	Take Pride in Our Roots	Unity	Sense of Duty in Citizens
Women and Children	Aatmanirbhar Bharat	Cultural Pride	Unity in Diversity	Water
Inclusive Development				Lifestyle for Environment (LiFE)
Health and Wellness				
Tribal Empowerment				

(Source: https://amritmahotsav.nic.in/themes-2-0.htm)

From building modern infrastructure to fighting poverty, from gender equity to women-led leadership, from protecting the nation's borders to fighting Covid-19 and ensuring wellness; merely envisioning alone will not lead to materialization. Modi has needed to be able to inspire all stakeholders, create a sense of urgency and restore pride and self-esteem on an unimaginable scale, unprecedented in the history of independent India. And doing all this while dousing fires of petty politics and mudslinging takes courage and extreme steadfastness. Modi not only epitomizes this gumption but also has the ability to build a strong support system that has been delivering on this vision to the nation. One can draw a parallel with the philosopher King Janaka[23] who was known as the ideal ruler even as he led the life of a mendicant within the walls of his palace. Constantly seeking to make the life of his subjects better, Janaka stayed untouched and unperturbed by the riches or fame attached to royalty. Chanakya[24], in his *Chanakya Neeti*[25], the treatise on public administration, writes, 'To perform duties of the State with maximum efficiency, the functionaries of the State must learn to control their sensual needs, and maximize their internal potentials'.[26] Living this aphorism for the last five decades and more, Narendra Modi stands tall as a visionary leader not limited to the Indian subcontinent alone, but as a global statesman helping the world navigate through some of the most complex and critical challenges it has ever faced.

Leadership is a passionate and time-intensive commitment requiring a deep sense of purpose. Without a compelling and inspirational purpose, overcoming obstacles and maintaining focus can become challenging. A sense of purpose empowers individuals to identify values that lend meaning to risk-taking, providing both direction and the motivation to act. In the pursuit of purpose-driven leadership, authenticity takes centre stage. It's not merely about possessing a purpose; it's about embodying it with unwavering conviction and sincerity. Authentic leaders, driven by a higher calling, remain steadfast in the face of challenges, anchored in the enduring values encapsulated in their purpose. This commitment to living the identified purpose not only sets a leader apart but also inspires others to join the collective journey towards a shared vision.

At the heart of Modi's visionary leadership is his commitment to national service and the endeavour to elevate India to a developed nation. This commitment acts as the driving force that propels him forward, offering the clarity and resilience required to navigate complexities effectively. Modi's authenticity is evident not just in articulating a compelling purpose but, more significantly, in consistently and genuinely embodying that purpose. His steadfast dedication leaves a lasting impact, not only on the nation he leads but also resonating on the global stage.

II

The Personal Facets of Leadership

कोऽतिभारः समर्थानां किं दूरं व्यवसायिनाम् ।
को विदेशः सविद्यानां कः परः प्रिय-वादिनाम् ॥

ko'tibhāraḥ samarthānām kim dūram vyavasāyinām |
ko videśastu viduṣām kaḥ paraḥ priyavādinām ||
—Panchatantra 2.57

No task is impossible for a competent person, no place is distant for a businessperson, no land is foreign for educated persons, no one is a stranger for persons with good communication abilities.

~

Narendra Modi's exceptional communication skills are pivotal to his leadership style, blending deep listening with persuasive oratory to inspire action and foster national unity. It stems from a deep conviction in the power of the people: Jan Shakti. Be it through verbal modes or non-verbal modes, Modi's messaging has been consistent and well-tailored, demonstrating his knowledge of the topics. As opposed to using speech as a tool for manipulation and generating compliance, his communication can be explained by the Indian model of *Sadharanikaran* or simplification. It uses the concepts of *sahridayata* and sanctity of *vak* (speech), where words are not used futilely, and conversations are seen as opportunities to generate a convergence of hearts. Through a mix of authenticity, strategic messaging and engaging storytelling, Modi's communication transcends mere rhetoric, embodying a transformative force that strengthens his leadership and galvanizes the nation towards shared goals.

~

Artful Mastery: Communicating to Lead and Nurturing Human Connections

In April 2016, Pullela Gopichand, a renowned badminton player and chief coach of the Indian national badminton team, was driven by an interesting belief in the universal importance of sport and the critical need to foster physical literacy. Concerned about the increasing focus on medals and victories, Gopichand feared that the true essence and purpose of sports were being neglected. Recognizing the significance of this issue, he decided to take his concerns to someone who could make a real difference—Prime Minister Narendra Modi.

Determined to present his case effectively, Gopichand meticulously prepared a presentation, eschewing digital aids for a more direct approach. After securing an appointment, he was invited to Parliament House for a meeting with PM Modi.

The meeting, initially uncertain in duration, turned out to be a profound interaction. PM Modi warmly welcomed Gopichand, with whom he requested a photograph before diving into the discussion. This gesture set a friendly tone for the meeting. Invited to share his thoughts, Gopichand embarked on a detailed exposition of his views, speaking uninterrupted for nine minutes—a duration longer than he had anticipated, given the advice he had received about the limited attention span typical of such high-profile meetings.

This interaction revealed PM Modi's exceptional listening skills. Despite the tight schedule, indicated by an aide's interruption signalling the next meeting, Modi gestured for the conversation to continue, extending the meeting beyond the initial seven-and-a-half minutes to about fifteen minutes. This extension was not just a matter of courtesy but a marker of genuine interest in Gopichand's message.[1]

The encounter between Pullela Gopichand and PM Modi was illustrative of more than just a shared interest in sports and physical literacy. It highlighted PM Modi's deep listening skills, his ability to give undivided attention and his warmth in one-on-one interactions. For Gopichand, this meeting was a powerful demonstration of the Prime Minister's leadership qualities—not just as an orator but as a listener who values and respects the opinions of others, even extending discussions to ensure comprehensive understanding and engagement.

T.V. Somanathan, the finance secretary of the Government of India, recalls a similar experience in a crucial meeting convened by the Prime Minister, which he attended as the then joint secretary in the Prime Minister's Office (PMO). Alongside his junior colleague Brajendra Navnit and other PMO officers, the discussion centred on the critical state of the public sector electricity distribution companies, or DISCOMs.

DISCOMs in India have long battled financial instability, operational inefficiencies and infrastructural challenges, necessitating governmental intervention and restructuring efforts to restore stability. The primary cause of their crisis was financial distress, largely due to underpriced electricity, compounded by high transmission and distribution losses and inefficient billing and collection practices. Political pressures to subsidize electricity for certain sectors further aggravated the revenue shortfall and debt accumulation.

Moreover, DISCOMs encountered significant technical and commercial losses due to antiquated infrastructure and power theft, which were exacerbated by operational inefficiencies and regulatory delays. In response, the Government of India initiated a bailout in the early 2000s, culminating in the Electricity Act of 2003. This legislation spearheaded reforms to enhance operational efficiency, ensure cost-reflective tariffs and extend electricity access, aiming to rejuvenate the sector.

Despite these reforms, DISCOMs' financial health remained precarious, prompting this meeting to be convened. The meeting, which included key ministers and officials like Power Minister Piyush Goyal and Finance Minister Arun Jaitley, focused on the persistent challenges facing the power sector. The Prime Minister attentively absorbed the power ministry's plea for a bailout akin to the 2003 initiative. The Reserve Bank of India (RBI) advocated for the government's intervention to restructure loans and authorize increased borrowing by state governments. The power ministry accordingly proposed allowing states to take over a substantial part of the DISCOM debt by relaxing the 3 per cent fiscal deficit ceiling. The expenditure secretary expressed concerns that such a move might only perpetuate a cycle of inefficiency unless the power sector and DISCOMs committed to substantive reforms. He pointed out that something similar had been tried a decade earlier; loans were taken over by states but eventually, DISCOMS continued to incur losses, resulting in the present predicament. Giving states the easy option of relaxing the borrowing limit would not promote any real reform as it would not require any hard choices or changes in the functioning of DISCOMS.

The Prime Minister, fully engaged with these discussions, recognized that inaction was not a viable option, as it could precipitate a power crisis with far-reaching implications for India's burgeoning economy and the daily lives of its citizens. He wanted to know how relief could be given without creating conditions for the cycle to repeat. Faced with what appeared to be a classic case of a need for relief versus creating perverse incentives, the Prime Minister sought practical, innovative solutions from the team. In this context, Brajendra Navnit, the junior-most officer in the room, boldly proposed allowing state governments to enhance their borrowing capacity, but with a condition: in the future, if the DISCOMs continued to incur losses, these losses would automatically be counted as a part of the 3 per cent fiscal deficit. This would provide short-term relief, but if the states did not carry out improvements, they would face budget constraints. Such a measure would provide strong motivation for reform. Eventually, this balanced approach was agreed upon, aiming to provide financial relief to DISCOMs while maintaining fiscal discipline among the states.

PM Modi's attentiveness to varied viewpoints, insistence on innovative, out-of-the-box solutions, and creation of a conducive environment for junior officers to contribute ideas exemplifies his approach. This meeting not only showcases Modi's deep listening skills but also his willingness to foster a collaborative and innovative problem-solving environment, and this led to the launch of the transformative UDAY scheme.[2]

Cabinet colleagues, senior bureaucrats and political associates vouch for the Prime Minister's ability to listen without getting distracted. This not only allows the people conversing with him to feel comfortable and confident but also reaffirms that they are encouraged to present their views without hesitation. Many of PM Modi's associates who meet with him regularly are aware that he values people who tell him the truth and not just what he wants to hear. The Prime Minister is also very auditory in his learning style, and this further complements his ability to listen. He rarely interrupts when a person speaks even when the person's inputs are mediocre, presentation ordinary or the idea silly. He waits until they finish, evaluates their input objectively and then speaks his mind. By not speaking early on in meetings, the PM gives the advantage to the entire group to say what it wants to, without prejudice or trying to align with what he thinks.

Deep listening is just one part of PM Modi's leadership abilities. The Prime Minister possesses exceptional oral communication abilities that have played a significant role in shaping his political influence and leadership style. Known for his eloquence and compelling oratory, Modi has a unique talent for connecting with diverse audiences on national and international platforms.

One of his notable strengths is his ability to convey complex, intricate ideas in a clear or accessible manner—be

it while addressing a large gathering or engaging in one-on-
one discussions. His speeches often incorporate anecdotes,
metaphors and real-life examples, allowing him to effectively
communicate his vision and policy objectives. Furthermore,
Prime Minister Modi has a commanding presence and an
engaging speaking style that effortlessly captivates his listeners.
His speeches are marked by conviction and confidence, instilling
a sense of assurance and trust in his audience. This charisma is
a powerful tool that enables him to rally support and mobilize
public sentiment behind his initiatives. National Security
Adviser Ajit Doval attests to the profound impact of Modi's
personal magnetism, stating that he is yet to encounter anyone
who leaves a conversation with PM Modi without being deeply
inspired and moved. Leadership expert Warren Bennis had
once stated, 'Charisma is not the cause, but the consequence of
effective leadership'.[3]

Modi's versatility in language is also noteworthy. He is
proficient in several languages, and this enables him to connect
with citizens across the linguistic diversity of India. This
linguistic dexterity underscores his commitment to inclusivity
and accessibility in communication. His speeches reflect his
deep understanding of cultural nuances and regional sentiments.
He demonstrates a keen awareness of the specific concerns
and aspirations of different communities, allowing him to
tailor his messages to resonate with diverse demographics. His
speeches—whether delivered during election campaigns, rallies,
radio broadcasts like *Mann Ki Baat*, in Parliament, or to the US
Congress—are consistently insightful and deeply inspirational.

Initiated in October 2014, *Mann Ki Baat* (MKB), or Talks
from the Heart, is Prime Minister Modi's monthly radio
programme, for which the inauguration coincided with the
transformative Navaratri festival.[4] This widely embraced
initiative has surpassed historical benchmarks in popularity
and outreach[5], including 32nd American President Franklin
Roosevelt's famed Fireside Chats. Strategically scheduled for
maximum impact, the programme is broadcast on the last

Sunday of every month. It reaches an impressive 96 per cent of
the Indian populace and transcends linguistic boundaries with
translations.[6] Modi's optimistic tone and focus on uplifting
narratives cultivate hope and positivity. He has used this
programme to announce and motivate people to take part in
development campaigns like Swachh Bharat Abhiyan (Clean
India Campaign), Beti Bachao, Beti Padhao (Save the Girl Child,
Educate the Girl Child), the Amrut Scheme (Scheme for Urban
Infrastructure Transformation), Start-up India, Stand-up India
and many more. It also serves to update the public on crucial
foreign policies and international engagements.

In his radio addresses, Prime Minister Modi employs a
blend of Diffusion Theory and Participatory Development
Communication. Diffusion Theory, pioneered by American
scholar Everett Rogers, follows a top-down approach in
disseminating knowledge and practices. This theory explains
how, over time, an idea or product gains momentum and
diffuses (or spreads) through a specific population or social
system. The result of this diffusion is that people, as part of
a social system, adopt a new idea, behaviour or product. PM
Modi has utilized *MKB*, for example, to inform people of new
applications and technologies through which they can move
towards a 'Digital India'. This approach allows individuals to
transition from relying on traditional practices to adopting
innovative solutions, ultimately leading to a more developed
and technologically advanced way of life.

While on the one hand the diffusion theory is vertical and
top-down in its orientation, the participatory model, on the other
hand, stresses the importance of the cultural identities within
local communities and of democratization and participation at all
levels. Through *MKB*, the PM has attempted to demystify public
governance and policy issues, ensuring that citizens feel engaged
with the larger, macro-level development narratives of the nation.

PM Modi has also been successful in democratizing
information and reducing information asymmetries—where
certain knowledge bases have historically been the monopoly

of elites. He also uses *MKB* as a platform to bring about a collective national identity amongst citizens and create a spirit of oneness and appreciation for several national symbols and events.

A range of communication channels, including social media platforms, websites, public gatherings, political networks and direct correspondence to his office, afford him the means to gauge the prevailing sentiments of the populace. This allows him to tailor his messages to resonate with their concerns, underscoring the importance he places on public input.

The effectiveness of his communication strategy rests on three key elements: trustworthy content, unwavering consistency, and a focus on the needs of citizens.[7] Above all, these foundations are elevated by the Prime Minister's personal magnetism and the genuine sense of trust that he exudes. The non-partisan nature of this communication approach guarantees it faces minimal criticism while delivering maximum impact and value.

Khadi, a handspun and handwoven fabric from India, embodies a rich blend of cultural heritage, ecological mindfulness, and a movement towards economic independence. Initially made from cotton, khadi has expanded to include silk and wool, all spun on a traditional *charkha*. Its significance transcends its materiality, representing a philosophical commitment to self-sufficiency, as championed by Mahatma Gandhi during the fight for Indian independence. Gandhi's endorsement of khadi was not merely about fabric but a call to embrace swadeshi values—prioritizing local goods over foreign imports as a form of peaceful protest against the colonial rule.

This fabric symbolized a rejection of the industrial goods that underpinned British economic dominance, encouraging a return to traditional craftsmanship as a means of asserting economic autonomy. Today, khadi's appeal lies not only in its artisanal quality and sustainability but also in its potential for widespread adoption, which remained largely untapped.

Recent years have seen a remarkable resurgence in khadi's popularity, largely attributed to the significant endorsement of the Prime Minister on different platforms. For example, in the last eight years, production in the khadi sector increased by 191 per cent, with an increase in sales of 332 per cent, after the PM's verbal support of the product in one of the early *MKB* episodes.[8] This revival underscores the enduring legacy of Gandhi's teachings and the contemporary relevance of khadi in promoting sustainable fashion, supporting local artisans and fostering a more self-reliant economy.

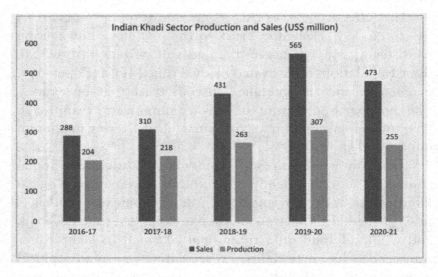

(Data Source: Ministry of Micro, Small and Medium Enterprises)

The ideas pitched by the PM have also become trendy movements many a time and reflect the enormous emotional and intellectual influence of his messages on the common people. A good example of the participatory model of communication was displayed by the launch of the #SelfieWithDaughter campaign, initiated by a sarpanch (village head) in a small remote village of Haryana because he was inspired by the Beti Bachao, Beti Padhao scheme. The PM fully supported the campaign and in an *MKB* episode he encouraged everyone to participate. He stated:

I request you all to take a selfie with your daughter and post it on #SelfieWithDaughter. And do not forget to post a tagline around the theme of 'Beti Bachao Beti Padhao' with it, whatever be the language, it can be in Hindi, English, your mother tongue or your native language. And I promise to re-tweet the most inspirational tagline with you and your daughter's selfie. We can turn 'Beti Bachao Beti Padhao' into a mass movement.[9]

Prime Minister Modi consistently emphasizes three central themes in his communications. The first theme is Jan Shakti—or the empowerment of the people—which underscores the significance of robust democratic values extending beyond electoral participation; the second is the imperative to alter societal mindsets; and lastly, there is the conviction to reconnect India with its civilizational heritage.[10]

Connecting people to a purpose by channelling their passions is the epitome of leadership. Modi's communication ability has been honed in such a way that people feel intimately connected to the requests made by their leader. In a country as big as India with a population of 1.4 billion, it is no easy feat. For the younger generation, he champions the concept of *vikaas* (development), tapping into their entrepreneurial spirit. Simultaneously, he seamlessly engages with the rural population through the Swachh Bharat initiative, aligning it with the overarching aspiration of development. The ability to unite diverse groups of people, each at different stages of life, around a shared vision necessitates the effective transmission of both emotions and ideas.

Nurturing Human Connections

The rich heritage of Indian civilizational literature offers deep insights into the art of effective communication, detailing various indigenous communication models. However, contemporary studies on communication often overlook these models, focusing instead on Western theories like the Shannon Weaver model[11], Theresa and Gaby's Communication Theory[12], or Elisabeth Noelle-Neumann's spiral of silence model.[13] The Western-centric understanding of communication generally neglects the ancient Indian model of Sadharanikaran. This model, literally meaning, 'simplification without loss of essence', has been around in various forms for over 3500 years and is rooted in the works of the ancient spiritual master, Abhinavagupta[14] and Bharata Muni's *Natya Shastra*.[15]

Sadharanikaran, derived from Natya Shastra, represents an ancient Hindu approach to conveying deep *bhaavas* (personal emotions) and fostering a shared understanding or sahridayata (consensus). This model emphasizes the importance of the relational and social aspects of communication, focusing on the collective rather than individual perspectives. It posits that effective communication requires not just the transmission of information but also a collective emotional and social transformation. Central to this concept is the idea that genuine communication is anchored in 'compassion with affection', and it acknowledges the potential for miscommunication across different social and cultural settings. Unlike individual-centric models, Sadharanikaran's relational approach is particularly relevant for effective communication within interconnected communities.

Sadharanikaran places its primary emphasis on sahridayata (which literally means a convergence of hearts); it seeks to identify a shared orientation, commonality and mutual understanding between communicating parties or groups. According to this model, sahridayata hinges on two distinct groups: the *preshaka* (sender) and the *prapaka* (receiver). The model underscores the significance of bhaava and *sandarbha* (context). The concept of communion, derived from the Latin term 'communis', meaning 'common understanding', also denotes the same principle. There is a communion in conversation, and the depth of this communion is contingent upon the potency of the emotional and mental state of the communicators and the context (social, cultural, situational, etc.) in which communication is taking place.

At the sender's end, there lies *abhi-yanjana* (an encoding). This refers to how language (verbal or otherwise) is used to convey an idea. Once decoded by the receiver, it transforms into *rasavadana* (decoding), encapsulating the essence of the message. The model additionally acknowledges that a *sandesha* (message) must traverse a *sarni* (akin to a channel or bridge). From sender to receiver, a message's quality can be affected by external *dosha* (noise or other distractions)[16], as well as the channel's quality. Once the *rasa* (essence) is comprehended by the receiver, it prompts *pratikriya* (feedback), concluding the communication process within the Sadharanikaran model. This model, as previously mentioned, rivals the comprehensiveness of any other established communication model. Regrettably, most contemporary literature on communication describes the process using similar terminology, while often overlooking this ancient Indic account of it.

Sadharanikaran

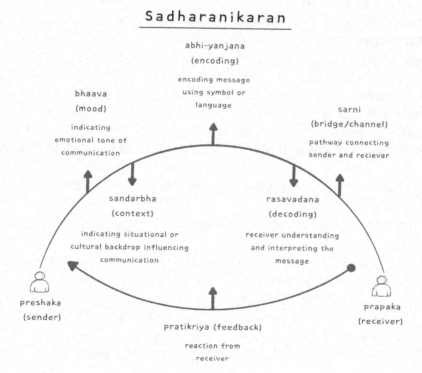

abhi-yanjana
(encoding)

encoding message
using symbol or
language

bhaava
(mood)

indicating
emotional tone of
communication

sarni
(bridge/channel)

pathway connecting
sender and reciever

sandarbha
(context)

indicating situational or
cultural backdrop influencing
communication

rasavadana
(decoding)

receiver understanding
and interpreting the
message

preshaka
(sender)

prapaka
(receiver)

pratikriya (feedback)

reaction from
receiver

The modern (Western) theory of communication is broadly split into the 'process'[17] school of thought, which focuses on the persuasive ability of communication channels and the 'semiotics'[18] school of thought, which focuses on 'interactional research,'[19] grounded in the Marxist world view of class, domination, conflict, etc. There is a distinct 'strategic' edge to both these approaches, reflecting post-World War II origins. As is the case with many things, it is the vision that informs the agenda for the evolution of a discipline. When the vision of communication is persuasion by any and all means possible, the resultant communication strategy is also tailored as per that notion. It is the building of a narrative to ensure a competitive advantage. The impact of this can be seen in the idea of 'narrative wars' in the age of social media. Communication in this cultural milieu is indistinguishable from manipulation.

The Indian philosophy of communication diverges markedly from the goal of strategic manipulation. Instead, it aligns more closely with a philosophical school of communication. In this context, the word 'communication' is revered as sacred, embodying the concept of *Shabda Brahman*—a timeless, cosmic resonance that symbolizes the *rta* (underlying order) of the entire universe. According to this notion, the universe itself originated from *pranava* (Om)[20], the primordial sound, underscoring the vital role of sound in both creation and existence. As a cultural norm, words are held in high regard and are not to be used lightly. This is reflected in the preference for the oral tradition over written communication during the Vedic age in Indian history.

In the words of Robert T. Oliver[21]:

> In Western rhetoric the assumption is that the speaker seeks to manipulate a change in the reactions of his listeners. His aim is (however gently) to coerce agreement from them. In the view of ancient Asian rhetoric, the speaker seeks from his audience, not agreement, but acceptance. The nuance of difference is small, but it is significant. The speaker does

not expect from them an active grappling with his ideas and feelings to determine whether or not—and with whatever kinds of modifications—they should be approved; what he seeks is to win their concurrence.[22]

In ancient India, the exploration of rhetoric was a collective journey towards enlightenment, where both the speaker and the listener aimed to discover a universal truth that embraced them and all other things. In contrast, the Western tradition places emphasis on purpose and persuasion, often manifesting as a perpetual struggle between a speaker striving for dominance and a listener defending their own beliefs. Orthodox Indian thought, however, veered towards a different path which prioritizes the avoidance of both purpose and persuasion, thereby relinquishing the notion of conflict. Finance Minister Nirmala Sitharaman elucidates how when one engages with PM Modi's words, an underlying theme of unification becomes evident. She not only highlights his unwavering focus and presence in conversations, but she also notes his gentle and compassionate approach when offering suggestions or opinions. His sole objective in conversing seems to lie in attempting to fathom the encompassing unity shared by both him and the audience.

According to this Indian perspective, any disparities are perceived as mere illusions. The presupposition of a unified identity is accepted without question, and any apparent contradictions are seen as shortcomings arising from individual limitations in character and understanding, acknowledged by both the speaker and the listener. Oliver astutely articulates that this understanding of communication resonates with the core philosophy of the Upanishads and that it embodies a rhetorical viewpoint, which has exerted a profound and enduring impact on Indian society and the Indian mindset.[23]

Detractors of Modi talk about him remaining silent in circumstances where a response is anticipated, particularly in the aftermath of significant events covered by the media.

However, few understand the profound value he places on *vak*. To Modi, every utterance stems from a place of truth and unwavering conviction. He believes that people shape their own realities and internal truths based on their knowledge and experiences. But for him, speaking from the realm of vak is more than mere words; it is a sacred act, imbued with deep meaning. Vak represents *ninya vachamsi*[24] (truth) and reflects one's inner integrity.

The Rig Veda delves into the concept of *satya-vak* (true-speech), reflecting the vision of the rishi, the seer. It is through this elevated form of vak that the rishis articulate the true essence of objects, as is unveiled to them in *kavyani kavaye nivacana* (sublime poetry).[25] Those who have engaged closely with Modi can discern this quality in his conversations. PM Modi's understanding of the multifaceted dimensions of human life, ideals and aspirations echoes the rishi-vision from the Rig Veda, demonstrating his deep insight. In the Rig Vedic tradition, vak is a medium through which rishis express their spiritual experiences, adeptly using words. Vak, as depicted in the Rig Veda, is truthful, illuminating and inspires *cetanti sumatinam* (noble thoughts)[26], highlighting its significance and purity.

Throughout history, leaders such as Narendra Modi, Nelson Mandela, Barack Obama and Angela Merkel have deeply understood the significance of impactful communication. Their messages carry weight because they are rooted in universal truths, which these leaders have deeply internalized. Their profound empathy extends far and wide, reflecting a remarkable level of understanding and compassion. Rajnath Singh and Anurag Thakur, both Cabinet colleagues of PM Modi, attest to the depth and expansive scope of their conversations with him. They recount experiences from personal interactions and various Cabinet meetings where Modi's engagement was marked by a level of absorption, intensity and focused attention that remained undistracted. Similarly, Sri Sri Ravishankar, the founder of The Art of Living Foundation, acknowledges the

Prime Minister's exceptional capacity to grasp complex ideas
presented to him with minimal distortion. He sees this as a
testament to PM Modi's inner strength—the power of the spirit.

Ramachandra Roddam[27] elaborates on the diverse
manifestations of the power of vak. He identifies individuals
with the compelling ability of *sammohana* (attraction) in
speech, often seen in great orators whose words hold a
captivating sway. Some possess a remarkable knack for debate
and argumentation, an extension of their spellbinding oratory,
coupled with the capacity to immobilize opponents. Then there
are those who, while perhaps not as riveting in their delivery,
display scholarly mastery, deftly navigating the nuances of
their domain. This expertise indicates a deep immersion in
a specific field. Lastly, Roddam describes a select few who
possess the rare talent to offer insights that cut through mental
clutter, freeing the listener's mind and leaving them in a state
of reverent wonder. Their impact stems not from the resonance
of their voice, but from the profound weight with which
they expound upon ideas and concepts that flow in a liminal
stream, intricately linked to the human mind, yet tantalizingly
elusive. This capacity is akin to a laser beam that illuminates
a mysterious point in the vast darkness, a point that is well
within the listener's line of sight yet shrouded in a mystical veil.
Smriti Irani, another Cabinet colleague of Modi's, also talks
about how the PM is like a sponge, absorbing knowledge and
information that comes from all sides and from all kinds of
people. He never pretends to be an expert and is ever willing
to keep learning. It is this humility coupled with the desire to
learn new things that she feels makes him a great leader.

In addition to his profound capacity for attentive listening
and precise communication, PM Modi recognizes the
significance of non-verbal communication, a vital aspect for
everyone, and especially crucial for politicians. His choice of
attire, such as the long flowing beard he sported a few years
ago and the coats crafted from recycled materials, serves as

symbolic expressions conveying specific messages, well-suited for the occasion. His donning of the *pagdi* (turban) during Independence Day speeches is another notable example. The turban has long been a significant emblem for Indian men, though its adoption has waned among the urban, English-educated classes. In ancient Indian society, the style and quality of one's *paagh-paaghdi* (turban) and *saafa* (head cloth for turban) were indicative of an individual's stature and character. It represented valour, pride and honour. Placing it atop one's own head is deemed an act of courage and placing it atop another's head is deemed as a sign of honour, respect and dignity. While its importance has endured among the rural population of India, Modi's choice to wear it also underscores his consistent commitment to the development of rural India. The way it is draped further conveys the resolute and decisive nature of the person adorning it. In ancient times, an individual's paagh-paaghdi and saafa could reveal whether they were brave or timid, upright or dishonest. It is non-verbal demonstrations such as these that enable PM Modi to effortlessly forge a strong connection with the masses. The thoroughness of his communication mirrors the prowess of King Sugriva's minister in the Ramayana, Hanuman[28], who is known for his wit, devotion, resilience and strength.

In the Kishkindha Kanda[29] of the Ramayana, Hanuman exemplifies the Sadharanikaran model in his communication, encompassing elements such as his modulation, tone, body language and more. To illustrate, when Hanuman introduces himself to the brothers Rama and Lakshmana, the latter who is vigilant for potential threats, initially harbours doubts about Hanuman's trustworthiness. However, Rama subsequently provides Lakshmana with reasons to believe that Hanuman is a sincere individual. Rama, a proficient grammarian, explains to Lakshmana that despite Hanuman's lengthy discourse, not a single grammatical error can be found in his sentences. Hanuman's demeanour and gestures convey politeness and gentleness, and his speech exhibits a richness, depth, confidence and distinction that are all well-balanced. In praising Hanuman's vocal delivery, Rama notes that Hanuman's voice resonates distinctly from his chest, mirroring his character, and that his tone is harmonious and falls within the mid-range pitch. Hanuman's style of communication is convincing, concise and spontaneous, while his speech is scholarly, yet easily comprehensible. Consequently, Hanuman presents himself to be a person of integrity rather than a deceiver, earning Rama's trust.

Communicating to lead entails more than the mere act of hearing or speaking the right words at the opportune moment. While Sadharanikaran offers a comprehensive theory of communication, MIT researcher Otto Scharmer introduced a framework called 'Theory U', which emphasizes how attentive listening can serve as a potent leadership tool. This approach integrates systems thinking, mindfulness and collective action to tackle complex challenges and facilitates transformative change. Within 'Theory U', listening assumes a central role as a foundational practice for delving into deeper levels of awareness and comprehension. It transcends surface-level word perception, demanding an open mind and heart to genuinely grasp others and the larger system in play.

Prime Minister Modi exemplifies these outstanding communication skills, encompassing the multifaceted abilities crucial for effective leadership. His proficiency in setting a clear vision, building trust, inspiring others, mediating conflicts, providing constructive feedback and navigating change, underscores his mastery of this pivotal aspect of leadership. Through open and direct communication, he fosters an environment of trust and collaboration, enabling his team to achieve its highest potential. His adeptness in addressing internal and external stakeholders underscores the significance he places on effective communication. During crises, his clarity and reassurance serve as a guiding light, instilling confidence in the nation.

What sets his oratory apart is its innate ability to inspire and motivate. Each address carries a distinct motivational undertone, invoking a collective sense of duty and responsibility. Whether it is drawing examples from local folklore or regional heroes, PM Modi speaks in a manner that appeals to the collective identity of a diverse population, fostering a spirit of inclusivity that is crucial for a pluralistic society. This motivational force empowers citizens to actively participate in the nation's development journey, instilling a newfound confidence in their own agency.

Yet, it is not just the words themselves, but the deep-seated conviction that underlies them which truly defines Modi's communication style. His unwavering belief in his vision infuses his speeches with an authenticity that resonates with people across the spectrum. This authenticity builds trust and credibility, solidifying his position as a leader who speaks from the heart and acts with steady resolve.

Strategically, PM Modi's communication is a finely-honed tool. His messages are purposefully crafted, tailored to specific audiences and timed for maximum impact. This strategic approach ensures that his words resonate precisely where they are needed, further amplifying their influence.

On the international stage, PM Modi's linguistic prowess and cross-cultural communication skills have been instrumental in fostering diplomatic relations. His ability to articulate India's interests and priorities in a global context has enhanced the country's standing in international forums.

Prime Minister Modi's communication abilities are more than just eloquence; they are a transformative force that drives his leadership. This is best summed up by National Security Adviser Ajit Doval:

> Through his words, [Prime Minister Modi] not only articulates his vision but also ignites a collective sense of purpose, empowering citizens to actively participate in the nation's growth story. His communication is the medium through which he fosters unity, inspires action, and influences public sentiment, both at home and on the global stage. It is this unique blend of inspiration, conviction, and strategic finesse that defines Modi's leadership as a force to be reckoned with.

उद्यमः साहसं धैर्यं बुद्धिः शक्तिः पराक्रमः।
षडेते यत्र वर्तन्ते तत्र देवः सहायकृत् ॥

udyamaḥ sāhasaṃ dhairyaṃ buddhiḥ śaktiḥ parākramaḥ ǀ
ṣaḍete yatra vartante tatra deva sahāyakṛt ǁ
—Mahasubhashita Sangraha 6882

*Hard work, risk taking, patience, intellect, strength and prowess
are six human qualities, which, if they are present in an individual,
even God extends help.*

~

Narendra Modi's leadership style is emblematic of principles deeply rooted in India's spiritual and philosophical heritage, characterized by integrity, empathy, fearlessness, positive thinking and a strong sense of duty. His commitment to public service, underscored by a life of renunciation and dedication to the nation's welfare, mirrors the ethos of ancient Indian teachings. His motto in life has been the motto of his mentor Guruji Golwalkar: 'This life is a sacrifice to the nation; everything is dedicated to it, nothing belongs to me.' His ability to connect with people, his compassion for the less privileged, and his relentless pursuit of knowledge and self-improvement are qualities that not only define his governance but also inspire a vision of a progressive and inclusive India. Through his actions and decisions, Modi embodies a leadership style that is both transformative and deeply resonant with India's enduring values and aspirations for the future.

~

Essential Traits: The Mosaic of Integrity, Tenacity, Resilience and Commitment

In the tapestry of India's spiritual and cultural heritage, the Mahabharata stands as a monumental epic, weaving the story of a profound struggle between two cousin factions that forever altered the ethos of Indian civilization. At the heart of this saga is Bhishma Pitamaha[1], originally named Devavrata. His transformation into Bhishma, a name meaning 'frightful', stems from a solemn vow of lifelong celibacy made in the flush of youth. This vow, steeped in sacrifice, set forth a chain of events spiralling towards the epic's climactic war. Despite the repercussions of his promise, Bhishma's legacy endures in the hearts of many Indians, a beacon of renunciation, unwavering commitment, integrity and the power of resolve.

In the Indian ethos, renunciation, or vairagya, is not just a virtue but the cornerstone of true leadership. This principle underlines the ascetic discipline where personal desires and accolades are forsaken for the greater good. Such a path, arduous and rarely trodden, is illuminated in the annals of history and philosophy. It is this very essence of vairagya that resonates in the life journey of the Prime Minister. From forsaking a domestic life for the quest of potential monkhood to immersing himself in the public's service without the respite of holidays, his life mirrors the ethos of self-sacrifice. He walks the path laid by his mentor, Guruji Golwalkar[2] of the RSS, who professed, '*Rashtraya swaha; idam rashtraya idam na mama*', which translates as 'this life is a sacrifice to the nation; everything is dedicated to the nation, nothing belongs to me'[3]—an ode to living life as an homage to the nation, where personal identity dissolves into the service of the collective.

The modern lifestyle places a premium on the enjoyment of sensual pleasures. Viewed from that perspective, Modi's life may appear needlessly austere from afar, but this view disregards the cycle of crests and troughs that accompanies the modern lifestyle. Each session of bashful indulgence is followed by a bout of deprivation, and the remedy for that loss—often through ever-increasing indulgence—only leads to a spiralling path towards self-debasement. The original purpose of holidays, derived from 'holy days', was for the worship of deities and work towards self-transcendence. According to Eastern spirituality, leisure time must be used for contemplation and reflection, to pursue higher spiritual goals and to recover one's humanity.

Not known to take breaks amidst responsibility, Modi is known to utilize his leisure time in a unique way through his 'Meet Myself' programmes. He has ventured off to some unknown place and just silently observed nature. This method of reclusiveness is not unknown in India and is practiced by many across the world to help reorient their bearings. PM Modi's Kailash Mansarovar Yatra[4] post his first election victory as an organizer in 1987, or his seventeen-hour long streak of meditation in Kedarnath, are all seeded in this principle of rta (cosmic order) alignment.

While this may provide the appearance of a sterile approach to life devoid of joy, it is the time-tested method for removing fetters in the experience of true joy. According to thought leader Ram Swarup[5]:

Renunciation is not opposed to joy; rather, they go together. The world cannot be enjoyed by greedy possession; it is enjoyed by generous renunciation. Therefore, the Vedic teaching is - enjoy by renunciation, by self-giving. True joy finds its fulfillment and culmination in renunciation; renunciation of all that is false, unreal, crooked, and dark.

When craving and desire (kamachhanda) are renounced, it brings concentration; when ill-will is renounced, it brings joy. When mental defilements (kleshas) of various descriptions are given up, different powers (indriyas) like faith (sraddha), energy (virya), mindfulness (smriti), concentration (samadhi) and wisdom (prajna) are born in the soul.[6]

Indian philosophy emphasizes *indriya nigraha*, or control of the senses, and this forms the bedrock for renunciation. In a seductive world filled with tempting opportunities, one needs to practice self-control to cultivate integrity and keep hungers in check.

Even the harshest critics of the PM acknowledge his individual integrity. PM Modi has shown his resolve in demonstrating integrity at every stage, whether it is running the national government for nearly a decade without a whiff of any financial irregularity—using technologies like Direct Benefit Transfers (DBT) to minimize leakages—or dismissing corrupt public servants. Integrity is a complex concept, embodying a range of moral and ethical standards that influence a person's actions in all life areas. True integrity involves being honest, just and upright in every interaction and decision. It is characterized by a consistent adherence to one's moral values and principles. Moreover, integrity involves accountability, accepting responsibility for one's actions and their outcomes, whether positive or negative. Respect for others is also a crucial aspect of integrity, which includes valuing other people's rights, beliefs and property.

Courage often walks hand in hand with integrity. Standing up for what is right, especially in the face of personal loss, criticism or unpopularity, is a hallmark of integrity. Lastly, integrity demands impartiality. It calls for decisions and actions that are fair and unbiased, uninfluenced by personal gain. Prime Minister Modi's steadfast commitment to inclusive development, as seen in his conviction in Sabka Saath, Sabka Vikaas, Sabka Vishwas (together with all, development for all, for the trust of all), cutting across caste, creed and religious lines, is a testament to this aspect of integrity.

Once, during his tenure as the chief minister, an interviewer asked him how much he has done for the state's Muslims. He replied, 'Nothing.' The aghast interviewer then asked how much he has done for Hindus, and he replied, 'Nothing.' He then explained to the confused interviewer that he doesn't identify his state's citizens by their religion or caste, but to him they are all Gujaratis, the only identity that matters.[7] Today, he has expanded this to include every Indian, irrespective of caste, creed, religion, language or geography. This deep-rooted conviction of the PM was explained by him during the inauguration of the Statue of Equality[8], a monument dedicated to the eleventh-century saint Shri Ramanujacharya[9]:

> There should be the development of everyone without discrimination. Everyone should get social justice without discrimination. The India of today is making a united effort to make those who were oppressed for centuries the partners in development with complete dignity.[10]

Personal integrity significantly contributes to character development, and when paired with empathy, it greatly enhances the expression of leadership. It is said of Rama, the legendary king of India and protagonist of the Ramayana[11], that he would visit his subjects in the kingdom of Ayodhya even when he was just a prince and would listen to their stories. Even if not in a position to help directly, he would be genuinely moved by their stories, sharing their joys and sorrows. This helped Rama build personal connections and endeared him to their hearts. So, when his father invited any opposition to Rama's coronation, the verdict was unanimous: Rama must be crowned the next king.

Connecting to people, getting to know them, and engaging in compassionate action forms the bedrock of public leadership. Addressing a group of information technologists at an event titled '*Mai Nahin Hum* [Not Me, Us]' the PM spoke about the source of inspiration. Inspiration, he said, does not simply come from reading books and quoting great leaders. One must place themselves in a situation where genuine empathy can originate. Citing an example of taxi drivers, he said that his approach has been to strike up a conversation with taxi drivers after alighting from the ride. Having the conversation after the ride involves a wilful devotion of time, as opposed to during the ride where the passenger and driver are obliged to travel together. In this conversation, he'd ask the drivers about their life, their work, their ability to put bread on the table and handle other expenses, etc. Through these conversations, he would not only open the hearts of other human beings to himself, but it also made him truly understand his privileges in life. This is the foundation of empathetic service, he said.[12]

This spirit of connectedness can be seen in the numerous visits PM Modi made to the new building of the Indian Parliament during its construction to encourage the workers. He would remind them that they were not simply creating a building but that they were creating history, and he congratulated them with shawls and mementos when the building was completed.[13] There is power in being appreciated by leaders. By tying his praises to the service rendered for the nation, Modi perfectly utilizes interactions to instil patriotism and duty to service in his fellow citizens. Whether it is engaging with athletes, celebrating the Diwali festival with soldiers posted to border areas, consoling the players of the Indian cricket team after they lost the 2023 World Cup finals, motivating the engineers who are building the Vande Bharat trains, or checking in with citizens who benefit from government programmes, PM Modi uses every opportunity that presents itself to engage and connect with people from different walks of life.

While empathy refers to the ability to understand and share the feelings of another person, compassion goes a step further than empathy. It is not only understanding someone's pain, but it is also about alleviating that pain. Compassion involves a desire to act—to support or help the person suffering.

Varesh Sinha, a former Gujarat bureaucrat, recalls an incident showcasing Narendra Modi's compassion during his tenure as the chief minister. In the middle of a meeting, a sudden noise at the window caught everyone's attention. Modi, discerning that a bird had possibly hit the window and was injured, immediately paused the meeting. He swiftly directed the forest department and animal healthcare professionals to attend to the bird, temporarily putting official matters aside to prioritize the bird's welfare.[14]

This act is reflective of the ethos in Indic scriptural wisdom, where *karuna*—or compassion—is more than an emotional response; it's a life principle shaping actions, thoughts and attitudes towards others and the environment. The Bhagavad Gita speaks of compassion as a divine quality that should be cultivated. It is seen as an expression of the underlying unity of all beings, rooted in the belief that all life is interconnected and part of the same divine reality (Brahman).

Karuna is also central to Buddhist teachings and is considered one of the four *Brahmaviharas* (sublime attitudes), along with *metta* (loving kindness), *mudita* (empathetic joy) and *upekkha* (equanimity). The desire to relieve the suffering of others is born out of karuna. The Dalai Lama frequently speaks of compassion as essential for human happiness and world peace.

Sublime attitudes under Buddhism
(Brahmaviharas)

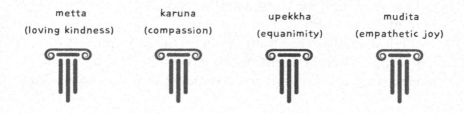

metta	karuna	upekkha	mudita
(loving kindness)	(compassion)	(equanimity)	(empathetic joy)

Jainism also places immense emphasis on compassion, which is integral to its core principle of *ahimsa*. The practice of ahimsa (non-violence), driven by compassion, emphasizes not just the avoidance of physical harm but also the importance of kind thoughts and actions towards all beings. The idea of seeing oneself in all beings and all beings in oneself promotes a compassionate approach to life. Compassion is not just an individual moral virtue, but it is seen as essential for the welfare of society and the world at large.

In Narendra Modi's leadership approach, compassion serves as a critical element, mirroring the teachings emphasized in his style. By fostering a supportive and empathetic work culture, he enhances team collaboration and job satisfaction. Smriti Irani, a Cabinet minister in PM Modi's government, recalls how the PM in 2014 called her and inquired about her son's health when he was admitted into a hospital.[15] She describes Modi as '. . . a leader who doesn't mollycoddle but knows when his subordinates need support.' She also says that he is almost like the head of a family in that aspect.

Similarly, Kuniyal Kailasanathan, a former bureaucrat, remembers Modi's personal gestures of condolence and concern during his family's challenging times. Additionally, as Ghulam Nabi Azad, the leader of the Opposition in the Upper House, approached retirement in August 2022, Prime Minister Modi gave him an emotional farewell. He expressed his gratitude for Azad's assistance during the evacuation of Gujarati pilgrims caught in a terror attack in Kashmir. 'Posts come, high offices come, power comes and how to handle these, one must learn from Ghulam Nabi Azad Ji. I would consider him a true friend,' the PM said.[16] It is evident that the PM's expressions of compassion span beyond political lines.

The CEO of NITI Aayog[17], B.V.R. Subrahmanyam (BVR) narrates an instance where he experienced, first-hand, how Modi's empathy and compassion lead to public action. The PM Vishwakarma scheme[18] was announced by the PM in his 2022 Independence Day speech. Addressing the nation, he said that this scheme would help skill millions of artisans who work with their hands in rural villages and who are not covered under any preexisting social protection scheme. The annual budget announced by the finance minister for 2023–24 also laid out the details of the scheme; but as it turned out, the people covered under the scheme were just categorized as artisans, without delving into the specific professions in which they worked.

Due to initial confusion surrounding the categorization of the scheme's beneficiaries, there was a risk that many people already covered under various other ministries' schemes might be duplicated in the Vishwakarma scheme. Around this time, the scheme's design was transferred to NITI Aayog, the apex public policy think tank of the Government of India, and BVR decided to directly approach the Prime Minister for clarity on the issue.

Coming back from a whirlwind tour of Karnataka, and while preparing for the upcoming state visit to the United States, the PM had been engaged continuously for twenty-two hours when BVR approached him, saying he urgently needed fifteen minutes of the PM's time. In a discussion that spanned forty-five minutes, the PM listened to BVR calmly and shared his views on how and why the scheme would need to be implemented. He said that every village had a collection of people without whom the village could not function optimally. They are the cobblers, blacksmiths, washer men, etc. who don't get covered under any scheme. He gave the example of Basvaya communities of Gujarat, a set of people from eighteen different professions whose name Basvaya literally means 'one who helps set up the village'. Asking for the scheme to be tailored for such communities, he gave all the directions to go about doing it. He said that State support was critical considering the context of technology and the possibility of large corporations over-running the role and utility of small artisans. Today, over 4,00,000 artisans have successfully registered under this scheme and are drawing the benefits.

This is the philosophy of Antyodaya in action and can only be enacted by a person with empathy. Antyodaya is the concern one shows to the person at the last mile and ensuring that the benefits of all development interventions reach them. To be fully aware of the needs of people around him and their contributions, accord recognition to the same, and connect with them emotionally and empathically is how his compassionate leadership expresses itself for public good. This empathy extends beyond policymaking; it is reflected in his interactions with people from all walks of life, resonating with their aspirations and struggles, thereby creating a unique emotional bond with the citizenry.

The personal qualities of a leader play a crucial role in shaping their leadership style and effectiveness. These qualities not only influence how leaders perceive and respond to challenges but also affect how a leader is perceived by their followers. The personal motto of the PM since his *karyakarta* (volunteer) days has been fourfold: '*pag mein chakkar* [be active, don't sit idle, and be fast in your actions]', '*jeebh mein shakkar* [always say good things, don't be bitter]', *sir pe barf* [work with a cool head]', '*aur dil mein haam* [and have courage in your heart]'.[19]

In alignment with this thinking, Harvard Business School professors Nitin Nohria and Paul Lawrence present a compelling exposition on the underpinnings of human behaviour in their seminal work *Driven: How Human Nature Shapes Our Choices*, particularly in the context of leadership. The authors describe how the brain evolved over time and how the four primary innate drives are hard-wired in the brains of all humans. They explain how these drives interact with human culture, emotions and skills, and how they shape the choices one makes. Their thesis posits that four cardinal drives are central to understanding and influencing human actions and decision-making processes, and how this plays out within the context of organizational life and leadership.

The first of these, the 'Drive to Acquire,' encompasses not merely the pursuit of material possessions but extends to the acquisition of status, power and influence. In an organizational leadership context, this drive is manifested in the aspiration for both personal and collective success. Leaders adept at engaging this drive effectively employ strategies that set ambitious organizational goals, recognize achievements and foster an ethos of continuous advancement. Such leaders adeptly utilize this drive as a catalyst for team motivation, thereby cultivating an environment where success and achievements are pursued and celebrated. Whether it is relief work after a natural disaster, the successful and timely establishment of a new Parliament building, the Bharat Mandapam[20] which was used to host the G20 summit of 2023, the completion of the Yashobhoomi[21] convention centre, or events like Vibrant Gujarat, the PM has been known—ever since his pracharak days—to set ambitious targets and stiff deadlines for his team, which lead to great accomplishments for the betterment of the nation.

In concert with this is the 'Drive to Bond,' which highlights the fundamental human need for establishing and nurturing social connections. Leadership that effectively responds to this drive focuses on building strong interpersonal relationships within the team, thereby fostering a sense of belonging and collaboration. Such leaders create a supportive and inclusive work environment, where team members are valued and a collective spirit is nurtured, enhancing team morale and loyalty. The PM's ability to connect with people across all levels aligns with this drive to bond, where the focus is on building meaningful relationships and fostering a community spirit.

The 'Drive to Learn' focuses on the pursuit of knowledge and personal growth and development. It highlights the existence of an innate human curiosity and a desire for self-improvement. Leaders who effectively harness this drive to learn engage their teams in work that is both meaningful and purposeful. They ensure that team members recognize the relevance of their roles and how these contribute to the larger organizational goals. By fostering an environment that encourages learning, intellectual growth and meaningful engagement, such leaders promote a culture of innovation and excellence. In the dynamic landscape of modern leadership, the capacity for constant learning and comprehension emerges as a cornerstone for effective leadership.

Vasu Patel, an overseas member of the RSS based in the United States, vividly recalls Prime Minister Narendra Modi's voracious appetite for knowledge. Reflecting on Modi's visits to the US in 1993, he remarked:

> Throughout our travels, whether on the metro, bus, or subway, Modi was constantly engrossed in reading. He had this remarkable habit of absorbing every piece of history he could find, even if it was just a snippet on a wall. His thirst for knowledge was evident; he sought to learn as much as possible, even during brief conversations or short visits.[22]

This insatiable curiosity extends to more contemporary discussions, as noted by Ajay Sood, the principal scientific adviser to the Prime Minister. He expresses admiration for Modi's relentless quest for understanding, highlighting discussions ranging from the National Research Foundation to quantum computing and green hydrogen. Modi's unyielding commitment to staying informed is a defining trait of his leadership.

In the dynamic and complex arena of global politics, the PM's leadership journey epitomizes the power and necessity of constant learning. Beginning as a regional political figure, Modi recognized, early on, the importance of staying informed and relevant in a rapidly evolving world. His leadership trajectory has been marked by a relentless pursuit of knowledge, ranging from understanding global economic trends to embracing technological advancements. This commitment to staying abreast of new developments has enabled him to craft policies and strategies that resonate not only within India but also on the global stage.

A significant facet of his leadership has been fostering a culture of innovation. His push for initiatives like Digital India showcases how his openness to new ideas and learning from global best practices has spurred technological and digital growth within the country. This approach reflects his belief in the power of innovation to drive national progress.

He also demonstrates how learning about diverse cultures and perspectives is vital for effective governance in a country as vast and varied as India. His policies and public addresses often reflect an understanding of and appreciation for India's diverse cultural tapestry, showcasing his empathy and inclusiveness.

Effective communication[1#] has been a hallmark of Modi's leadership style. His ability to articulate his vision and connect with a wide range of audiences, domestically and internationally, is a testament to his continuous learning and adapting to newer communication strategies. This skill has been crucial in rallying public support and conveying India's stance on various global platforms.

Adaptability and resilience[2#], fostered through continuous learning, have been evident in Modi's handling of challenges, whether they are economic reforms, environmental issues, the Kashmir issues or the Covid-19 pandemic. His ability to pivot strategies in response to changing circumstances reflects a leadership style that is dynamic and responsive.

Modi's enthusiasm for learning and self-improvement has served as an inspiration to many. His journey from humble beginnings to leading the world's largest democracy is a powerful narrative that motivates individuals to pursue knowledge and growth relentlessly.

In his role as a national and international leader, Modi's informed and knowledgeable approach has built credibility and trust. His expertise in various domains, from governance

---

[1#] Refer to chapter Artful Mastery: Communicating to Lead and Nurturing Human Connections.

[2#] Refer to the chapter Navigating Change: The Essence of Adaptive Leadership.

to international diplomacy, has earned him respect on both national and international fronts.

In an age defined by swift technological evolution, leaders such as Modi understand the critical need to remain pertinent. Their relentless quest for knowledge not only keeps them abreast of current trends but also shapes their decisions and strategies, ensuring they are both timely and future-oriented. This approach is pivotal in navigating the complexities of modern governance and maintaining effective leadership.

The fourth drive, the 'Drive to Defend' relates to the instinctual need for self-preservation and the protection of close affiliates. In leadership, this drive is translated into the creation of a secure and stable environment for the team. Leaders fulfilling this drive act as guardians, defending their team's interests and upholding organizational values. They provide security and stability, ensuring that the team operates within a safe and supportive environment.

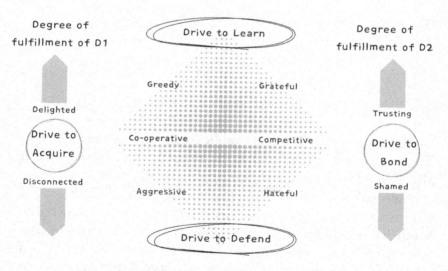

Derived emotions arrayed on a four-drive grid

(From *Driven: How Human Nature Shapes Our Choices*
by Nitin Nohria and Paul Lawrence)

Nohria and Lawrence's framework provides a nuanced understanding of the motivational forces that underpin leadership dynamics in organizations. There are very few leaders who can be mindful of these drivers and who can use them wisely and intentionally in the various contexts in which they operate. While the drive to learn seems to be the dominant one for Modi, he demonstrates a rare combination of all four drives that he thoughtfully puts together to express his leadership actions.

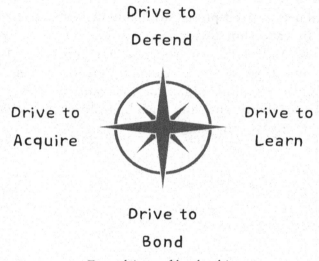

Four drives of leadership

Despite the overwhelming public approval ratings of over 75 per cent and global popularity that PM Modi enjoys, he is also vilified and criticized by sections of the media (domestic and global) and by his political rivals. Right from his chief minister days to his elevation as the Prime Minister of India, Modi has maintained an equanimous streak throughout and has consistently earned the trust and respect of the 1.4 billion citizens of the country. His forbearance stands as a hallmark of exemplary leadership, a quality that is crucial in navigating the intricate landscape of guiding others. It is patience, the strength of restraint and the wisdom of tolerance that he displays—all of which are essential attributes for any effective leader.

At the core of forbearance in leadership is the virtue of patience, especially in the face of adversity. Leaders invariably face challenges and setbacks, and it is their forbearance that enables them to remain composed. In the face of adversity, which is not uncommon in the complex landscape of Indian politics and governance, Modi has demonstrated a remarkable level of patience. His tenure has seen various challenging situations, from economic reforms to handling national crises. Through these, his ability to remain composed, avoiding impulsive reactions and, instead, opting for measured, strategic responses, speaks of his forbearance. Leading a nation as diverse as India requires an understanding of various perspectives and the ability to accommodate differing views.

The PM's leadership in this regard has often involved balancing multiple interests and making decisions that are aimed at the broader goal of national interest. He pursues *shreyas*—that which is beneficial in the long term, over *preyas*—that which might seem fleetingly pleasing but is deleterious in the long term. This principle is vividly reflected in initiatives such as the Pradhan Mantri Kisan Samman Nidhi (PM–KISAN) and the Pradhan Mantri Ujjwala Yojana (PMUY). PM–KISAN, for instance, not only provides immediate financial support to farming families for their agricultural and household needs but also lays the groundwork for a more sustainable financial environment that aims at doubling farmers' incomes over time, in concert with additional agricultural schemes. Likewise, PMUY is designed to deliver immediate benefits by offering subsidized cooking fuel, with the long-term objective of protecting the health of women and children from the hazards of smoke and pollution.

Furthermore, Modi's approach to mistakes and failures aligns with the qualities of a forbearing leader. Rather than a punitive approach, there is an emphasis on learning and improvement. This attitude fosters a culture where team members and administrative officials are encouraged to take initiative and innovate, knowing that errors in the pursuit of progress are part of the journey.

In the Vana Parva[23] of the Mahabharata, in a conversation between Bali[24] and his grandfather Prahalad[25], Bali asks if *teja* (energetic, or filled with vitality) is better, or *kshama* (forgiveness). Prahalad replies, neither. A wise man uses either of the traits depending on the circumstances. Constant forgiveness is a sign of weakness, whereby people lose respect of their friends, enemies and the public. Such a person would be ignored, a condition worse than death for honourable people. On the other hand, people who never forgive will be hated and shunned by all, being seen as a 'snake inside the house'. Prahalad elucidates that first offences—offences committed out of insufficient knowledge or error in judgement—must be forgiven after proper examination and depending on the gravity of the error. Offences done with full cognizance of ill consequences must be punished, as that is crookedness.[26]

Forbearance also manifests in managing provocations with unruffled composure. The realm of high office is fraught with high-pressure situations and provocations. Both, National Security Adviser Ajit Doval and Defence Minister Rajnath Singh talk of how Modi exhibited forbearance while handling scenarios like the 2017 Doklam crisis[27] or the 2016 surgical strikes[28] with a level head, preventing escalation and focusing on constructive resolution. The ability of leaders to remain calm in the storm is a beacon for their teams—it promotes a culture of stability and rationality.

The foundation of forbearance is laid with shraddha, which loosely translates to 'faith'. Faith in the Indian context does not refer to an ordinary, unquestioned belief which is familiar to the Western modes of thinking; it is rooted in *apta vakya*, trustworthy statements. Across generations, Indian sages and gurus, who devoted themselves to realizing the ultimate Truth, conveyed their wisdom in this way. Thus, their statements serve as the edifice for faith for anyone beginning on the path. More than a century ago, Swami Vivekananda said, 'Faith, faith, faith in ourselves, faith, faith in God—this is the secret of greatness'.

Another crucial definition of shraddha is faith in self, that is self-confidence. Without unwavering faith in oneself, accomplishing any task becomes difficult, irrespective of a person's talent. Swami Sarvapriyananda[29] of Ramakrishna Math[30] defines faith as having three constituents: self-efficacy, self-responsibility and self-direction.

Self-efficacy is the ability to be undaunted in the face of challenges and proceed with a 'let me try' attitude. The difference between failure and success is many times the difference between trying and abandoning. Many of the schemes brought about by the PM have been considered too ambitious and unrealistic (such as the Digital India campaign), yet their success proved the detractors wrong. As former US President John F. Kennedy said in his address announcing the lunar missions to the nation, 'We choose to go to the Moon in this decade and do the other things, not because they are easy, but because they are hard; because that goal will serve to organize and measure the best of our energies and skills, because that challenge is one that we are willing to accept, one we are unwilling to postpone, and one we intend to win . . . '[31]

Self-responsibility is the ability to take ownership for one's conditions in life. According to Swami Sarvapriyananda, the seven components of self-responsibility include taking responsibility for one's desires, quality of work, effective communication, expenditure of time, behaviour, values and state of happiness. Self-responsibility is a trait that requires a leader to not only acknowledge their role and duties but also to take ownership of their actions and their consequences, both positive and negative. Self-responsible leaders do not shy away from making tough decisions, nor do they blame others when challenges arise. Instead, they stand firm, learn from their experiences, and use these lessons to guide their team towards success.

Swami Sarvapriyananda goes on to say that the most important part of shraddha is to have self-direction and it is a pivotal attribute in the expression of leadership. It embodies an individual's capacity to set personal goals, make decisions and take initiative without the need for external guidance or pressure. Leaders who exhibit high levels of self-direction are often more adaptive, able to navigate through uncertainty and change with confidence and resilience. Self-direction is not just about steering one's own course; it's about illuminating the way for others, making it a cornerstone of effective leadership. Modi's diary entry from an early age showed his highest ideal: *sarve api sukhinah santu* [may the whole world be happy!] A tall calling, but one that his actions show he is relentlessly working towards.

Shraddha (faith)

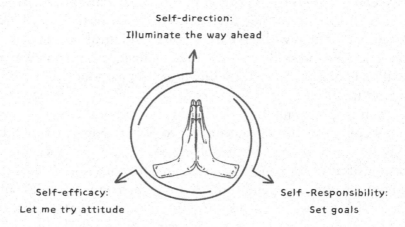

Self-direction:
Illuminate the way ahead

Self-efficacy:
Let me try attitude

Self -Responsibility:
Set goals

The transformative power of faith in leadership weaves through the very fabric of effective governance and organizational success, transcending beyond the realms of religious beliefs. It is this unwavering conviction in a set of principles, values or a vision that distinctly characterizes influential leaders. This faith, deeply ingrained in a leader's psyche, becomes a driving force that shapes not only their actions and decisions but also the collective spirit of their organization or community.

Leaders like Narendra Modi, imbued with a strong sense of faith in their vision, possess a unique ability to inspire others. This faith is not just their personal guiding light; it's an infectious force that resonates with people, providing them with a sense of purpose and direction. The leader's belief in their vision becomes a rallying call, galvanizing team members and stakeholders to commit to a shared goal. The energy and motivation derived from this faith are palpable, transforming the vision from an abstract concept into a tangible objective that people strive towards with enthusiasm.

This same faith instils a remarkable resilience in leaders, empowering them to withstand challenges and setbacks. When faith forms the foundation of their mission or values, leaders navigate turbulent times with a steadier hand. Moreover, a leader's steadfast faith in their values and principles cultivates trust and credibility. People naturally gravitate towards leaders who are consistent in their beliefs and who act in accordance with those beliefs. When team members trust their leader's convictions, they are more likely to follow them willingly and with confidence.

In decision-making, too, faith offers a guiding light. Leaders who possess a clear and unwavering belief in their principles find decision-making less daunting. Their faith provides a moral or ethical compass, guiding them towards choices that align with their core values and the broader mission of the organization.

Furthermore, faith naturally breeds optimism and a positive organizational culture. Leaders who exhibit a strong belief in their mission and values tend to create an environment imbued with hope and positivity. This optimistic outlook is a powerful driver that propels an organization forward, particularly during times of uncertainty or transformation.

PM Modi's leadership is infused with this kind of faith. His vision is inspired from Swami Vivekananda's vision of a future India which is happy and prosperous, a guru to the world. Modi's belief in the potential and capabilities of Indians stems from this vision. This is particularly evident in his vision for a 'New India', a narrative that encapsulates his aspirations for the nation's progress and prosperity. Under his leadership, this vision of hope has transcended into various initiatives aimed at economic growth, technological advancement, citizen engagement and social empowerment—instilling a renewed sense of optimism across the country.

Coupled with this sense of faith and hope is Modi's unwavering positive thinking. In his own words, he sees the glass neither as half full or half empty, but 'completely full always, filled in half with water and in half with air'.[32] His approach to leadership, especially in the face of adversity, highlights how a positive outlook can be transformative. Be it tackling economic challenges or steering the nation through the Covid-19 pandemic, Modi's focus on solutions and opportunities rather than problems exemplifies how positive thinking can effectively navigate a country through crises and uncertainties.

Positive thinking in leadership is more than just having an optimistic mindset; it's a powerful tool that shapes the entire spectrum of a leader's influence and effectiveness. It guides leaders like Modi to see opportunities where others see obstacles, to find potential in challenges, and to envision success even in the face of adversity. This mindset is not about ignoring difficulties or avoiding reality; rather, it's about approaching situations with a constructive attitude, focusing on solutions rather than dwelling on problems.

Leaders who embrace positive thinking set a tone of hopeful resilience. They instil a sense of possibility and confidence within their teams. Whether it is about becoming a five trillion-dollar economy, producing green hydrogen, putting a person on the moon, or ensuring a house for every Indian family, such ambitious targets seem much more attainable when they are inspirationally presented to the country by the PM. His ability to handle his charisma with humility and responsibility, coupled with the trust he enjoys from those around him, makes his positive thinking infectious. This attitude permeates throughout his teams, fostering an environment where challenges are viewed as opportunities for growth and learning.

Positive thinking in leadership also plays a crucial role in decision-making. Leaders with a positive mindset are often more open to different perspectives and ideas. They are willing to take calculated risks, understanding that growth often requires stepping out of comfort zones. This openness to new possibilities enables leaders to make decisions that are not only bold but also informed and balanced.

The impact of positive thinking extends to the way leaders handle setbacks and failures. Instead of being disheartened by failure, leaders who think positively view failures as valuable learning experiences. Whether it is the Chandrayaan–2 lunar mission[3#] or losing a cricket match, one can see how Modi can effortlessly analyse what went wrong, extract lessons, and move forward with a renewed sense of purpose. This approach not only helps in overcoming immediate setbacks but also builds long-term resilience within the team.

In times of change or uncertainty, the value of positive thinking becomes even more pronounced. Leaders like Narendra Modi who remain positive during such times act as beacons of stability and hope. His leading by example during the Covid times demonstrated how one can navigate through uncertainty with a calm and optimistic attitude. This not only helped maintain people's morale but also helped steer the country safely through the turbulent waters of change. Such leaders are not only able to stay positive, but their positiveness also spreads to those working closely with them. Bibek Debroy, the chairperson of the Prime Minister's Economic Advisory Council (PMEAC) mentions how he always leaves a meeting chaired by the PM feeling inspired, positive and filled with hope. People like Modi

---

[3#] Refer to Chapter **Leading with the Soul:** The Intersection of Leadership and Spiritual Growth.

are not just able to see the silver lining amidst the dark clouds, but also inspire their teams to work towards expanding this silver lining until the dark clouds are crowded out.

In exploring the landscape of modern leadership and positive thinking, the work of American professor and organizational behaviour expert Richard Boyatzis offers pivotal insights, particularly his concept of Positive Emotional Attractors (PEAs)—states of mind of people that are used to describe leaders like Modi. This idea forms the crux of Boyatzis's research on Intentional Change Theory[33] and Resonant Leadership[34], providing a nuanced understanding of how positive emotions and psychological states can profoundly influence leadership and organizational behaviour.

	Positive emotional attractor (PEA)	Negative emotional attractors (NEA)
Psychological	Greater sympathetic influence Release of oxytocin and vasopressin associated with social bonding Decreased blood pressure Higher heart rate variability	Greater sympathetic influence Release of epinephrine and norepinephrine to mobilize defenses: release of cortisol Increased pulse, blood pressure and rate of breathing Lower heart rate variability
Neurological	Default mode network (DMN) neurogenesis	Task positive network (TPN) Inhibited neurogenesis
Emotional	Positive affect: hope, joy, amusement, elation	Negative affect: defensiveness, guilt, shame, fear, anxiety
Cognitive	Enhanced working memory and perceptual openness	Decreased executive functioning; Limited field vision/perception
Relationship	Global attention Promotion focus Learning orientation Resonant (in tune with each other)	Local attention Prevention focus Performance orientation Dissonant (out of sync or distant)

Source : Boyatzis, R.E., Rochford, K., & Taylor, S.N.(2015)

Characteristics of positive and negative emotional attractors

(From R.E. Boyatzis, K. Rochford, and S.N. Taylor, 'The role of the positive emotional attractor in vision and shared vision: toward effective leadership, relationships and engagement', *Frontiers in Psychology*, 06, 2015, https://doi.org/10.3389/fpsyg.2015.00670)

At the heart of Boyatzis's theory lies the concept of PEAs, states that evoke positive emotions, inspire psychological openness, and are characterized by feelings of hope, optimism and the realm of possibilities. These PEAs are not just fleeting emotional experiences; they are crucial in motivating individuals towards meaningful change and personal development. Boyatzis's Intentional Change Theory posits that enduring change in individuals—be it leaders or employees—unfolds through a process that is initiated and sustained by these positive emotional experiences. It is through PEAs that individuals can envision a desirable future, engage with their strengths, and kindle intrinsic motivation for growth and change.

Moreover, Boyatzis's work illuminates how positive thinking facilitates effective learning and development. In this positive emotional state, individuals are more receptive to new ideas, more inclined to engage in experiential learning, and can harness their creative potential more fully. This contrasts sharply with the effects of Negative Emotional Attractors (NEAs), which often lead to defensiveness and a narrowing of perspective amongst such people and those they influence.

In the context of leadership, Boyatzis, along with his collaborators such as Annie McKee and Daniel Goleman, emphasizes Resonant Leadership, a style deeply intertwined with PEAs. Resonant leaders like Modi are those who create emotional connections and foster a positive environment, activating PEAs within their teams. This kind of leadership is not just about achieving short-term goals; it's about cultivating an atmosphere that promotes sustained growth, well-being and a sense of shared purpose. It is this kind of thinking that enables the PM to think big, make grand plans and strategize for the next twenty-five years of *Amrit Kaal*.

Boyatzis extends the application of PEAs to the sustainability of change and well-being in personal and organizational realms. PEAs are instrumental not only in initiating change but also in maintaining continuous development and preventing burnout. This balance is essential in the often high-stress environments of public office. Whether it is conducting *Chintan Shivirs* (togetherness events and strategic retreats) within the PMO and all ministries or driving his teams to explore process change through Kaizen[35], many such change initiatives are driven by PM Modi's PEA thinking.

Another defining aspect of PM Modi's leadership is his
fearlessness. The state of 'no fear' or *abhih*, finds reference in
the Rig Veda and the Upanishads[36] where it is often cited as a
quality attained through spiritual knowledge and realization.
The Taittiriya Upanishad speaks of *abhayam* (fearlessness) as
a supreme state that is achieved through spiritual knowledge.
Similarly, the Mundaka Upanishad mentions fearlessness as a
trait of those who have attained true knowledge. Fearlessness is
a profound attribute in the realm of leadership and is a quality
that goes beyond mere bravery; it signifies a deeper level of
courage that is interwoven with wisdom, foresight, and an
unwavering commitment to principles. In its core, abhih is not
just the absence of fear but the ability to confront, embrace and
transcend it. It's about leaders facing uncertainties, challenges
and potential threats not with trepidation but with a composed
and assured demeanour. This form of fearlessness stems from a
sense of security that comes from a deep-rooted confidence in
one's values and convictions. It's about being steadfast in the
face of adversity without being swayed by popular opinion or
temporary setbacks.

Leaders embodying abhih demonstrate an exceptional
ability to make difficult decisions. In moments where others
might falter under pressure, these leaders stand resolute. This
decisiveness, born out of fearlessness, often requires making
tough choices for the greater good, sometimes even at the
cost of personal loss or unpopularity. Time and again, Modi
has demonstrated a readiness to take bold and risky decisions,
often in the face of significant opposition or criticism. From
politically courageous economic reforms like the Goods and
Services Tax (GST) and Demonetization, significant policy
shifts like the abrogation of the Constitution's Article 370 to
revoke the special status previously accorded to Jammu and
Kashmir,[4#] and withdrawal of the Farm Laws, to personally

[4#] Refer to the chapter Navigating Change: The Essence of Adaptive
Leadership.

courageous decisions such as risking his life to unfurl the Indian national flag in Kashmir disregarding terrorists' diktat, Modi's public life has been characterized by decisions that reflect a blend of courage and conviction. His fearlessness, particularly in decision-making, underscores a leadership style that is not afraid to take risks in pursuit of what he believes is the nation's best interest.

A fearless leader serves as a pillar of strength for their team, particularly in times of crisis or change. Their unshaken confidence and calm in the face of daunting challenges can be a powerful motivator for their team members, encouraging them to approach their own tasks and responsibilities without fear or hesitation.

Abhih in leadership is also closely linked with integrity (as was discussed earlier). Fearless leaders are often those who stand firm for ethical and moral principles, even when it is inconvenient or risky to do so. Their fearlessness is not just in facing external challenges but also in upholding their inner values, making them exemplary role models. In the face of opposition or criticism, a leader's abhih is particularly tested. It's in these moments that such leaders display their true mettle, maintaining their course and staying true to their vision, undeterred by the noise and distractions around them.

Prime Minister Narendra Modi's leadership style is a complex blend of various personal characteristics, each contributing distinctively to his unique approach to governance. His mix of integrity, faith, optimism, courage, empathy and compassion shapes his leadership, significantly influencing India's growth and progress. These traits form the basis of his disciplined service mindset, one that is not swayed by the allure of power, is focused on action without attachment to outcomes, and is always ready for serving selflessly or stepping aside when needed.

In the Indian perspective, as demonstrated by Modi's life, these attributes are replicable and originate from a belief in an unchanging, eternal essence—a fundamental Truth which

underlies ever-changing reality. For aspiring leaders or spiritual
seekers, the key is to serve and be guided by this mantra from
the Brihadaranyaka Upanishad[37]:

asato maa sad gamaya,
tamaso maa jyotir gamaya,
mrityor maa amritam gamaya (1.3.28)

Lead me from the untruth to truth,
from the darkness of ignorance to the light of knowledge,
and from death to immortality.

Modi's approach and philosophy align with Adi
Shankaracharya's[38] teaching in verse 11 of his timeless poem
'Bhaja Govindam', which warns against pride in wealth, youth
or power, as time swiftly takes them away. It encourages
a detachment from the illusory world and the pursuit of the
eternal truth.

maa kuru dhana jana yauvana garvam
harati nimeshhaat kaalah sarvam
maayaamayamidamakhilam budhdhva
brahma padam tvam pravisha viditvaa

Do not be arrogant about your wealth, fame, or power,
for time will snatch all in the blink of an eye.
Free yourself from the illusion of the world of
Maya (illusory nature)
and attain the timeless Truth (state of Brahman).[39]

These qualities have not only defined Prime Minister Modi's
tenure, but they also promise to shape his enduring legacy in
India's political history.

यदा संहरते चायं कूर्मोऽङ्गानीव सर्वशः ।
इन्द्रियाणीन्द्रियार्थेभ्यस्तस्य प्रज्ञा प्रतिष्ठिता ॥

yadā saṃharate cāyaṃ kūrmo'ṅgānīva sarvaśaḥ |
indriyāṇīndriyārthebhyastasya prajñā pratiṣṭhitā ||
—Bhagavad Gita 2.58

One who can withdraw the senses from their objects, just as a tortoise
withdraws its limbs into its shell, is established in divine wisdom.

~

The spiritual and temporal realms are often considered being opposite to each other. However, performance of duty with a sense of detachment can help a person progress on the spiritual path as well. Narendra Modi's leadership journey is marked by an unwavering commitment to serving the nation, demonstrating resilience and maintaining equanimity in the face of both triumphs and challenges. Modi's practices of yoga, meditation, and his adherence to spiritual teachings like those in the Bhagavad Gita have shaped his approach to governance, emphasizing the importance of selfless service, integrity and compassion. Through his actions, Modi exemplifies a *karmayogi*, leading with a sense of higher purpose and inspiring a vision that seeks to uplift the lives of millions, emphasizing the interconnectedness of all beings and the importance of acting without attachment to outcomes. This unique blend of spirituality and leadership not only defines his tenure, but also offers a model for enlightened leadership in the modern world.

~

Leading with the Soul:
The Intersection of Leadership and Spiritual Growth

On the evening of 23 August 2023, at approximately 6 p.m., all eyes across India were fixed on their television screens, anticipating the lunar lander Vikram's historic descent on to the South Pole of the moon. Previous attempts, including India's Chandrayaan–2 mission[1], had fallen short of achieving a soft landing in this challenging location. There was no guarantee of a successful landing this time, and a failure could have drawn ridicule from critics, both in India and overseas. However, Vikram executed a flawless landing, igniting widespread joy and celebration throughout the nation. The dedicated scientists at the Indian Space Research Organisation (ISRO) were jubilant, and Prime Minister Modi—who was witnessing the event live from Johannesburg, South Africa, while attending the BRICS summit—conveyed his warmest wishes and congratulations.

After a brief stop in Athens, Greece, the Prime Minister promptly headed to Bengaluru—the headquarters of ISRO—and with unwavering pride, he proclaimed, 'India is on the Moon, we have our national pride placed on the Moon . . . This is today's India—fearless and relentless. This is an India that thinks innovatively and explores the uncharted territories to illuminate the world. This India will pioneer solutions to the most pressing global challenges of the 21st century'.[2]

It was only a few years earlier, in September 2019, that the Prime Minister had flown down to ISRO to watch the Chandrayaan–2 landing fail, leaving the then Chairperson K. Sivan and his colleagues in tears, visibly despondent. But the Prime Minister was not willing to see this as a failure. For him, such attempts were precursors for future success. The PM shifted the narrative of success from just a successful soft landing of Vikram to an endless pursuit of science requiring lifelong experimentation. The PM showed great maturity, spontaneity, wisdom and leadership. He wonderfully articulated how the mission was about learning and therefore the concept of success or failure was limited to whether one learns from the situation or not.[3]

The Prime Minister had then said:

'Resilience and tenacity are central to India's ethos. In our glorious history, we have faced moments that may have slowed us, but they have never crushed our spirit. We have bounced back again and gone on to do spectacular things. This is why our civilization stands tall.' 'As important as the final result, is the journey and the effort. I can proudly say that the effort was worth it and so was the journey. Our team worked hard—travelled far, and those teachings will always remain with us. The learnings from today will make us stronger and better.[4]

During both landings—'success' or 'failure'—what stands out is the conviction of beliefs and equanimity displayed by the Prime Minister. To remain unaffected by the outcome of either Chandrayaan–2 or Chandrayaan–3 is the spirit of equanimity that those working closely with Modi repeatedly mention.

This quality of equanimity is best described in verse 48 of Chapter 2 in the Bhagavad Gita[5]:

yoga-sthah kuru karmani sangam tyaktva dhananjaya
siddhy-asiddhyoh samo bhutva samatvam yoga uchyate

Perform your duty equipoised, O Arjuna,
abandoning all attachment to success or failure.
Such equanimity is called yoga.

In this chapter, Lord Krishna[6] imparts the message of
maintaining inner calmness and balance amidst life's challenges
and dualities. He advises Arjuna to perform his duties without
attachment to the results, and to treat joy and sorrow, gain
and loss, success and failure, all with equanimity. This teaching
encourages a state of emotional equilibrium and spiritual
harmony for individuals to navigate life's ups and downs with
grace and wisdom. *Samatvam* refers to this evenness of mind—
the state of maintaining mental balance and stability in the
face of various life situations, pleasant or challenging. Lord
Krishna teaches that one should approach success and failure,
pleasure and pain, with the same level-headedness, without
allowing one's emotions to be swayed excessively by external
circumstances.

This state of equanimity is widely considered a crucial
component of spiritual growth and it can be achieved only
when a person is able to take an unbiased helicopter view of
a situation, their role, and the actions required in a specific
moment of time. Learning to remain unaffected by emotions,
mindfully separating from them, and acting with poise and
balance is an expression of leadership that finds description
both in psychology and in spiritual traditions.

Viktor Frankl, an Austrian neurologist, psychiatrist and
Holocaust survivor, is renowned for developing logotherapy, a
psychotherapeutic approach to wellness centred on discovering
meaning in life. His significant contribution is often associated

with the concept known as 'the space between stimulus and response'.

In his influential work, *Man's Search for Meaning*, Frankl elucidates how individuals possess the agency to select their responses to external stimuli, even in the most daunting and dire situations. He posits that between the stimulus (external event) and our reaction, there exists a gap or space. Within this space lies our liberty to choose our response. This capacity to determine our attitude and response to any given circumstance constitutes a fundamental aspect of human freedom and dignity. This principle lies at the heart of logotherapy.

By acknowledging the space between stimulus and response, individuals can exercise their capacity for self-awareness and conscious choice, ultimately discovering meaning and purpose even amid adversity and suffering. From a leadership perspective, Frankl's teachings advocate for individuals to pause and reflect before reacting impulsively. By doing so, they can make more deliberate and profound choices in response to circumstances.

This practice takes years of disciplined effort and is similar to what the Indian saint Ramana Maharshi[7] has aptly called 'witness consciousness'. Witness consciousness is the state of being an impartial observer or witness to one's own thoughts, emotions and experiences. It requires one to be objective and non-judgemental. It comes from the recognition that there is a deeper, unchanging awareness that underlies the ever-changing stream of thoughts and sensations. By cultivating this state of witness consciousness, individuals can disidentify from the transient phenomena of the mind and ego and come to realize their true nature beyond the limitations of the physical body and the egoic self. This practice of witness consciousness is considered a powerful tool for attaining self-realization and experiencing a state of inner peace and transcendence, which also makes it invaluable in the exercise of identifying and using the 'space' that Viktor Frankl talks about, and ultimately, in the practice of Enlightened Leadership.

Witness Consciousness

impartial observer, witness
to one's own experiences

being objective and
non-judgemental

Such persons who have attained the state of unwavering consciousness are described as *stitha-prajna* in the Bhagavad Gita. Lord Krishna explains that such an individual is free from attachment and desires, remains unperturbed by external circumstances and perceives the divine presence in all beings. He further elucidates that the nature of self-realization is rooted in disciplined practice, detachment and devotion. He teaches that through this self-awareness, one can attain a state of equipoise and, in the process, experience the supreme bliss of union with the divine.

Sri Sri Ravishankar[8], a spiritual leader in India, describes how Narendra Modi embodies this spiritual evolution through his leadership actions. Whether it is the expression of the power of discernment or of detachment, he highlights Modi's single-minded focus on India's development, while also keeping the larger global interests in mind. This is a determined approach that was most evident even when a personal tragedy struck the Prime Minister. Narendra Modi was very close to his mother

Hiraben Modi, and he made it a point to visit her every year on his birthday and seek her blessings. On 30 December 2022, after a short stay in the hospital, his mother passed away at ninety-nine. Heartbroken but steady, the PM performed the last rites[9] of his mother as condolences kept pouring in from all quarters. After cremating her mortal remains, the PM resumed his work, much to the surprise of those unacquainted with his work ethic. 'PM Narendra Modi will join scheduled programmes in West Bengal via video conferencing,' the PM's office tweeted. This was perceived as a message to the party colleagues to carry on with their work and not allow the PM's personal tragedy to come in the way of their public duties.

In his tribute to his mother, one can glean hints of PM Modi's apparently strange behaviour towards the most cherished person in his life: 'A glorious century rests at the feet of God . . . In Maa [mother] I have always felt that trinity[10], which contains the journey of an ascetic, the symbol of a selfless karmayogi and a life committed to values'.[11]

The Indian world view has always regarded seva, or selfless service, as the highest virtue in a leader. Service towards others even at the expense of personal convenience has been exalted as the pathway for self-unfoldment and self-transcendence, the most vociferous proponent of which, in modern times, was Swami Vivekananda. He declared that in a country such as India where the population is materially famished, it would serve no good to aim for personal liberation alone. Rather, spiritual enlightenment must be attained in the service of others, through the path of *karmayoga*.[12]

Describing the PM's work ethic, his ability to learn from all situations, his deep sense of duty and a non-attachment to the power of his office, Minister of Finance Nirmala Sitharaman recollects the section from the Mahabharata, popularly known as the Vyadha Gita[13], to describe her observations of him.

The Vyadha Gita tells the story of a young renunciate who, after years of austerities alone in the forest, develops supernatural powers. One day, he goes into town to beg for alms and is asked to wait by a woman at whose house he had approached. Filled with conceit, he imagines cursing her for the delay. However, the woman reads his mind and chides him for such thoughts. Amazed, the monk asks how she could read his thoughts, to which the woman responds that she is not aware of any such power; all she does is dedicatedly serve her husband. She then directs him to a *vyadha* (butcher), who can explain the mysteries of life to him.

The monk goes as asked and is horrified to find the man cleaving and cutting meat. But the butcher too reads his mind and asks him to wait. A little later, when the monk asks him about the source of his powers, the butcher replies that he simply does his duty towards his parents and society dedicatedly, and that he remains unattached to his job or station in life. He tells the monk, 'I neither know your yoga, nor have I become a *sannyasi* (renunciate), nor did I go out of the world into a forest; nevertheless, all that you have heard and seen has come to me through the unattached doing of the duty which belongs to my position'.[14]

While this sense of duty and detachment is easy to appreciate as an essential for the exercise of enlightened leadership, it takes a lot of mindful effort and discipline to live it daily. Eknath Easwaran[15] discusses the opportunities and challenges that one faces in doing this.[16] He views the control of the mind as one of the key steps in the entire spiritual journey. He mentions how sensuality, ill will towards others, anger, laziness and restlessness can come in the way of one's inner progress. Sensuality in the Buddhist tradition is not about moral judgement. It refers to the human tendency to become entangled in the impressions of one's senses and to become attached to what brings sensory pleasure or pain, removing one's real freedom of choice. Ill will is not just about negative thoughts and feelings about others. It is also about blaming others when things go wrong, judging others and carrying resentment in the mind about those whom one dislikes. Restlessness arises out of the inability to keep the mind still. It takes away focus and scatters one's attention all over the place. It can mean different things, including a lack of focus, boredom, worrying over consequences of one's actions, and the inability to be at peace with oneself.

By immersing oneself fully in the present task and avoiding internal and external distractions, individuals can enter the state aptly described by Mihaly Csikszentmihalyi as a state of 'flow'.[17] This concept explores the pinnacle of human experience achieved through complete absorption and deep focus. In this state, action seamlessly merges with awareness, creating a sense of timelessness and heightened performance. Csikszentmihalyi outlines key conditions for experiencing flow, including defined goals, immediate feedback and a balance of challenge and skill.

In Hindu philosophy, the concept of *shuddha sankalpa*, or purity of intention, stands as a critical prerequisite for such profound experiences of deep focus and awareness. Shuddha sankalpa signifies a resolute, unwavering and lucid dedication to a specific goal or objective. Embracing shuddha sankalpa aids in honing the mind's focus and harmonizing one's actions with a higher purpose. For Prime Minister Modi, it embodies a pledge to purity, sincerity and wholehearted dedication to his chosen path of national service.

One of the critical emotions that people in high places who work under constant pressure need to watch out for is anger and its different manifestations, which comes in the way of this experience of 'oneness'. Hardik Shah, the private secretary to the Prime Minister, narrates how he has never seen the PM express anger or irritation towards anyone. Another close associate, Hasmukh Adhia—who has also served as Modi's Principal Secretary when he was the Chief Minister of Gujarat—recounts how in all the time that he has known the PM, he has never seen Modiji lose his temper despite the gravest provocation.

Once when queen Draupadi asked king Yudhisthira about his non-anger even during adverse turn of events, the king replied, 'A person who does not get angry even in the face of angry people, saves not only himself but others as well from great fear. He becomes a healer to both himself and others, in removing people's faults. Be one weak or strong, during the time of hardships, one must always find refuge in kindness and mercy. The sages are of the unanimous opinion that a kind, forgiving person is always victorious'.[18]

Anger stands as a prominent source of human suffering. Actions fuelled by anger not only lack rationality and proportionality but, upon reflection, often leave the doer burdened with regret and susceptible to various other negative consequences. In the Bhagavad Gita, Arjuna asks Krishna why individuals are compelled to commit wrongful acts, even unwillingly, as if by force. Krishna elucidates that it is desire, or *kama*, that drives individuals to actions they would otherwise avoid with clear judgement. Unfulfilled desires, born from passionate attachment to worldly objects, give rise to anger. This anger is a destructive adversary, consuming all in its path, and it is one of the three gates leading to *naraka* (hell, symbolizing torment and suffering), the other two being *kama* and *lobha* (greed).

The Gita prescribes self-discipline, mindfulness and detachment from worldly pursuits as remedies to overcome anger. It emphasizes the importance of finding inner peace and maintaining equanimity even in challenging situations, with the assertion that managing emotions, including anger, is vital for spiritual growth and self-realization. In the Bhagavad Gita, Lord Krishna advises Arjuna to recognize the signs of anger within himself as an initial step towards addressing it. In this, he emphasizes the value of mastering one's emotions, including anger, by refraining from impulsive reactions. This, Krishna suggests, can be achieved by cultivating a sense of detachment from the outcomes of one's actions. By not becoming overly attached to specific results, one can reduce the likelihood that they might succumb to anger when circumstances don't align with expectations.

Continuing his counsel to Arjuna, Krishna promotes forgiveness and compassion towards others, even when provoked. He imparts the wisdom that harbouring resentment and anger harms the individual more than the target of the anger. Krishna elucidates how engaging in practices like yoga and meditation can calm the mind, alleviate stress and nurture inner peace. This, in turn, facilitates self-awareness and the practice of self-control. In the words of modern-day sage Aurobindo[19], 'Not to be disturbed by either joy or grief, pleasure or displeasure, by what people say or do, or by any outward things, is called in yoga a state of *samata*—equality to all things. It is of immense importance in sadhana to be able to reach this state'.[20]

Daniel Goleman, the renowned American psychologist and author, is widely recognized for his extensive research on emotional intelligence and its profound impact on personal and professional success. His seminal book, *Emotional Intelligence: Why It Can Matter More Than IQ*, delves into the critical role that emotions, self-awareness and self-control play in our lives. Goleman echoes the wisdom found in the Bhagavad Gita, stressing the significance of recognizing and effectively managing emotions—particularly anger—in our daily interactions. He describes emotional intelligence as the ability to comprehend and govern one's own emotions while empathizing with others and contends that it stands as a pivotal determinant of personal and professional triumph. Goleman's body of work underscores the imperative of being attuned to anger and skilled in navigating it, as an integral facet of emotional intelligence. He strongly emphasises self-regulation, which encompasses the capacity to manage impulses, navigate distressing emotions, and effectively adapt to shifting circumstances. Meditation and yoga stand as powerful instruments in the journey towards achieving and maintaining an enhanced level of self-awareness and self-regulation. These ancient practices offer a pathway to deeply connect with one's inner self, fostering a profound understanding of one's thoughts, emotions and reactions.

Prime Minister Modi isn't just a vocal proponent of yoga; he's been a dedicated practitioner for several years. Amidst his bustling daily schedule, he ensures to incorporate yoga, *dhyana* and *pranayama* into his routine. While yoga has gained global popularity, it's often misunderstood as mere physical exercises for fitness. The true essence of yoga is expounded in the Yoga Sutras attributed to the sage Patanjali and is considered a foundational text of classical yoga philosophy. These sutras (principles) present a comprehensive framework for achieving mental and spiritual well-being. Though not explicitly focused on psychology, they provide profound insights into emotional well-being, the mind and consciousness.

Sutra 1.2, *Chitta Vritti Nirodha*, encapsulates the core of the entire text, elucidating how yoga involves calming the fluctuations of the mind. It suggests that by achieving stillness of the mind, one can attain inner peace and tranquillity. In Sutras 1.12–1.16, Patanjali underscores the significance of *abhyasa* (practice) and vairagya (renunciation) in attaining mental equilibrium. Through regular practice and the relinquishment of attachment to external outcomes, one can diminish the impact of emotional oscillations. Patanjali identifies five root causes of suffering or *kleshas*: ignorance, egotism, attachment, aversion and clinging to life. By recognizing and addressing these underlying sources of emotional turmoil, individuals can work towards enhanced emotional well-being.

In what is commonly known as Ashtanga Yoga, Patanjali delineates the eight limbs of yoga: *yama* (ethical principles and restraints), *niyama* (observances or practices), *asanas* (physical postures), pranayama (breath control), *pratyahara* (withdrawal of the senses), *dharana* (intense concentration), dhyana (meditation) and samadhi (enlightenment, state of bliss). The combination of these practices is intended to purify the mind and nurture qualities such as compassion, contentment and self-discipline, all of which contribute to emotionally balanced leadership. Individuals who diligently incorporate these practices into their daily routines, begin to exhibit heightened emotional intelligence, empathy, self-mastery, resilience, presence in the moment and sensory restraint. Their leadership style and decision-making would reflect a profound understanding of broader contexts and an intentional connection with various stakeholders. Incidents like the one described earlier at ISRO and the personal experience of several senior public leaders associated with the PM are a testimony to this.

Ashtanga Yoga

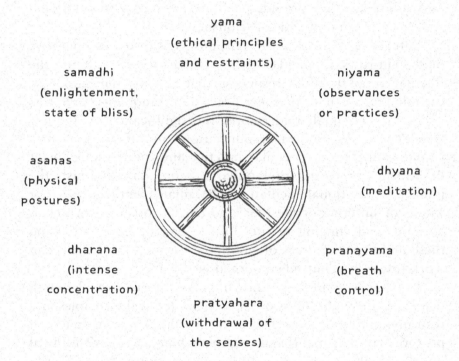

yama
(ethical principles
and restraints)

samadhi
(enlightenment,
state of bliss)

niyama
(observances
or practices)

asanas
(physical
postures)

dhyana
(meditation)

dharana
(intense
concentration)

pranayama
(breath
control)

pratyahara
(withdrawal of
the senses)

The neuroscience of leadership is an emerging field that delves into how the brain functions within leadership roles, and how leaders can leverage neuroscience findings to heighten their effectiveness. The limbic system, a pivotal component of the brain, plays a central role in processing emotions. Leaders who adeptly navigate their own emotions and demonstrate empathy towards others tend to excel in their roles. In addition to emotional intelligence, a leader's capacity for social cognition—comprehending the thoughts, feelings and intentions of others—is now regarded as indispensable for effective leadership. Leaders who accurately discern and respond to the social dynamics within their teams are better positioned to make sound decisions and cultivate robust relationships.

Moreover, reflective thinking, sustained curiosity and a commitment to lifelong learning constitute pivotal facets of effective leadership. The brain's neuroplasticity allows for reorganization and adaptation, emphasizing the significance of continuous growth and development. Leaders who are able to leverage this neuroplasticity are able to acquire fresh skills and quickly adapt to evolving environments.

Neuroscientific research has also unveiled the detrimental effects of chronic stress on the brain. Astute leaders can apply stress management techniques like mindfulness and meditation, to preserve cognitive function and decision-making prowess, particularly in high-pressure situations. The prefrontal cortex, recognized as the hub for executive functions and decision-making, is notably affected by stress and unregulated limbic system activity, leading to a decline in decision-making effectiveness.

Integrating insights from neuroscience into leadership practices empowers leaders to make more informed decisions, foster stronger relationships and cultivate healthier work environments. It underscores the notion that leadership transcends mere authority, and instead, entails deep comprehension and positive influencing of the human brain and its behaviour.

The Dalai Lama's profound interest in neuroscience has spurred his active involvement in various experiments related to prefrontal cortex development. Through collaborative efforts with scientists and researchers, several studies have been conducted on meditation and its effects on the brain.

One particularly noteworthy experiment[21] involved seasoned Tibetan Buddhist monks, known for their extensive meditation practices. The study closely examined shifts in their brain activity, with a special focus on the prefrontal cortex. This region of the brain governs attention, concentration and emotional regulation. The findings indicated that consistent meditation practice had the potential to induce alterations in brain function, leading to heightened activity in the prefrontal cortex. This area is not only associated with executive decision-making but also with qualities like empathy, compassion and emotional well-being. Additionally, experiments unveiled the presence of qualities such as determination, detachment and discernment in these monks. While these attributes signify spiritual growth, they are also crucial for effective leadership expression.

Teresa de Cepeda y Ahumada[22], later to become loved in the Christian world as Saint Teresa of Jesus, wrote in her autobiography that the vital quality for spiritual growth is *determinacion*—determination, decision and will. 'Those who have this determination,' she declares, 'have nothing to fear.' Determination and spirituality complement each other in powerful ways. Spirituality often involves a deep sense of purpose, meaning and connection to something greater than oneself. This can provide a strong foundation for determination, as it offers a sense of direction and inner strength.

The intent of PM Modi to make India a global power, to ensure that every Indian's life is socially and economically included, and his ability to stay determined and unaffected by distracting criticisms, reflects his deep spiritual evolution. When someone is spiritually determined, they draw upon their beliefs and values to fuel their resolve in pursuing their goals. This can lead to a greater sense of purpose and a willingness to overcome obstacles with a sense of calm and resilience. Moreover, spirituality can provide a source of comfort and perspective during difficult times, which can be crucial in maintaining determination in the face of adversity. It can also foster a sense of interconnectedness with others and the world, which can inspire a desire to make a positive impact.

According to his Cabinet colleague and the home minister of India, Amit Shah, 'Narendra Modi is among those leaders who work relentlessly and determinedly. I have known him for many years. Since the last thirty years, he has not taken a single vacation or leave even for a day, and he works over eleven hours a day.' The PM's hard work, focus and discipline demonstrate his dedication to making his vision a concrete reality—that of making India a leading country in the changing world.

Besides his resolute determination, Prime Minister Modi also exemplifies a profound sense of detachment and dispassion. This was evident in the passage and subsequent withdrawal of the Farm Laws. On 20 September 2020, the Farm Laws were passed by the Upper House of the Parliament amid vigorous opposition. The bill encountered significant opposition from the opposing parties before it was ultimately passed by Parliament.

Recognizing that a significant portion of India's population relies on the agrarian economy, PM Modi was keenly aware of the need for substantive reforms in this sector. Drawing from his experiences as an RSS pracharak, he witnessed first-hand the deep-rooted influence of traders and middlemen in the agricultural system, resulting in the systemic exploitation of farmers. His aim was to liberate farmers from vested interests and implement changes that could revolutionize India's agricultural landscape, ensuring fair compensation for their hard work. He was deeply committed to doubling the farmers' income in the shortest period of time, and doing everything possible to improve the agricultural sector has been one of the key focuses of his administration.

Despite the Farm Laws' intent to benefit farmers with small and marginal landholdings, two major concerns arose among them. First, the apprehension that the new laws might undermine the Minimum Support Price (MSP)[23] and the *mandi* system.[24] Second, the fear that corporate entities would dominate and set terms that could lead to the exploitation of farmers.

During his *Mann Ki Baat* on 29 November 2020, the PM expressed his unwavering commitment to the laws and their potential impact, stating, 'The agricultural reforms in the past few days have also now opened new doors of possibilities for our farmers . . . These reforms have not only served to unshackle our farmers but also given them new rights and opportunities'.[25]

But this was not to be as the farmers embarked on a year-long protest, primarily in the Delhi–Punjab–Haryana region. They rejected the government's proposal to amend the laws and vowed to escalate their protest until the laws were entirely revoked. Despite numerous rounds of talks and Supreme Court intervention, a concrete resolution remained elusive. As the protests escalated, with road blockades causing significant disruptions to the economy and concerns of national security, on 19 November 2021, the Prime Minister announced the repeal of the Farm Laws.

In his address to the nation, he humbly acknowledged:

Today, on the eve of Guru Nanak's Prakash Parv[26], while apologizing to the countrymen, I want to say with a sincere and pure heart that perhaps there must have been some deficiency in our efforts, due to which we could not explain the truth like the light of the lamp to some farmers.[27]

Throughout this tumultuous period, the PM is said to have maintained remarkable composure, refraining from casting blame or losing patience. While he remained steadfast in his conviction regarding the laws and the ambition to double farmers' incomes, he also stayed detached from the political ramifications of their withdrawal. His foremost concern was to earn the farmers' trust and safeguard the nation's integrity and security. Colleagues marvelled at his equanimity, observing how he continued to discharge his responsibilities with unwavering focus while keeping his ego under control.

Spiritual teacher and founder of California's Blue Mountain Centre of Meditation Eknath Easwaran has discussed how a person on the spiritual path and beyond the pull of the outer world can experience a closing down of the senses where all identification with the body, senses, mind and ego dissolve. While living with a dissolved ego may sound like the road to oblivion, in practice, it emerges as the road to love, vitality and as an overflowing, ever-present sense of joy.[28]

The PM's withdrawal of the Farm Laws also reflects his ability to let go of all personal demands on life. Only when people can renounce desires for personal pleasures and profit, does their suffering alleviate. When one is detached and able to let go of actions with a selfish intent, they inherit the enormous power embedded in the depths of the unconscious mind, as well as the trust and respect of the people around them.

In the Bhagavad Gita, Lord Krishna advises Arjuna to act selflessly, without being overly concerned about success or failure. By doing so, an individual can maintain equanimity in the face of challenges and remain undisturbed by external circumstances. This state of non-attachment, or *asangatvam*, allows for a deeper connection to one's true self and the ultimate reality. In essence, asangatvam in the Bhagavad Gita encourages individuals to perform their duties with dedication and sincerity, while staying detached from the fruits of their actions. This forms the basis of karma yoga.

Detachment in leadership is not about being emotionally disconnected or insulated from the emotions of others. It refers to the ability to maintain a level-headed and objective perspective, even in emotionally charged or challenging situations. It involves a leader's capacity to separate personal emotions from decision-making and to remain focused on the greater good. A leader who practices detachment can make rational, unbiased decisions that are based on facts and the best

interests of the team, organization or country. This quality can
be particularly valuable in crisis management or in situations
where tough decisions need to be made. A good leader knows
when to show empathy and connect with their team while still
maintaining a level of objectivity.

As one can see from the Farm Laws incident, detachment
in leadership is about finding a middle ground where a leader
can make clear-headed decisions while still being attuned to the
emotional needs of others. Practicing detachment in everyday
scenarios is not easy. Relationships today—whether personal,
professional or political—are often transactional and driven
by selfish considerations. Understanding and connecting to
the larger purpose of life is a critical driver of leadership, and
it is usually crowded out in the narrow demands that one's
ego makes of a person. Only a spiritually detached person
can appreciate what Swami Vivekananda said about being
'detached while being attached' and 'attached while being
detached'. A person detached from the demands of one's own
personal ego also learns to be unconditionally loving and giving
of oneself with no expectation, of any kind, in return. They
feel liberated performing their daily actions and operate with
the total sense of freedom. In the words of the Buddha, it is
such people who can draw up from within, the deep creative
resources required for the work on hand. It is such people who
can truly love everyone and perform their duty with clarity of
purpose and purity of focus.

It is also important to note that action at this level requires
the quality of discernment, which is aptly captured by Eknath
Easwaran as being pure detached love in action. Adi Shankara,
the great Advaita philosopher-saint of India, describes the
ability to discern the real from the unreal in his philosophical
treatise, *Vivekachudamani*. He discusses the importance of
viveka (discernment) for the spiritual aspirant. In the spiritual
context, discernment refers to the ability to distinguish between
the eternal and the transient, the real and the unreal. The text
emphasizes the importance of discerning the Brahman (ultimate
reality) from the *maya* (illusory nature). It teaches that true

wisdom lies in recognizing the impermanence and limited nature of worldly pursuits, and in seeking a deeper understanding of the eternal truth that underlies all of existence.

The sense of discernment, as emphasized in texts like the Vivekachudamani, can significantly enhance the practice of leadership in several ways. Discernment, in this sense, allows a leader to see beyond surface-level issues and recognize the deeper underlying truths. This clarity allows for a more focused and purposeful approach to leadership. It enables a leader to discern the values and principles that are truly important for decision-making and identify choices that are ethical and moral. By discerning between short-term gains and long-term achievements, a leader can make more informed decisions that lead to sustained success and growth. This ability to recognize what is truly important provides a leader with the resilience necessary to manage adverse circumstances. Discernment helps a leader distinguish between temporary setbacks and enduring challenges. It enables them to stay composed and navigate through difficult times. The ability to discern, coupled with an observer's view, enables a leader to consider multiple viewpoints and make well-informed choices that benefit the entire team, organization or country.

Leaders with a keen sense of discernment are less likely to be swayed by external pressures or personal interests. They are more likely to lead with authenticity and maintain integrity. A discerning leader can recognize the unique strengths and potential in team members, delegate effectively and empower individuals to contribute their best. Discernment helps leaders recognize changing circumstances and adapt accordingly. This agility is crucial for a leader's ability to stay relevant and effective in dynamic environments. With clear focus on the big picture, discernment can also help a leader transcend personal ego and prioritize the collective good, fostering a selfless approach to leadership. When team members see a leader making discerning decisions based on a clear understanding of what truly matters, it fosters trust and confidence. Trust is the foundation of strong relationships between leaders and their team members. It fosters a positive work environment and encourages open communication, allowing for more effective collaboration and teamwork.

A sense of discernment arising as an outcome of spiritual evolution equips a leader like Modi with the ability to see beyond the superficial and transitory to make wise, ethical and enduring decisions that benefit their cause in the long run. In her book, *SQ: Spiritual Intelligence*, Danah Zohar writes about the concept of spiritual intelligence (SQ) as a fundamental form of intelligence alongside cognitive intelligence (IQ) and emotional intelligence (EQ). She argues that SQ is particularly vital, as it enables one to access higher-order values, meaning and purpose, guiding their decision-making and actions. A critical concept introduced by Zohar is that of moral imagination. This entails the capacity to envision ethical and purpose-driven solutions to complex problems.

Leaders with a high SQ are known to navigate ethical dilemmas, making decisions that align with their values and the greater good, even in challenging situations. People with a high SQ are rooted in deeply held principles and operate from a moral compass with a sense of purpose that extends beyond personal interests. This style of leadership fosters trust, authenticity and a commitment to the greater good. Leaders with developed SQ possess a heightened ability to envision a better future and derive profound meaning from their work. They inspire others by articulating a compelling vision that resonates on a deeply intrinsic level, motivating teams to work towards shared goals with a sense of purpose and fulfilment.

This heightened spiritual awareness enables Modi to face triumphs and challenges with equanimity. His steadfast composure stems from his understanding that true success lies in remaining centred amidst life's ever-changing circumstances. Meeting him, one is often impressed with his deep sense of presence and how this presence affords him the ability to stay calm and objective, cognizant of the role he needs to play in the moment. Eckhart Tolle, a well-known spiritualist and author, discusses the 'power of now', and how the present moment is where true power and transformation lie. Tolle sees the 'power of now' as a state of heightened awareness and presence, where one is fully engaged with the current moment without being dominated by the incessant chatter of the mind. In this state, individuals can experience a profound sense of peace, joy, and a deeper connection to their true essence and inner being. Tolle encourages practices such as meditation, deep breathing and mindfulness exercises to help individuals access and harness the 'power of now' in their daily lives. When challenges arise, leaders who remain calm and centred provide a stabilizing influence for their team.

Narendra Modi's distinctive approach to leadership can be envisioned as a sacred spiritual journey, an expedition of the soul that continually unfolds and evolves. His leadership isn't merely a role he fulfils; it is an expression of his innermost self, and a reflection of his profound spiritual quotient. Grounded in timeless principles of selflessness, compassion and unity, Modi's leadership serves as a guiding light for those who seek to lead from a place of deep spirituality. His journey stands as a testament to the enduring power of spiritual leadership, offering a unique perspective that emphasizes the unity of the material and the spiritual realms in the pursuit of a better world. His leadership journey is not merely a series of actions but a profound spiritual odyssey. With an unwavering focus on selfless service, Modi has dedicated himself tirelessly to a higher purpose—the betterment of society and the nation at large. Embodying a deep sense of duty and responsibility, he perceives his role as integral to the larger tapestry of India's growth and development.

Above all, Modi's actions are steeped in a profound spiritual understanding of the interconnectedness of all beings. He views his role as a means of serving a higher purpose, tirelessly working to uplift the lives of the Indian people. Narendra Modi epitomizes the qualities of a karmayogi who leads with selflessness, integrity and compassion, leaving an indelible mark on the nation's progress and development.

III

Public Leadership and Adaptability

यः काममन्यू प्रजहाति राजा पात्रे प्रतिष्ठापयते धनं च ।
विशेषविच्छ्रुतवान्क्षिप्रकारी तं सर्वलोकः कुरुते प्रमाणम् ॥

yaḥ kāmamanyū prajahāti rājā pātre pratiṣṭhāpayate
dhanaṃ ca |
viśeṣavicchrutavān kṣiprakārī taṃ sarvalokaḥ kurute
pramāṇam ||
—Vidura Neeti Shloka 85

That king who renounces lust and anger, who bestows wealth upon proper recipients, and is discriminating, learned and active, is regarded as an authority of all men.

~

Narendra Modi's leadership style is a profound blend of ancient Indian wisdom and modern governance principles, emphasizing self-reliance, citizen engagement and global responsibility. His approach to governance transcends traditional political paradigms by incorporating elements of Indian civilization, such as the concepts of cosmic order (rta), sacrifice (*yajna*), austerity (tapasya), cosmic debt (*rna*) and dharma into public service. Modi's strategies, including his emphasis on *Janbhagidaari* (People's Participation) and *Atmanirbhar Bharat* (Self-Reliant India), highlight a shift towards empowering citizens, enhancing their engagement in governance, and fostering a sense of national pride and self-confidence. PM Modi's vision for India is not just about economic growth or technological advancement but about crafting a society that is rooted in its cultural ethos while boldly facing the future. This synthesis of traditional values with a forward-looking agenda aims to position India as a global leader, contributing to worldwide peace and prosperity, and fulfilling the vision of India as a Jagadguru (world mentor).

~

From the Podium to the People:
Decoding the Essence of
Public Leadership

On 20 May 2014, a significant turning point unfolded in Indian history. The Bharatiya Janata Party (BJP) secured a victory in the national elections, marking the conclusion of the decade-long tenure of the Manmohan Singh government. As Narendra Damodardas Modi, the Prime Minister-designate, arrived at the hallowed halls of the Parliament, he approached the entrance with a gesture of deep reverence. Bowing down, his forehead gently touched the steps, offering homage to this esteemed Institution and its members. Prostration is a venerable Indian tradition, signifying profound respect for elders, teachers and religious leaders. In temples, it symbolizes a devotee's submission to the Divine. Narendra Modi often alludes to the Parliament as the 'Temple of Democracy', viewing it as the living embodiment of the collective will of the people. His prostration stands as a testament to his aspiration to serve his fellow citizens with this spirit. It also reflects his unwavering dedication to collaborate with Parliament, uphold the laws of the land and engage with the spirit of cooperative federalism.

During his maiden Independence Day address in 2014, Modi stated, 'I have come here, not as a *pradhan mantri*, but as a *pradhan sevak*.' He perceived his role as Prime Minister as more of a service role rather than a position of power and authority. He saw it as an opportunity to fulfil his aspiration to serve his fellow countrymen. This declaration of being a pradhan sevak is the undercurrent that frames his expression of public leadership.

In an era marked by increasing complexity and ever-evolving challenges, the understanding of public leadership is expanding, both within academic discourse and, more crucially, in the public's collective imagination. It now encompasses a broader spectrum of cultural, social, technological and spiritual dimensions, alongside the political and administrative realms. It is attributed to individuals or groups with the means and intent to generate 'net societal benefit'.

Typically, public leadership is defined as: 'Mobilizing individuals, organizations and networks to formulate and/or enact purposes, values and actions which aim or claim to create valued outcomes for the public sphere. Here, the focus is not only on individual actors but also on processes and practices which shape the attention and resources of others about publicly agreed or sought goals and actions. It is not solely about public-office holders but about those who shape public debate and action'.[1] German philosopher Jürgen Habermas conceived of the public sphere as an arena, open to all citizens, where individuals can debate and shape public matters and challenge values, decisions and activities in the market, the State and civil society.[2] While the debate keeps growing and the definition expanding, public leadership is now getting equated with 'Public Services Leadership'.

In practice, public leaders have become synonymous with holders of public office. This is a powerful cognitive shift, where people in authority are naturally assumed to be leaders even when they may not be so. The most critical aspect of this change is how the person with both de jure[3] and de facto[4] powers views their role, responsibility and authority. If the public office representative is not attuned to this cognitive shift, it can lead to tremendous stress in the whole system and by extension, in society.

The meeting convened by PM Modi in December 2019, and the subsequent actions he has initiated, exemplify this comprehensive expression of public service leadership.

This meeting was centred around him informing the Cabinet about the outbreak of the coronavirus infection in the city of Wuhan, China. Those were the early days and very little was known about the infection, which was mostly restricted to China. Several ministers, including the then health minister, Harsh Vardhan and the current health minister of India, Mansukh Mandaviya, had participated in the meeting. Most attendees had not heard about the issue and could not appreciate why the PM was talking about preparedness for a challenge that did not seem to be India's problem. The Prime Minister wanted the country to be prepared and was beginning early discussions on the possible consequences of this viral outbreak, which seemed to be acquiring pandemic proportions. He spoke about a containment strategy that would require action across several ministries.

Cabinet Secretary[5] Rajiv Gauba vividly remembers this meeting and the profound impression it left on him. He was struck by the Prime Minister's unparalleled grasp of the issue, which far surpassed that of the others present. In the subsequent months, the meticulous planning unfolded in unprecedented ways. It began with the enforcement of the longest lockdown in world history and extended to galvanizing citizens to take ownership of their roles. The PM orchestrated a seamless collaboration among diverse ministries—from health to civil aviation, railways to finance, steel to defence and more. In Rajiv Gauba's experience, he had never witnessed such a large-scale crisis being managed with such remarkable effectiveness.

The PM's tireless efforts extended to coordinating with state chief ministers, providing them unwavering support in their fight against the pandemic. This included repurposing numerous public sector entities to produce crucial medical supplies. Additionally, a non-profit entity—PM CARES[6]—was established, solely dedicated to enhancing the healthcare infrastructure and preparing for similar contingencies in the future. The PM also spurred scientists into action, urging them to accelerate vaccine development, while simultaneously reassuring the citizens. Every facet of the crisis was anticipated and addressed, from the economic stimulus package to the distribution of free food grains, from the daily monitoring of national response to the evacuation of stranded Indian citizens from foreign shores.

It comes as no surprise that the world, at large, now lauds India's efforts in managing the pandemic and the subsequent recovery, despite significant scepticism on account of the humongous challenges it faced. India stands as the sole nation in continuous economic recovery and currently ranks as the fifth largest economy globally. Mansukh Mandaviya reflects on how crisis management, under the PM's guidance, was not solely driven by visionary and strategic thinking, but that it was also deeply rooted in securing the welfare of society and catering to the essential needs of the common people.

Even as a child, Narendra Modi was moved by disasters and wanted to respond to them in the best possible way. When he was studying in high school, the Narmada River had flooded, and several parts of Gujarat were affected. To lessen the impact on communities, Narendra Modi decided to set up a tuck shop in his school and send the profits earned to support relief and rehabilitation activities. The location of the disaster, or the extent of any natural calamity, was never a deterrent for his response. Even recently, as the Prime Minister, he ensured that the Indian government responded as soon as he received news of the earthquake in Türkiye,[7] and a medical contingent was deployed for care and relief.

The idea of societal welfare is deeply embedded in the role of the State and is part of the *bharatiya* tradition. It is seen as the very purpose for which the ruler is endowed with the 'power' to rule. In the Mahabharata, Vidura[8]—a well-known intellectual figure worthy of respect and emulation—describes five kinds of power: the *prajna bala* (intellect); the *abhijata bala* (innate abilities of the ruler); *dhana bala* (economic power); the power of *amatya-bala* (good counsel) and *bahu bala* (physical power), which is considered the basest. The foremost power, according to Vidura, is the power of the intellect—one's *buddhi*[9]—which is used for discernment. Possessing a surplus of intellectual acumen simplifies the acquisition of other forms of power. With intellect, man can control a huge elephant or a fiery lion. Vidura elucidates that one can safeguard and harness this intellect by withdrawing the influence of the five senses to foster its growth.

Five kinds of power described in the Mahabharata

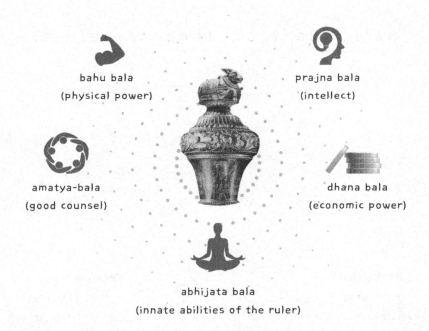

bahu bala
(physical power)

prajna bala
(intellect)

amatya-bala
(good counsel)

dhana bala
(economic power)

abhijata bala
(innate abilities of the ruler)

The *Arthashastra*[10] describes the power of the ruler as three essential *shaktis* (loosely translated as 'power' in this context). They are *utsaha shakti*, the energy or passion of the king or leader; *mantra shakti*, the power of counsel; and *prabhava shakti*, the power of material resources. How the Bharatiya point of view is different from mainstream thinking is through the nature of these powers and their ordering. Mantra shakti is seen as superior, with utsaha shakti coming next, followed by the material. A similar idea is seen in the Vedic description where the power of the will (in this case, *iccha shakti*) generates the enabling conditions for power; then comes the power of knowledge (*jnana shakti*); followed by the power of action (*kriya shakti*). While all manifestations of power are interrelated, Indic thought presents a clear hierarchical relationship, and Indic thinking lays emphasis on the 'softer' and 'smarter' application of power by the ruler to ensure *loka sangraha* (universal welfare). Contrarily, traditional Western thinking clearly celebrates the notion of 'material' or 'hard power'.

Arthashastra's three essential shaktis

mantra shakti
(the power of counsel)

utsaha shakti
(the energy or
passion in a person)

prabhava shakti
(the power of
material resources)

Ensuring welfare of all beings not only requires deep concern for the 'other' but also a heightened sense of self-discipline and a personal agenda that is devoid of selfishness. Prime Minister

Modi's focus on Antyodaya—the welfare of the person at the last mile—draws inspiration from a verse found in the Bhagavad Gita, 'Those who rejoice in the welfare of all creatures under one's care, those who rejoice in the prosperity of one's countrymen and by extension the world, those for whom this is a priority are *sarvabhūtahite ratāḥ* [welfare of all beings]'.[11]

The state of governance, in any country, results from the equilibrium that in turn emerges from tensions among four 'powerful' forces that operate in a given political ecosystem. In electoral democracies, the citizens elect their representatives to form the government. This form of political leadership draws its strength and mandate from the will of the people and the leaders commit to delivering on the promises made during their election campaign. The head of the government and their Cabinet guide the party in power to legislate and make appropriate rules and policies, and they design the appropriate programmes in service to the people. The policies and programmes implemented by the government cannot exist in a vacuum. They require formal structures and institutions populated by the permanent executive to deliver adequate services to the citizens. Domination of any one of these forces determines and shapes the governance that emerges. When political leadership is strong and powerful without the active engagement of the citizens, governance tends to be on the authoritarian side of the spectrum. When the citizens are disengaged and dependent on the government and political leadership, the result is a patronizing State, with little or no accountability for either performance or good governance. When political leadership ignores the needs of the common citizens or when policymaking gets captured by powerful forces, rules are crafted to favour an elite few. When institutions that are expected to deliver to citizens are weak, unaccountable and ineffective, governance becomes the casualty, and the citizens suffer for the same. Even if the political leadership intends to deliver on good governance, it would be difficult with weak or ineffective institutions.

Over the last seventy-five years, India has seen the evolution
of the role of the State due to the changing political, social
and economic contexts in the country. The asymmetries of
information and power that typically exist position the State
at the top of a hierarchy and leaves very little room for citizens
to participate and engage. Typically, citizen engagement
spreads across the spectrum from abject dependency on the
State to holding the State fully accountable for its actions.
Electoral dynamics and State-supported subsidies in India
have also created a culture of entitlement where there is little
to no incentive for citizens to engage with the State beyond
participating in elections.

Daniel Bell, in his influential work *The Cultural Contradictions
of Capitalism*, introduces an alternative perspective on the
fundamental challenge of public leadership. He posits it as
the stress between four distinct and autonomous realms, each
governed by its exclusive operational logic:[12]

- The political realm: Driven by the logic of expansion
  through legitimacy and intending to appear as
  representative of the will of the majority. The political
  realm encourages widening the support base through
  measures that may contradict efficiency, values or self-
  expression.
- The realm of markets: Operating through the logic of
  efficiency and focused on input-to-output calculations.
  Due to its focus on efficiency and generating surplus for
  stakeholders alone, this realm is fundamentally at odds
  with the inclusive expansionism of politics.
- The realm of society: Upholding collective ideals such
  as equality and equity, functioning as the preserver of
  societal values.
- The realm of the individual: An individual seeks self-
  expression and creative fulfilment.

Bell's thesis centres around the idea that the cultural aspects
of capitalist societies, particularly those driven by consumerism

and individualism, eventually undermine the very work ethic and ethos of rationality and efficiency that originally propelled the economic success of capitalism. In essence, the cultural sphere, with its emphasis on self-expression, personal gratification and hedonism, clashes with the economic sphere, which relies on discipline, rationality and deferred gratification. This contradiction, according to Bell, leads to a tension where the pursuit of personal and hedonistic values in the cultural domain undermines the social and economic structures necessary for a stable, efficient capitalist economy. The result is a society where cultural values are increasingly at odds with the requirements of a functioning capitalist economy.

Cultural Contradictions of

Capitalism

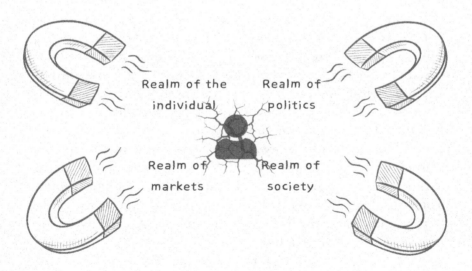

Realm of the individual

Realm of politics

Realm of markets

Realm of society

A public leader today has to straddle the contradictions of all the four realms and still deliver results. This is further compounded by the impact of globalization where the interests of transnational actors compete with, and override, the dynamics of domestic democratic politics, including, in many cases, the sovereignty of nation states. Balancing the cultural context of India and promoting civilizational pride without losing sight of the growing national economy is the unique contribution of Modi.

Dani Rodrik[13] refers to this dynamic as the 'inescapable trilemma', where the trifecta of nation state, democracy and globalization are mutually incompatible. He postulates that any leader or nation can only strive to prioritize two of the three realms. According to Rodrik's trilemma, achieving deep global economic integration while maintaining strong nation states means compromising on democratic principles, as decisions beneficial for global markets may not align with the wishes of the local electorate. Conversely, combining democracy with strong nation states often leads to protectionist policies, which can hinder global economic integration. Lastly, aligning global integration with democracy can weaken the autonomy of nation states, as global economic rules might override national policies. It is within this complex web of electoral democracy, geo-strategic hierarchies and the aspirations of 1.4 billion incredibly diverse people that one must study the leadership of Narendra Modi and glean lessons for the future.

Such a study of the PM's leadership will likely lead to the understanding that at the core of his great success is the tremendous civilizational awareness he holds, which forms the bedrock of his vision and action. He taps into the quintessence of timeless principles and traits that permeate Indian history. From Abraham Lincoln to Lee Kuan Yew to Narendra Modi, these foundational truths across cultures speak directly to the responsibilities of leadership.

In the Indian civilizational context, this entire idea of complexity is encoded into a few conceptual tenets. As a keen student of civilizational thought, Modi is not just aware but a highly accomplished *sadhak* (practitioner) of the Indic tenets of rta (cosmic order), yajna (sacrifice), tapasya (austerity), rna (debt) and dharma. These tenets are explained below:

Rta embodies the concept of an inherent harmony, a cosmic cadence in the natural world. The sun is exactly at the distance it should be from the earth for life to be possible and the intense creative activity in each cell is representative of the creative force that animates planetary scale evolution (*yatha pinde, tatha brahmande*[14]).

Yajna underscores the multi-layered sacrifices that uphold the cosmic order. The cyclical journey from life to death and nature's transformative process of every substance bear testament to this eternal yajna.

Tapasya is an innate yearning within humans for greater expansion. Recognition of the divinity within each person is considered the pinnacle of this expansion. This speaks to why Modiji uses the *divyang* metaphor to generate public awareness about our responsibility towards the 'specially abled', where the spirit of this divinity is expressed in thought, word and deed.

Rna entails a cosmic debt. A debt a person carries towards the universe, towards the five elements, towards the ancestors, towards the biosphere and towards all living things.

Dharma is the behaviour that upholds all the aforementioned principles. It has universal and context-specific attributes. It factors the third and fourth order consequences and, more critically, puts the onus of that responsibility on the individual. When karma (action) is not guided by dharma, rta is not maintained, yajna is unperformed, tapasya stops yielding fruits and rnas remain underpaid. This leads to a decline in the order of the world and anarchy prevails.

6 Indic Tenets for a Leader

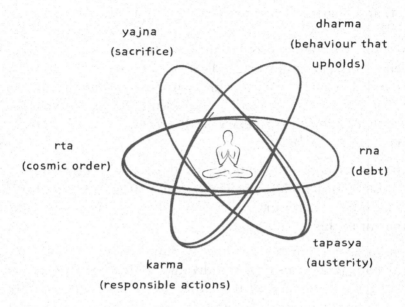

As a leader seeped in Indian civilizational consciousness, one can see how Modi draws from these ideas to deal with the complexities of public leadership. When he urged the upper middle class to forgo cooking gas (Liquefied Petroleum Gas [LPG]) subsidies for more precise targeting, he appealed to the loftier ideal of yajna, encapsulated in the Give It Up campaign.[15]

In his steadfast global leadership on environmental issues, he bases his approach on the concepts of the pancha maha-bhutas (the five primordial elements) and rna (debt). This perspective is evident in the COP declarations, the Delhi Declaration at the G20 in 2023, and in the establishment of action-oriented collaborative platforms like the International Solar Alliance. During political rallies, he elevates the public perception of leadership to one of duty and sacrifice—evoking the image of a fakir or a yogi to embody the spirit of a land and its people who inherently value spiritual asceticism and seamlessly integrate it into every facet of the secular world. This philosophical foundation, deeply ingrained with this civilizational ethos, sets the stage for understanding the transformative shifts Modi has initiated in the broader spectrum of governance and public welfare.

Historically, the public sector has primarily been responsible for providing goods and services for the welfare of the public. However, with the introduction of privatization and deregulation in India during the 1990s, the private sector significantly expanded its capacity to cater to the needs of various stakeholders through services that were otherwise provided by the government. Additionally, civil society and non-governmental organizations have played an active role in complementing state efforts to ensure services reach those in need. However, during the pandemic, the Prime Minister catalysed a new paradigm of trust-based citizen partnership that he has termed *Janbhagidaari*.[16] This initiative represents a significant shift towards leveraging collaborative efforts between the government and citizens to navigate through crises, underscoring a novel approach in governance that builds on the nation's civilizational principles and adaptively responds to contemporary challenges.

When citizen engagement is strong and democratic traditions are the driving force of political leadership, the result is an authorizing environment that forces the political and executive systems to deliver good governance. Over the last many decades, India has operated as a provider state, where citizens were treated as mere recipients of welfare with little or no say in matters that affected their development. In this context, one should view the emergence of a new kind of public leadership that Prime Minister Modi has been displaying. He demonstrates conscious and proactive leadership, encouraging citizens to partner both formally and informally with the State in governance and development matters. He has successfully shifted the State from legislating rules based on mistrust of the citizens to ones based on trust.

This change is evident in his various efforts, such as allowing citizens to self-attest copies of legal documents, nominating unrecognized individuals for civilian awards and involving citizens in shaping the education policy. This new approach emphasizes active citizen participation, encapsulated in the concept of Janbhagidaari, which translates as people's participation or partnership. The PM has publicly acknowledged that citizens are the central purpose of his governance model, and this would be the mantra that the bureaucracy has to keep in mind in delivering goods and services.

Shifting the role of the State from a provider to that of a partner in an environment that is driven by a culture of subsidies and revdis[17] is easier said than done. Operating in this rapidly altering ecosystem requires risk-taking and a courageous mindset to meet the growing and complex demands of stakeholders with differing needs and perspectives. It requires skills of collaboration, adaptiveness, credit sharing, partnership, persuasion and conflict resolution, along with a nuanced and practical understanding of disruptive innovations, digital arenas, big data management and emerging technologies. It is this ability of Modi that allows him to prepare citizens on one side and, on the other, open the State apparatus for scrutiny. This is no easy task and requires the demonstration of public leadership of a very high order. Prime Minister Modi has not only built enormous credibility and trust amongst the citizens but is also willing to risk his political capital in urging the citizens to go beyond being silent recipients of doles in a welfare state to becoming active citizens demanding good governance.

Traditionally, governance structures in India have borne the responsibility and authority to make decisions that directly impact the lives of citizens. The introduction of Janbhagidaari shifts the focus towards placing the needs and concerns of citizens at the heart of decision-making processes. This initiative aims to provide citizens with access to information, services and resources, actively involving them in the policy formulation process. For this model to succeed, a significant shift in mindset is required among the millions of civil servants nationwide who are engaged in public service. The Prime Minister's efforts to reduce asymmetries of power and information challenge the existing status quo, which is a difficult adjustment for many. Such a transformation demands major systemic changes, a process that can be unsettling. This move towards a more transparent and collaborative governance model not only underscores a fundamental change in how authority and responsibility are perceived but also paves the way for a more engaged and informed citizenry.

The primary objective of Janbhagidaari is to enhance citizen participation in the decision-making processes that directly impact their lives and to foster a stronger bond between citizens and the government. The constant exhortation made by the PM to the citizens, calling them to reciprocate and shift their mindsets from regarding the State as a provider to interacting with it as a well-informed and engaged partner, reflects his conviction in building a vibrant and engaged democracy. His call for citizens to not only participate in the political, social and economic aspects of their community but to also hold public servants accountable demonstrates his visionary intent.

From Provider to Partner

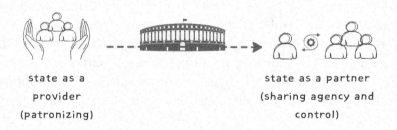

state as a
provider
(patronizing)

state as a partner
(sharing agency and
control)

Democracy and governance are not accidental occurrences but have to be intentionally nurtured and delivered. This can happen only when citizens operate with a sense of responsibility, when they have the required incentive to participate, and when the government is both responsive to, and respectful of, their participation. Over the last few years, there has been a growing movement towards increased citizen participation in various aspects of India's governance process. Whether it is the MyGov[18] platform, the Prime Minister seeking inputs from the people for his annual Independence Day speech or seeking suggestions from citizens for the annual budget—one can see the openness and desire to reduce the information and power asymmetries that have been barriers to the expression of a confident and self-reliant citizen.

The evolution of Indian democracy is evident in the Prime Minister's deliberate efforts to place citizens at the core of all development initiatives. His emphasis on citizen-centricity should be viewed as a crucial component of the social agreement he is currently forging between citizens and the systems responsible for public service delivery. This social contract stems from his conviction in citizen rights, and it is now incumbent upon citizens to join him in this celebration of democracy as India enters the 'Amrit Kaal'.[19] Nowhere else in the world has a leader endeavoured to transition institutional control and agency from predominantly state-driven to a shared partnership with citizens. While this is work in progress and will require years of sustained efforts in sensitizing the State apparatus and preparing citizens to participate responsibly, the intent, vision and political will displayed by Prime Minister Modi is commendable.

Driving State actors to engage with citizens is only one side of the equation. Arousing passion to engage citizens requires a deep understanding of their psyche, needs and capabilities. Binding 1.4 billion people with the common cause of nation-building requires a charismatic public leader who can present a vision that is engaging and exciting. Building faith in the collective potential of the population is a continuous process and requires a leader who can tirelessly demonstrate conviction in the process and make it attractive for citizens to engage. Building national pride in the culture and civilization, while infusing self-confidence and strength in citizens of a post-colonial nation, requires leadership that is, at once, inspirational and pragmatic. Whether it is through the International Yoga Day, or his call for citizens to be a part of Team India for a New India, the PM has been consciously and continuously encouraging Indians to take pride in Indian matters.

The ability to combine national priorities and the personal needs of the citizens is another unique ability of Modi's, which is exemplary of the requirements of public leaders today. The Prime Minister has committed to green leadership[20], reflected in the ambitious targets that he has set for India to be met by 2070. Meeting this COP[21] target is only possible by providing deliberate leadership and adequate budget and policy support. The PM has invested time and resources on green jobs[22], on the National Green Hydrogen Mission[23], on phasing away old vehicles using fossil fuels, and on prioritizing solar and wind energy, all to usher in a LiFE (Lifestyles for Environment) economy.[24]

The Prime Minister's strong emphasis on personal responsibility for leading an eco-friendly lifestyle reflects the ecological sensitivity deeply rooted in ancient Indian scriptures such as the Yajur Veda.[25] For instance, the Yajur Veda illustrates this respect for nature by mandating that even for the simple act of cutting a small branch from the Palasa tree, also known as the Flame-of-the-Forest (Dhak, *Butea monosperma*), a student is required to seek permission with a respectful invocation: '*O palasa! I need to cut your branch for the purpose of yajna for the gods.*' This ancient practice underscores a profound reverence for the natural world, emphasizing that every act of taking from the environment should be considered and respectful.

Balancing the need for energy self-sufficiency with the imperatives of economic growth and environmental sustainability presents a formidable challenge. Careful and deliberate allocations are crucial to achieving this equilibrium. PM Modi is clear that India's development cannot be a blind imitation of Western models, but instead, should be based on the interests of the planet and people. This approach not only respects India's rich cultural heritage but also aligns with global efforts to promote sustainable development.

The indigenous cultures around the world treat nature as sacred through its worship of rivers, mountains, rocks, trees and animals. In India, everything one experiences is considered inherently divine and treated with reverence. It is also part of the cultural psyche to see earth as the mother, and to understand that one cannot exploit her without repercussions. PM Modi's mandate for the G20 of 'One Earth, One Future, One Family' is another example of his commitment to not just India's development but to strategically aligning the civilizational and cultural strength of the country with global interests.

Development goals and initiatives need to ensure that the immediate, everyday needs of citizens are met, while also setting the foundation for building and maintaining momentum for sustained growth over the next many decades. While most public leaders are driven by 'Short Termism'[26], it takes political courage to expend one's capital on balancing the 'long term' interests of a nation too. The challenge that any head of government faces is making decisions that are consistent with the responsibilities of leadership. They have to take the next election and the next news cycle into account without losing sight of the coming generation. There is a kind of courage and risk-taking adventurism required, which PM Modi does not hesitate to show. One cannot hope to be a leader without *dhairya* and *shaurya*—courage and valour. A person at this level has to be willing not just to accumulate one's political capital by going along and doing what is popular but must be ready to spend it to get something meaningful done.

Many public leaders and policymakers are passionate about social issues and have the best intentions in trying to advocate for reform or implement policy change to address them. But translating good intentions into good decisions is not always as easy as it seems. Public policy is the result of decision-making that is constrained by complex interactions between political preferences, embedded institutions and limited resources. For many policy choices, the correct course of action is unclear. In certain instances, the choices themselves may be hard to identify. Effective policymaking requires the ability to analyse situations systematically, deal with uncertainty, make trade-offs among conflicting interests, account for other values and institutional characteristics, and develop a strategy for working with other parties to achieve the chosen objective.

Bringing in policies that can be championed electorally, scientifically sound, administratively feasible and politically sustainable is a fine balancing act that requires a nuanced appreciation for the perspectives of all stakeholders. The style of leadership that drives this kind of policymaking needs to be embedded in a grounded knowledge of people at the grassroots. Leaders need to have the acumen to pick the right team to lead the execution of these policies, and the political courage to take risks. Having worked for several decades with different kinds of stakeholders, having experienced communities at the grassroots and having maintained a willingness to consult and listen to Cabinet colleagues and senior bureaucrats gives Prime Minister Modi the unique advantage to drive citizen-centric policies and programmes that also align with the larger vision of a developed nation. Calling citizens to adopt the *Panch Pran* (five pledges) for India's collective development is not just timely but a fundamental foundation for ensuring the Amrit Kaal (Era of Elixir). Urging citizens to take pride in India's civilizational strengths, stay united with a sense of national duty and shed all traces of colonial thinking underscores the importance of these pledges.

Social development is a long-drawn-out generational process that is painstakingly slow. It is driven by stable policy support that the government in power is expected to provide. This necessitates that programmes and schemes are not driven by political exigency but by the ground realities that prevail. A growing economy can sustain and thrive only with a sensitive, understanding, and stable government made up of leaders capable of developing well-thought-through, long-term policies. The government also needs to understand that the poor and the socially excluded no longer need elaborate and complex safety nets in the form of sops and subsidies. They need a State that can ensure that their human and social capitals are steadily and consistently expanded over periods of time—long enough so that all citizens can participate in wealth creation. This is the only way to ensure economic dividends are accessible for all. This understanding is reflected in PM Modi's continued focus on citizen-centric governance, ease of living, atmanirbhar (self-reliance) and building an inclusive economy that addresses the needs and concerns of the person to the last mile. While this undercurrent of Antyodaya is a critical element, one must also bear in mind that the dignity of the citizen is not just in being accommodated in government schemes and doles but that each citizen is an active and engaged participant in the economic narrative.

Prime Minister Modi has the unique ability to connect India's civilizational past with the present without losing sight of what the future should be. The PM has been incessantly working towards building on India's civilizational DNA without romanticizing it, and crafting pride in what Indians have, while staying focused on building today's potential for a better tomorrow. Demonstrated in the symbolic representation of good governance by installing the Sengol[27] in the new parliament; ensuring that the Parliament is future-ready both in terms of physical space and technology and spreading the sense of achievement for having it built in less than three years, the Prime Minister pushes for the nation to learn from the past to craft a future that all can be proud of.

This foundational paradigm conceived by the PM is now getting institutionalized through his call for an 'Atmanirbhar Bharat'. Many people perceive the word 'atmanirbhar' in a limited way, relating it to the concepts of self-reliance and self-sufficiency. To get a comprehensive understanding of PM Modi's thinking of atmanirbhar, one needs to appreciate the context of India today, look at it from a historical and civilizational lens and see how India is getting ready to take her place as a thought leader for shaping the world's future.

India's historical legacy is steeped in innovation and intellectual accomplishments, spanning governance, spiritual thought, education, healthcare, industry and trade and commerce. It has been a beacon of knowledge, drawing scholars from China and the Far East to its renowned universities. Its scientific and mathematical treatises were disseminated by Persian and Arabic scholars, leaving an indelible mark on the Western world. India traded its riches—spices, textiles and jewels—with the Middle East and the eastern coast of Africa. Pre-British India was the subcontinent of choice for academics, traders and travellers, boasting a distinguished guest list including Vasco da Gama, Faxian, Niccolò de' Conti, Ibn Batuta, Duarte Barbosa, Alberuni, Marco Polo, Hiuen Tsang and many others.

Centuries of colonization and several invasions from outside changed the context to one of self-doubt, inferiority, intellectual stagnation and a slavish mentality. India, at the time of Independence, was a country that represented all this and more. When the British left India, they did not just leave the country with political freedom. They left people who continued to think and behave like the subjects of the British Crown. For most Indians of that generation, becoming a citizen was a novelty and demanded a change in beliefs, values and practices. While it is easy to be dependent on a benevolent State, becoming a free thinker and operating with the spirit of citizenship requires conviction, discipline and hard work. This is possible only in an ecosystem that promotes self-respect, self-belief and facilitatory support. Unfortunately, the prevailing environment for several decades following Independence did not encourage the full expression of engaged citizenship. This not only accentuated the 'dependency' mindset but also left a large population of Indians feeling inadequate and diffident about their own capacities. Fast forwarding to current times, one can see that this is no longer the dominant narrative.

Today, a new generation of young, educated and self-assured individuals are shaping their own destinies and the destiny of India. This transformation should be viewed against the backdrop of India's elevated status on the global stage in recent years. The visibility and respect accorded to India and its people are direct outcomes of the numerous diplomatic endeavours undertaken by the Prime Minister in various countries. Whether through the evacuation of Indians from conflict zones, the *Vande Bharat* missions, the G20 presidency, or attempting to secure a permanent seat at the United Nations Security Council (UNSC), it is evident how this ecosystem has propagated a sense of pride and self-reliance within each Indian.

Moving towards self-reliance from the historical dependencies of the last several decades is more than just a paradigm shift. A change in mindset is required of citizens, as well as of the political class, and the bureaucracy. The Prime Minister is constantly pushing for this, beginning a few years ago with the launch of programmes like the Swachh Bharat Abhiyan, Startup India, Standup India, Yoga Day celebrations and Ayushman Bharat[28] (Healthy India). These programmes not only reinforced the reasoning behind why Indians must look to themselves for making India clean, healthy and economically independent as a country but also gave the necessary fillip through government support. Pride also manifests in many ways. Beyond the sentiment of having a clean environment, feeling healthy and transiting through world-class airports, joining the energy revolution and being a global thought leader also contributes objectively towards the expression of atmanirbharata. From the growing trust in government and its agencies, to identifying persons for civilian awards like the Padma Shri[29], one can see the undercurrent feeling of atmanirbharata gradually seep through the collective consciousness of the masses.

While it is very easy to limit our understanding of atmanirbhar to government programmes, one needs to take a comprehensive outlook and appreciate its evolution from a programme to a larger process, a way of life, a way of thinking, an emergence of a positive and constructive mindset. In a sense, what the Prime Minister is gently nudging towards is the evolution of Indians from being a subject to becoming a citizen. Whether in civil society, politics, economics, environment, international relations, global trade, healthcare and wellness or education; a volatile, uncertain, complex and ambiguous world is seeking answers to problems challenging its very sustenance. This experiment of atmanirbhar and the lessons that India is learning today can help usher in a new model of sustainable development and a world where equity, fairness, justice, dignity and citizen engagement are no longer fashion statements but a way of life itself.

Swami Vivekananda envisioned a revitalized India, seated majestically on a radiant throne, assuming the role of Jagadguru (world teacher) to all of humanity. India's atmanirbhar initiative transcends mere progress or development for the nation itself. It is equally about the betterment of the entire global community. When a nation, confronted with a unique set of challenges like India, taps into the boundless potential of its citizens and generously imparts this wisdom to the world, it paves the way for numerous other nations to emulate this model, fostering a legacy of peace and prosperity. This marks the metamorphosis of India into the beacon of wisdom and the universal mentor it is destined to become—a vision the Prime Minister tirelessly endeavours to achieve.

यद्यदाचरति श्रेष्ठस्तत्तदेवेतरो जन: ।
स यत्प्रमाणं कुरुते लोकस्तदनुवर्तते ॥

yad yad ācharati śhreṣhṭhas tat tad evetaro janaḥ ।
sa yat pramāṇaṁ kurute lokas tad anuvartate ॥
—Bhagavad Gita 3.21

Whatever actions great persons perform, common people follow.
Whatever standards they set; all the world pursues.

~

Exercising leadership requires a problem-solving attitude and the ability to generate hope in people that the problems are solvable. From his early days as Gujarat's chief minister to his tenure as Prime Minister of India, Narendra Modi has demonstrated an unwavering focus on citizen-centric governance, leveraging technology to enhance service delivery, and fostering a culture of participation (Janbhagidaari) among the populace. His initiatives, such as the Swachh Bharat Mission for cleanliness, Jan Dhan Yojana for financial inclusion and Make in India for economic growth, reflect a pragmatic and a systems approach to addressing India's challenges. PM Modi's leadership emphasizes the importance of a responsive government that prioritizes the welfare of all citizens, especially the marginalized, ensuring that the fruits of development reach the last mile. His focus on giving the work back to the people, and unleashing the latent power of the community, informed with a civilizational ethos, has empowered people to propel India's growth forward.

~

Inspiring Change, Igniting Hope:
Public Leadership as a Catalyst for Transformation

Prime Minister Modi has a unique ability to relate to people and respond to their needs empathetically. He has consistently displayed this from his days as chief minister. He was sworn in as the chief minister of Gujarat on 7 October 2001, replacing Keshubhai Patel, who was criticized for his handling of the Bhuj earthquake. Pramod Kumar Mishra, the current principal secretary to Prime Minister Modi, recalls the moment when the then chief secretary of Gujarat, G. Subba Rao, called to appoint him as the principal secretary to the incoming Chief Minister Modi. Although Mishra was apprehensive, having not held a similar position before, he was eager to understand the expectations of the new CM. The chief secretary conveyed Modi's criteria for selecting suitable officers: absolute integrity, teamwork skills and a willingness to embrace technology. To this day, these three criteria remain Prime Minister Modi's expectations for bureaucrats closely associated with his office.

Mishra also reminisces about how swiftly Modi acclimatized to the chief minister's role and promptly orchestrated a citizen-centric response to the earthquake's aftermath. Modi introduced an innovative initiative where secretaries from various ministries were mandated to spend weekends in different quake-affected villages, gaining first-hand experience and assessing the challenges faced by affected citizens. Every Monday, without fail, for several months, Modi meticulously reviewed progress, identified potential policy adjustments and promptly addressed field-level issues. This sustained effort ensured that the rehabilitation response not only provided immediate relief but also served as a blueprint for several states to emulate. Modi's inclination to not only create a model action plan but also to share it widely is characteristic of him even to this day. The Rehabilitation Plan was shared with then-Prime Minister Atal Bihari Vajpayee and ambassadors of various nations, exemplifying how countries could respond comprehensively, addressing immediate relief while bolstering communities for future events. This ethos aligns with this well-acknowledged verse from the Maha Upanishad:

ayam nijah paro veti | ganana laghu cetasam ||
udaracaritanam tu | vasudhaiva kutumbakam ||

Small minds engage in 'me' and 'mine' but for the magnanimous, the whole world is a family.

A notable characteristic of PM Modi, as remembered by Mishra, is his empathetic approach towards public servants. Mishra reminisces about an incident when the Chief Minister's Office received a request to issue a charge sheet[1] against a government employee on the verge of retirement. Curious about the delay and the timing of the disciplinary action, the CM asked Mishra for clarification. Modi emphasized the importance of addressing misconduct promptly while also ensuring that departing employees do not leave with resentment. Mishra, having worked closely with Modi, notes his consistent respectfulness towards civil servants, never resorting to public humiliation or raising his voice, even in cases of poor performance. Instead, Modi advocates for public recognition of good work and offers constructive feedback in private. In meetings, Modi makes sure that each individual feels respected and worthy, while at the same time, he observes if the body language of the staff members exudes clarity and confidence.

Rajnath Singh, the defence minister of India, also reminisces about the Prime Minister. He emphasizes his unwavering dedication to expediting India's journey towards becoming a developed nation and he commends the unique combination of equanimity and resolute decision-making prowess exhibited by PM Modi. This was most evident in the aftermath of the heinous terrorist attack in Pulwama, Kashmir. On 14 February 2019, a convoy of seventy-eight vehicles carrying over 2500 Central Reserve Police Force (CRPF) personnel fell victim to a terrorist attack. A suicide bomber targeted a bus carrying police personnel, resulting in the tragic loss of forty lives and numerous injuries. The entire nation seethed with anger, demanding an immediate response. However, navigating the complexities of international relations, the pressures of domestic politics, and acknowledging that this attack was yet another act of terror sponsored by Pakistan required careful consideration before any action could be taken. The government's resolve to eradicate terror emanating from across the border, while accounting for the potential consequences of any action, demanded courage, a clear strategic vision and a profound understanding of global affairs. All these facets were evident in the surgical strike conducted on terrorist camps in Balakot a few days later, on the 26th of the same month.

With superior intelligence and top-notch precision to avoid civilian casualties, the Balakot strike was an exercise in limited-scale offensive action. It achieved several milestones for India, demonstrating its munition capability, deflating the nuclear bluff of Pakistan, seriously affecting the terrorist infrastructure across the border, and changing India's image from that of a reticent country to a responsible and strong regional power. It displayed to the world that India could not only talk the talk, but walk the walk—in this case, by curbing terrorism, without giving in to volatile emotions.

Delivering on social development on one side, safety and security on the other, growing the economy and ensuring a respectful place at the global table is a never-ending task for any public leader. While political priorities set the direction to act, it is only a rare few who can balance multi-directional pulls and priorities to stay focused on what they have set out to do. Narendra Modi is not just determined to do this but is able to combine his larger vision of a developed nation with the pragmatic understanding that this momentum cannot be limited to just himself but needs to be institutionalized in the larger ecosystem of public administration.

Whether it is the capacity building of his council of ministers that he personally leads, or the Chintan Shivir[2], which the PM encourages all government ministries to undertake, he realizes that a building is only as strong as the foundation it rests on. The effective and efficient delivery of goods and services in the public sector relies on the people who oversee implementation. Working within a bureaucracy of which high performance and accountability is being asked, requires several established and well-entrenched systems to be re-examined. New attention on strengthening these systems often causes the individuals working within them to feel threatened, and exceptional managerial oversight and an ability to inspire change are required for reform. PM Modi's patience, perseverance, never-say-die attitude and conviction in the abilities of the system to deliver are essential to ensuring that civil servants are being held accountable for their performance and that their capabilities are continuously being developed.

Today, India stands at a pivotal juncture in its history where three influential forces are shaping governance and state capacity. Firstly, propelled by the surge in information and communication technology (ICT), people are now hyper-connected. Young Indians in small towns and villages are linked to the broader global community, and this exposure is influencing their aspirations and desires. Technology has been empowering today's citizens in India, and they no longer settle for the passive receipt of benefits from a patronizing government; instead, they actively assert their rights and set out to influence how the State impacts their lives. Secondly, this increasingly informed citizenry is driving the evolution of a more mature political system. Politicians from all sides now recognize the critical importance of delivering on their campaign promises, particularly in areas like healthcare, education, creating public infrastructure and social welfare. Lastly, the rapid advancement of new technologies is opening up governance possibilities that were unimaginable just a decade ago, and it is the duty of the State to harness these emerging technologies for the collective good, while also mitigating potential harms.

Operating in this dynamic ecosystem requires a new mindset and an evolving skill set. To keep up, leaders are expected to acquire new skills each day and operate in a learning ecosystem. This was the fertile ground on which the seed of Mission Karmayogi was planted. Mission Karmayogi—or the National Programme for Civil Services Capacity Building (NPCSCB)—encapsulates a change in the mindset of government officials from considering themselves as *karmacharis* to becoming karmayogis. The suffix '*chari*' refers to someone who simply does, while the suffix 'yogi' refers to one who is skilful and adept at what they do—consummately, being yoked to the task at hand and staying dedicated to *kartavya* (duty) with samatvam (equanimity).[5#] Another transition required of this new ecosystem is a change in the workplace from assigning individual responsibility to performance to diagnosing the constraints to performance and remediating them. The final transition required is moving the public HR management system and the corresponding capacity-building apparatus from being rule-based to role-based.[3]

In the wake of the Covid-19 pandemic, the world is confronted with a BANI (Brittle, Anxious, Non-linear and Incomprehensible)[4] reality, reshaping our perceptions of the future of work within government. The concept of

---

[5#] Refer to *Leading with the Soul: The Intersection of Leadership and Spiritual Growth*.

what constitutes a public good is undergoing a continual transformation, in tandem with the escalating demands and aspirations of citizens. Under the stewardship of PM Modi, India is steering towards a Minimum Government, Maximum Governance[5] paradigm, emphasizing broader stakeholder involvement. Prime Minister Modi perceives governance infused with technology as imperative, which is fundamentally altering how goods and services are provided in India. From initiatives like Aadhaar[6], Direct Benefit Transfer (DBT)[7], and Digilocker[8]; to platforms like the Centralised Public Grievance Redress and Monitoring System (CPGRAMS)[9] and MyGov[10], as well as innovations like faceless transactions and drone deliveries; advancements in online education and the establishment of a Digital University—India is steadfast in its pursuit of integrating technology into both governance and service delivery. To participate, a civil servant must not only possess unwavering dedication but also the proficiency of skills to fulfil this evolving mandate. While the world grapples with these transformations, India has undertaken the vanguard role in cultivating a future-ready civil service, committed to lifelong learning and poised to meet the expanding needs of citizens and the nation.

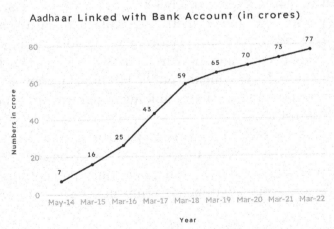

Aadhaar Linked with Bank Account (in crores)

Source: Unique Identification Authority of India

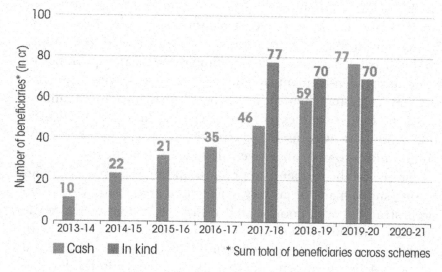

(Source: Direct Benefit Transfer Mission)

Democracy entails more than simply entrusting a government with a five-year contract. It is, in essence, Janbhagidaari— meaning, participation of the people. This call given by PM Modi encapsulates the essence of all programmes and initiatives introduced by him and his government over the past nine years. It draws from Narendra Modi's rich life experiences; from his upbringing in poverty to his tenure as an RSS pracharak; his role as the National Secretary of the Bharatiya Janata Party and his leadership as the chief minister of Gujarat. Each of the government's initiatives are firmly rooted in a foundational principle or value, serving as the bedrock upon which the Janbhagidaari programme stands. While addressing the National Training Conclave in New Delhi in June 2023, the PM delved deeply into the significance of how citizens perceive the State and its service delivery apparatus, emphasizing the criticality of fostering a trusting relationship between the various arms of the State and the citizens.

One can find the basis of Modi's citizen-centric thinking in one of his early experiences. During the challenging times of the severe drought in Gujarat, Narendra Modi, serving as an RSS pracharak, displayed exceptional resourcefulness and leadership in managing the transportation of food and fodder to the distressed areas. Understanding the critical importance of community involvement, Modi worked closely with residents, actively engaging them in the process of identifying available food and fodder sources within the region. This not only ensured that resources were used judiciously but also empowered the communities to play an active role in the relief efforts.

He asked the residents to prepare sukhdi, a simple and long-lasting snack made of jaggery, ghee and wheat flour. Modi then orchestrated a well-coordinated transport system to move the sukhdis and the fodder to the needy areas. He worked with vehicle owners, drivers and authorities to ensure timely and efficient delivery, prioritizing distribution based on the level of need in different regions. He made sure that the relief efforts were as effective as possible.

Modi was also pragmatic and empathetic in his approach. He asked the transporters to contribute the first trip at their own cost and promised to pay for the fuel for the second trip and the market rates for the subsequent trips. This way, he ensured that the transporters had a minimal financial loss and felt a sense of participation. He adapted to the changing situations and challenges, adjusting based on feedback and circumstances. In tandem with his grassroots efforts, Modi also engaged with government authorities, seeking their support and assistance in facilitating the transportation of fodder. This collaborative approach helped to streamline the process and overcome any bureaucratic hurdles that may have arisen. This kind of practical approach to solving public problems without losing sight of the private gains of the stakeholders involved forms a key element in Modi's approach to community engagement and citizen participation.

Prime Minister Narendra Modi's approach to governance is deeply influenced by the insights from *Minor Hints*, a guide on public administration authored by T. Madhava Rao, an influential administrator in the Baroda[11] province during Maharaja Sayajirao Gaekwad III's tenure (1875–1939). As per Rao, the first duty of the ruler was to promote the happiness of his subjects while recognizing that the Raj (government) is a public trust.[12] PM Modi has repeatedly spoken about his admiration for Maharaja Sayajirao Gaekwad III. He was recognized as a visionary leader in the history of India's princely states and was fondly referred to as the 'Progressive Maharaja'. Under his rule, Baroda State underwent significant modernization and development, and he implemented various reforms in education, infrastructure, industry and social welfare. He emphasized the importance of education and established a wide range of educational institutions, including the Maharaja Sayajirao University of Baroda. He also promoted women's education and initiated progressive measures such as free primary education for both boys and girls. Additionally, Sayajirao Gaekwad III introduced policies to improve agriculture, develop industries, and enhance the overall economy of Baroda State. He implemented land reforms, improved irrigation systems and encouraged industrial growth by attracting investments and establishing factories.

India has struggled for centuries with the challenge of maintaining public hygiene and waste management. Given India's geographical and population size, it requires that every individual take ownership and responsibility of both personal and public hygiene. Earlier programmes to tackle this issue focused more on state fiscal support and subsidies and failed to tap into the enormous community resources and personal pride of every citizen. This was what Modi did when he conceived and launched the ambitious Swachh Bharat Abhiyan on 2 October 2014, within a few months of taking office as the Prime Minister. The objective of the Mission was to change the centuries-old behaviour of open defecation and eliminate it, eradicate manual scavenging- and promote scientific solid waste management. On 2 October 2019, the 150th birth anniversary of M.K. Gandhi, the scheme was confirmed to have attained 100 per cent open defecation-free status for all villages, districts, states and union territories (UTs). It is currently in its second phase which is aimed at sustaining behavioural change and moving towards making waste management a community-driven initiative across the country. Recognizing Prime Minister Modi's commitment towards a cleaner and greener world, including the pledge to eliminate single-use plastic in India, the United Nations bestowed him with the 2018 Champions of the Earth Award, considered being the highest environmental honour globally. Prime Minister Narendra Modi also received the 2019 Goalkeeper Award, for the Swachh Bharat Abhiyan, also known as Swachh Bharat Mission (SBM), from the Bill and Melinda Gates Foundation in New York. The Foundation asserted that the SBM can serve as a model for other countries around the world.

Compared to its previous avatar of Nirmal Bharat Abhiyan[13], SBM was spearheaded by the PM himself through example (attributing dignity to cleaning) by repeatedly resorting to physically cleaning public places. Reflecting Gandhi's vision of India, the programme comprised citizen-engaged actions like contests to create the mission logo and present essays on Vision India[14], and engaged participation by elected representatives and government servants, thus creating mass awareness—a *jan andolan*. As a result, with the construction of 102.8 million toilets, rural sanitation coverage of almost 100 per cent has been achieved.[15]

SBM is not a scheme that was thought up overnight. It is the culmination of all the experiences Narendra Modi had before he became Prime Minister of India—it culminates his dreams since his RSS pracharak days. In a conversation with Assa Doron and Robin Jeffery, authors of *Waste of a Nation: Garbage and Growth in India*, Modi said that two experiences in his home state of Gujarat motivated and influenced his attitude towards social change and cleanliness and sanitation.

One was the massive floods of Morbi in 1979,[6#] killing thousands of people. The other was the panic over the suspected bubonic plague in Surat in 1994. In Surat, a huge cleaning-up operation was undertaken, and Modi was a part of this drive. The town was restored to its normal state and an epidemic was averted. As the chief minister of Gujarat, Modi said if change could happen in Surat and other places, it is possible elsewhere, so he focused on improving the hygiene and sanitation practices in urban and in rural areas. Open defecation (OD) being a centuries-old habit, made the implementation of SBM a challenging task because there was no demand for toilets before. About fifty-five crore people in villages were devoid of toilets. Modi was aware of the social and health risks to women and children in particular and knew that one of the reasons for girls dropping out from schools was lack of toilet facilities. Dignity of women was his priority.[16]

In Indian wisdom, *shaucha*, meaning 'cleanliness and purity', is seen as an essential component of living a *dharmika* life, and the Hindu texts have underlined its significance. As per Daksha Smriti[17], a person should always strive to maintain shaucha in whatever job he undertakes, because without such dedication to purity, all activities and works are futile.

The *Har Ghar Nal Se Jal* (Piped Water to Every Household) scheme announced on 15 August 2019 by the PM in his Independence Day speech is another programme that includes community mobilization and ownership. It aims to provide complete coverage of every rural household with a running water supply. Since Independence up until 2019, only 16.87 per cent of the 191.9 million rural households in India had tap water connections. As of February 2023, 57.56 per cent of households have been covered by the scheme.[18] It is not only centred around providing water resources to rural households,

[6#] Refer to the chapter Charting a Bold Course: Visionary Leadership in Action

but also augmenting local water resources through water-harvesting techniques, to ensure sustainability.

This scheme is informed by the PM's Gujarat days, in his role as the chief minister. Modi had then exhorted farmers to utilize drip irrigation to conserve water. He sold the idea to farmers by using a logic rooted in their lived experiences.

> Imagine trying to feed a baby by dunking it in a pail of milk . . . If your child is not well, his weight is not increasing, and you have one bucket of milk, and if your child is taking a bath in that milk, will his health be improved? No. If you want to improve the health of your child, you will have to give it a few drops of milk every hour. Then the milk will go into his body and good health will be there. If he simply bathes in the milk, the body will not get any benefit. In the same way, when you grow the crop on the farm, don't think that the floodwater will strengthen your plant. Only the drip will strengthen your plant, so if you want to strengthen your plant you will have to use the same technique which you are using for your children.[19]

In 2014, sixty-seven years after gaining independence, a significant portion of India's population still lacked access to basic banking services. This meant they had no means to save money or secure institutional credit. Integrating the economically disadvantaged into the formal financial system not only aids in expanding the official economy but also fosters a sense of dignity and self-worth among those who have historically been excluded.

On 28 August 2014, Prime Minister Modi launched the Pradhan Mantri Jan Dhan Yojana (PMJDY)[20] to confront this fundamental challenge of financial exclusion among the impoverished. During the launch, the Prime Minister emphasized that this initiative was not just about acquiring a bank account but also about eradicating financial marginalization. For those born into financial inclusion, a bank account may seem like a commonplace convenience. However, exclusion from the mainstream financial system goes much deeper than just the absence of a bank account or debit card.

Traditionally, financial inclusion is understood as the delivery of financial services at affordable costs to all sections of society, especially the disadvantaged and low-income segments. An estimated 1.4 billion working-age adults globally, who are unbanked or under-banked, have no access to the types of formal financial services delivered by regulated financial institutions.[21] The PM's promise of providing financial inclusion to all citizens of India is not about just new bank accounts alone. The financial banking system needs strengthening, including the opening of new branches in remote and inaccessible areas and novel initiatives like mobile banking solutions (mobile ATM vehicles, mobile banking agents and using post offices as banking institutions). More importantly, an inclusive financial system requires a shift in mindset amongst banking personnel to consider the poor, not as mere beneficiaries of a government led scheme but as partners in the progress of the nation. Setting in motion this enormous paradigm shift is possible because of the political will and commitment to the cause displayed by the Prime Minister and the regular reviews that he conducts to keep the pressure on.

The programme should be seen from the perspective of PM Modi, whose personal experiences have taught him that possessing a bank account transcends mere financial benefits; it also enriches social experiences. Financial inclusion acts as a significant equalizer, instilling a sense of importance in the economically disadvantaged and integrating them into the broader economic framework. Additionally, such inclusion fosters feelings of dignity and self-worth. To achieve financial inclusion for all, a major shift needs to take place in the frameworks which underpin both the banking sector and the entire society. The 'haves' need to accommodate and accept that it is their responsibility too, to include the 'have-nots' in the economic scheme of things. The 'have-nots' need to shed their apprehensions and suspicions of the fortunate few and appreciate the significance and benefits of integration. Financial inclusion should be seen as a tool to help climb up the social and economic ladder and not become dependent on a patronizing system.

The Indian economy has traditionally been driven by cash, and cash transactions normally go uncaptured in the formal system. Apart from enabling the shift to a more accountable formal economic system, digital payments also offer the opportunity for large-scale use, enable the ease of living for citizens and include more people into the financial system. The introduction of digital payment mechanisms also provides the foundational platform required for social protection payments to go directly into the bank accounts of the people who need them.

Considering the myriad welfare schemes in existence, the physical distribution of cash is expensive for the exchequer, the use of cash opens possibilities for leakages, promotes corruption and enables the undeserving to receive benefits. The Direct Benefit Transfer (DBT) system eliminated physical cash distribution channels and facilitated electronic transfers to be sent directly into bank accounts. The Aadhaar-seeding[22] of bank accounts allowed for identity verification, helping ascertain whether welfare benefits were being sent to deserving individuals.

'Jan Dhan Account–Aadhaar–Mobile,'[23] or 'JAM trinity' facilitates DBTs of welfare subsidies into bank accounts. The driving motivation was to increase account ownership and usage. As a result, the market segments that were typically underserved by the formal financial system have now been brought into its fold.

One of the important thrusts under JAM was to improve bank account ownership by bringing banking to the bottom of the pyramid. By government estimates, approximately

500.9 million individuals hold PMJDY bank accounts that have been opened since 2014, of which 282 million are women account holders.[24]

With the successful induction of citizens into the formal economy through bank inclusion, the next step was to conduct transactions digitally to control the grey economy[25] and enhance the ease of completing transactions. For this, a digital revolution was launched through the help of initiatives such as when the government brought Internet connections to 1,00,000 panchayat[26] villages; and the Unified Payments Interface (UPI).

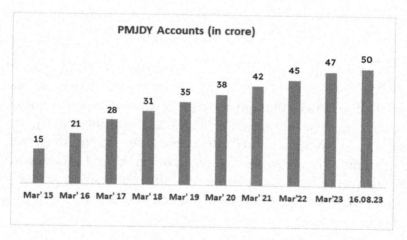

(Source: Press Information Bureau of India)

UPI is a digital payment platform in India that enables fast interbank transactions. Ever since its launch in 2016, UPI has achieved various milestones. In October 2019, it recorded one billion transactions in a month, proving many critics of Digital India wrong. Currently, UPI records over 10.5 billion transactions a month[27], proving to be a tremendous success story showcasing the power of the populace when the government enables it.

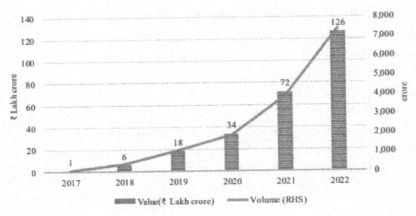

UPI transactions over the years

(Source: National Payments Corporation of India)

The Prime Minister's ability to combine the knowledge gained from his personal experience, the ability of the State to deliver and his conviction that no individual should be left behind, has shaped how all other schemes are formulated by the government. Whether it is affordable housing for the poor, programmes to augment incomes, or making India into a manufacturing hub, one can see the undercurrent of practical economics, strategic focus, political acumen, social protection and people-centricity as the foundational base.

A good illustration of this concept is the Make in India initiative. Launched in 2014, it is driven by four key features aimed at promoting entrepreneurship and economic growth. These features include New Processes, focusing on improving the ease of doing business and attracting foreign investment, with record Foreign Direct Investment (FDI) inflows of $83.6 billion in 2021–22 and a strong emphasis on supporting start-ups. New infrastructure, highlighted by the Production Linked Incentive (PLI) scheme across fourteen sectors, seeks to strengthen domestic manufacturing, create resilient supply chains and boost exports, particularly benefiting Micro, Small and Medium Enterprises (MSMEs). New sectors have been identified, such as semiconductors, with significant incentive schemes to encourage growth in these areas. Finally, a new mindset has transformed the government's role from regulator to enabler, fostering a more collaborative and supportive environment for industry. These processes collectively represent Make in India as a comprehensive strategy for industrial growth and innovation.

Make in India

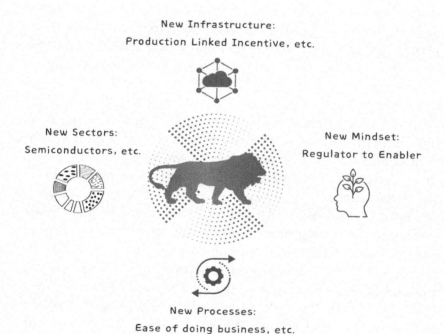

New Infrastructure:
Production Linked Incentive, etc.

New Sectors:
Semiconductors, etc.

New Mindset:
Regulator to Enabler

New Processes:
Ease of doing business, etc.

All these initiatives are amplified through personal investment from the top echelon, through continuous feedback, reappraisal and encouragement. A common perception of businesses becoming too big to fail—and thus curbing their risk-taking ability—was countered by the landmark Insolvency and Bankruptcy Code (IBC).[28] This allowed entrepreneurs to take risks with the confidence that they would not be hounded for genuine business failures, and assured banks that they would be able to retrieve their investments through asset dissolution or otherwise, without capital getting stuck. A result of this is visible in the number of unicorns[29] India created, which zoomed from eleven in 2016 when the bill was passed to sixty-eight in 2023.[30]

The One District One Product (ODOP) initiative is another manifestation of the Make in India vision. It facilitates the production and promotion of indigenous products from each district of the country and provides a global platform for the artisans and manufacturers of handloom products, handicrafts, textiles and agricultural and processed products, thereby further contributing to the socioeconomic growth of various regions in the country.

While programmes are usually conceived and implemented with political gains in mind, only a public leader with vision and farsightedness can envisage the current and future needs of a country and its citizens. It calls for a public leader with grounded experience, political courage and charisma to mobilize the masses, and a spirit of risk-taking adventurism to conceive of innovative ideas. Driving a programme with appropriate oversight, promoting programming directly to citizens in both physical and digital platforms, interacting with beneficiaries and seeking their inputs and participation, and ushering in new theories of change requires a new kind of leadership.

The Gati Shakti[31] plan is based on the principles of the 'Whole of Government' and 'Whole of Nation' and is testimony to the PM's conviction in it. Gati Shakti (Power of Speed) is a national master plan for multimodal connectivity, which brings together sixteen ministries, including Railways and Roadways, on a digital platform for integrated planning and coordinated implementation of infrastructure connectivity projects. The plan involves the coordination and cooperation of different government departments and agencies as well as the participation of the private sector and the people. On 13 October 2021 at Pragati Maidan, New Delhi, Modi laid down the vision of Azadi ka Amrit Mahotsav[32] and Gati Shakti and said:

> At the centre of this great campaign of Gati Shakti (speed and power) are the people, the industry, the business world, the manufacturers and the farmers of India. [. . .] The way the government dispensation has worked in the country for decades, people's perception of the government is all about poor quality, long delays, unnecessary hurdles and insult to public money. I am using the word insult because the successive governments were not concerned that even a single penny should not be wasted while using the public money which is given to the government in the form of taxes. It continued like this. The people had also become accustomed that the country would run like this. They used to get upset and become sad at the pace of the progress of other countries and were reconciled to the fact that nothing would change. Progress will be considered only when there is momentum, an impatience for speed and a collective effort.
>
> Leaving behind that old-fashioned government approach, India of the 21st century is moving forward. Today's mantra is – 'Will for Progress', 'Work for Progress', 'Wealth for Progress', 'Plan for Progress' and 'Preference for Progress'. Not only did we develop a work culture of completing the projects within the stipulated time frame, efforts are now being made to complete the projects before time. If today's India is committed to invest maximum for building modern infrastructure, it is also taking every step so that projects do not get delayed, there are no obstacles and work is completed on time.
>
> Along with the lack of political will, the country's infrastructure development suffered the most due to lack of coordination among government departments and

internecine tussle. We have seen tensions between the state governments and local bodies in this regard in states too. As a result, the projects, which should have been helpful in fuelling the economic growth of the country, become obstacles to the development of the country. Over time, these long pending projects lose their relevance and even their exigency. When I came to Delhi in 2014 with a new responsibility, there were hundreds of projects that were stuck for decades. I personally reviewed hundreds of such projects worth lakhs of crores of rupees. I brought all the departments and ministries of the government on one common umbrella platform and tried to remove all the obstacles. I am satisfied that now everyone's attention has been drawn to the fact that projects should not be delayed due to lack of coordination. Now the collective power of the government is being used to complete the schemes. Due to this, many projects which have remained incomplete for decades are being completed.

[. . .]

All these goals that I have listed are not ordinary goals. Therefore, the efforts and methods to achieve them will also be unprecedented. And they will get maximum strength from the PM Gati Shakti National Master Plan. Just as we have been successful in delivering the government facilities to the genuine beneficiary faster with the power of JAM trinity i.e. Jan Dhan-Aadhaar-Mobile, the PM Gati Shakti is going to do the same in the field of infrastructure. It is coming up with a holistic vision from infrastructure planning to execution.[33]

Prime Minister Modi's call for a Whole of Government approach, Less Government and More Governance, *Viksit Bharat* and Amrit Kaal reflect his beliefs and efforts throughout his leadership. Throughout these schemes and policies, a consistent theme emerges: the prioritization of women-led development by the Prime Minister, in line with his vision of empowering *Nari Shakti*, or women power. From expanding operational roles for women within the armed forces to enacting constitutional amendments to reserve one-third of all legislative seats for women, the Prime Minister has demonstrated a steadfast commitment to fostering a gender-just society. This dedication is further underscored by the notable presence of 43 per cent female enrolment in STEM (Science, Technology, Engineering and Mathematics) education, ranking among the highest rates globally.[34]

Coupled with instilling pride and nationalism, democratizing the approach, and giving it the foundation of civilizational ethos is a unique ability of the Prime Minister in shaping a clear and inspiring development narrative. Narendra Modi's public leadership stands as a testament to these enduring principles that have fundamentally transformed the course of governance in India. At its core lies an unwavering commitment to inclusive development, an approach that seeks to uplift every stratum of society. This commitment is underpinned by a focus on practical governance, eschewing rhetoric in favour of tangible, results-driven policies.

Moreover, Modi's leadership is distinguished by a keen sense of strategic planning, ensuring that each decision and initiative aligns with the broader vision for the nation. This forward-looking approach has not only spurred economic growth but has also positioned India as a dynamic force on the global stage.

Central to Modi's ethos is a deep concern for the well-being of all citizens, particularly those residing in the remotest corners of the country. This emphasis on the last mile ensures that the benefits of governance are not merely theoretical but reach those who need them the most. This is the kind of public leadership that leaders across the globe can emulate, to not just make stronger, more effective systems, but to ensure that these systems serve everyone and leverage everyone's ability to contribute to economic growth and social well-being.

श्लोकेन वा तदर्धेन तदर्धार्धाक्षरेण वा ।
अबन्ध्यं दिवसं कुर्याद्दानाध्ययनकर्मभिः ॥

ślokena vā tadardhena tadardhārdhākṣareṇa vā |
abandhyaṃ divasaṃ kuryāddānādhyayanakarmabhiḥ ||
—Chanakya Neeti 2.13

*Let not a single day pass without your learning a verse, half a verse,
or a fourth of it, or even one letter of it; nor without attending to
charity, study and other pious activity.*

~

There are two kinds of challenges a leader faces: technical challenges, which are easy to identify and quick to solve, and adaptive challenges, which require a protracted, innovative approach often accompanied by a change in mindsets. The revocation of the Constitution's Article 370 that granted special status to the Indian state of Jammu and Kashmir provides a brilliant example of adaptive leadership at work, where the state was transformed from a hotbed of terrorism into a success story in development. This move required PM Modi to navigate through a labyrinth of historical, political and social tensions, embodying the essence of managing adaptive challenges. It necessitated, to bring out this balance, ensuring that the change process neither stagnated due to complacency nor escalated into unmanageable conflict. A long-standing vision, coupled with a deft understanding of governance and proper stakeholder engagement, can manifest adaptive leadership that guides societies through transformative periods.

~

Navigating Change: The Journey of Adaptive Leadership

On 5 August 2019, the Indian government, under the leadership of Prime Minister Narendra Modi, made the decision to revoke Article 370, a provision in the Indian Constitution that granted a special autonomous status to the state of Jammu and Kashmir. Article 370 allowed the state to have its own constitution, a separate flag and considerable autonomy over internal matters, except for defence, communications and foreign affairs, which remained under the jurisdiction of the Indian government.

The revocation of Article 370 was accompanied by the reorganization of the state of Jammu and Kashmir into two separate union territories[1]—Jammu-Kashmir and Ladakh. The Indian government's decision to revoke Article 370 was primarily aimed at integrating Jammu and Kashmir more closely with the rest of the country and was a measure to address issues of development, security and terrorism in the region.

In an address to the nation on 8 August, just after the revocation, Prime Minister Modi stated:

As a country and as a family, you, and us, together we took a historic decision. A system which denied due rights to our brothers and sisters of Jammu-Kashmir and Ladakh; a system which was a huge hurdle in their development has now been eradicated. A dream which Sardar Vallabhbhai Patel had, a dream which Babasaheb Ambedkar had, the dream shared by

Shyama Prasad Mukherjee, Atalji and crores of citizens, has now been fulfilled.

A new age has begun in Jammu-Kashmir and Ladakh. Now the rights and accountabilities of all the citizens of the country are similar. I congratulate the people of Jammu-Kashmir, Ladakh and each and every citizen of the country.

Sometimes certain things of social life get so entangled with time that they are considered to be permanent. A sentiment of complacency develops, and it is thought that nothing is ever going to change. A similar sentiment prevailed for Article 370. Because of this, there was no debate or talk about the damage done to our brothers and sisters, our children in Jammu-Kashmir and Ladakh. Astonishingly, nobody was able to list the benefits that Article 370 delivered to the people of Jammu and Kashmir.[2]

While Narendra Modi and the Bharatiya Janata Party (BJP) had pledged in their election manifesto to repeal this article, many doubted the government's political resolve to follow through. They were aware of the personal, professional and political challenges associated with such a decision, recognizing the significant risks involved. Embracing this challenge demanded strategic planning, exceptional bravery, a willingness to put oneself on the line, the capability to effectively address risks and an unwavering sense of purpose. For Modi, this undertaking justified the risk, as the ultimate objective was national good. For someone accustomed to operating at the forefront of leadership in both personal and public life, seizing this opportunity to mobilize the people and address this formidable issue was a logical step.

This seemingly impossible task of reintegrating the state of Kashmir gains significance considering the background and root of the problem, which can be traced back to the Partition of British India in 1947, when the Indian subcontinent gained independence and was divided into two separate countries:

India and Pakistan. At the time of Partition, princely states[3] were given the option to join either India or Pakistan based on their geographical location and demographic composition. Kashmir, however, had a majority Muslim population ruled by a Hindu king, Maharaja Hari Singh. The Maharaja initially wanted to remain independent, but as tensions grew and violence erupted between Muslims and Hindus, he acceded to India in October 1947. Pakistan, however, disputed the accession, claiming that Kashmir should have been a part of Pakistan due to its Muslim majority.

This led to the first Indo–Pakistani war over Kashmir, which ended with a ceasefire in 1949 and a temporary division of the region. The ceasefire line, known as the Line of Control (LOC), divided Kashmir into Indian-administered Jammu and Kashmir, and Pakistan-administered Azad Kashmir. A portion of Kashmir, known as Aksai Chin, came under Chinese control.

Since then, India and Pakistan have fought several wars and engaged in numerous border skirmishes over Kashmir. Both countries claim the entire region as their own and have sought to gain control over it. The issue has been a major source of tension between the two nations and has had significant political, social and economic consequences for the people living there.

The Kashmir problem is complex and multifaceted, involving territorial disputes, religious and ethnic divisions and questions of self-determination. Various attempts have been made to resolve the issue through diplomacy and negotiation, but a lasting solution was yet to be achieved. In 1950, Article 370 of the Indian Constitution was introduced as a temporary provision, granting a special autonomous status to the state of Jammu and Kashmir.

The purpose of Article 370 was to provide a framework for the relationship between the Indian government and the state of Jammu and Kashmir. It was seen as a means to accommodate the distinct historical, cultural and religious identity of the region. Over the years, the special status accorded to Jammu and Kashmir under Article 370 became a topic of political and legal debate. Critics argued it had hindered the full integration of the state with the rest of India and impeded its development. They believed it created a sense of separation in identity and fuelled separatist sentiments in the region.

An insulated state with little or no federal oversight also encouraged a few elite families to enjoy the privilege of pelf and power at the expense of the common people. They controlled the political and commercial interests of the state and had developed deep stakeholding in ensuring that the status quo continued. Withdrawing the Indian Constitution's Article 370 not only disrupted their long-enjoyed power but also exposed their narrow self-interests and financial interests.

The armed forces and the police had to endure the conflict, aggravated by terrorists and separatists who stemmed from across the border. Long periods of violence against the Hindu minority (known as the Kashmiri Pandits) had created a generation of internal refugees and a deep religious divide. Kashmir, once famed for its culture, humanism, tourism and gentle lifestyle, was riddled with economic collapse, corruption, civil unrest and an environment of mistrust and misgovernance.

B.V.R. Subrahmanyam (BVR), the chief secretary of Jammu and Kashmir at the time of the revocation, recollects the days when this announcement was made by the Prime Minister and how well the PM handled the situation. It was June 2018, and BVR was working in his parent cadre state of Chhattisgarh as the additional chief secretary in charge of the Home Department. The chief secretary had just informed him that he was being relieved of his responsibilities in the state and had to report to the Government of India for an important responsibility. Subrahmanyam had just returned to the state after a long stint with the government and was a bit confused by this information. It was only later that he was informed that he had been appointed chief secretary of Jammu and Kashmir and had to report to his role immediately. Hurriedly packing a few clothes, he left the same night for Srinagar, the capital of Jammu and Kashmir.

A few days earlier, President's Rule[4] had been imposed in the state, a day after the BJP had pulled out of the government and ended its alliance with the Peoples Democratic Party (PDP). This coalition government headed by Mehbooba Mufti was unable to contain the growing terrorism and violence and resigned once the BJP withdrew its support. Most people were surprised that this coalition government had lasted as long as it had. The Prime Minister, believing in the necessity of democratic governance, had previously encouraged the BJP to align with the PDP, despite its perceived proximity to separatist factions.

A year before elections in 2014, Jammu and Kashmir had seen the worst floods in over a century. The Prime Minister had personally visited the state twice that year, in September and October, and had witnessed the damage first-hand, and the inability of the state government led by the then chief minister, Omar Abdullah to provide proper relief and rehabilitation to the people. It is likely that these visits are what prompted the PM to encourage a democratic government elected by the people of Jammu and Kashmir, hoping that a party associated with the terrorist elements could help convince them to allow peace to return to the Valley.

The killing of known terrorist Burhan Wani by the Indian security forces in 2016 was a watershed moment. The state was paralysed because of State-imposed lockdowns and hartals for nearly six months after that, and the inaction of Mehbooba's government was glaringly contributory. As a large number of government appointees were known terrorist sympathizers, the prospects for good governance and peace were bleak. The Government had to be dismissed by the president and the state assembly was placed under a state of suspended animation.

Governor N.N. Vohra, who had held several key senior roles in the Government of India earlier, was then tasked with governing the state with the President's Rule in place.

Several earlier attempts to solve the Kashmir issue had not been successful. Three full-scale wars, a continuous low-intensity conflict, internal refugees and terror campaigns within India supported by the Government of Pakistan had necessitated different responses over time. These long-drawn-out complex circumstances were more than just an emotional or a sovereignty issue. In the words of leadership expert Ronald Heifetz[5], this long-standing conflict dating back to the Partition of India was a combination of a 'technical problem' and an 'adaptive problem'. Heifetz defines technical problems as those that have straightforward solutions that can be deployed with a standard operating procedure. Many simple issues confronted daily fit into this category and many people effortlessly deploy solutions to such problems using their personal experience and knowledge. But there are a whole host of problems that are not amenable to just authoritative expertise or standard operating procedures. These problems cannot be solved by a top-down approach. Heifetz calls them adaptive challenges because they require constant adaptation—experimentation, discovery and adjustments from numerous places within an organization, community or country. Without learning new ways to work or changing attitudes, values and behaviours, people cannot make the adaptive leap necessary to thrive in a new environment. People are often quick to resist change because they are resisting the loss that inevitably comes with it. In Kashmir's case, some were resisting the loss of political power, clout and money. As religion was a primary concern, many feared losing their religious and cultural identities as well. The sustainability of adaptive and changing environments for effective problem-solving requires that the people involved in the problem are able to internalize the change.[6] In other words, for any meaningful change to occur, the people facing the problem need to also be the ones with the solutions.

Kind of challenge	Problem definition	Solution	Locus of work
Technical	Clear	Clear	Authority
Technical and adaptive	Clear	Requires learning	Authority and stakeholders
Adaptive	Requires learning	Requires learning	Stakeholders

Distinguishing technical problems and adaptive challenges

(From *The Practice of Adaptive Leadership* by Ronald Heifetz, Alexander Grashow and Marty Linsky)

Many people are unable to diagnose whether a problem is technical or adaptive, and they end up force-fitting technical solutions to adaptive problems, failing to resolve them. Many feel overwhelmed by the adaptiveness demanded in problem-solving and withdraw from exercising any leadership. Only a handful of leaders like PM Modi can be mindful, act as observers, and assess whether a problem is technical, adaptive or a combination of both. They then proceed to devise solutions that consider the various stakeholders involved and address the differing perspectives among them.

Leadership is about mobilizing oneself and others to do something that is societally constructive amidst enormous uncertainty. A leader needs to be aware of themselves, others, and the actions that are required in a specific moment of time.[7] Leadership requires the convening power to act, an appreciation of the context, motives and perspectives of the several stakeholders involved—what drives them and their engagement. A leader needs to be aware that several micro-experiments need to run constantly, and that these experiments may be productive or may prove counterproductive. They need to be able to stay dispassionate, take an observer's view, and recalibrate their actions in real-time.

Sakshi bhava is a term from Indian philosophy, specifically Advaita Vedanta,[7#] that refers to the concept of being an observer or witness of experiences. It is closely related with the idea of detached witnessing and self-awareness. The term is often used to emphasize the importance of recognizing oneself as the witnessing consciousness rather than getting entangled in the transient experiences of the world. It is the ability to be aware of the self and everything around us, all the time. In the overwhelming sensory world, we often get lost in whatever we see, feel, touch, hear and taste. One enters in sakshi, or the witness state, when the mind is not scattered and when one is absolutely in the 'here and now'.

Sakshi bhava requires that whatever happening in life be witnessed without the interference of emotions. By looking at every situation without involving our feelings, we can act rationally, detach from outcomes and realize that we are ultimately separate from the events occurring around us. This concept is not only limited to Advaita Vedanta but is also found in various other philosophical and spiritual traditions in India. Similar ideas are present in Buddhism, where mindfulness and detachment from phenomena are key components of the path to enlightenment. In yoga philosophy, the practice of *svadhyaya* (self-observation) and detachment from the fluctuations of the mind is also aligned with the concept of being a witness.

This concept is integral to Ramana Maharshi's teachings on self-awareness and the nature of the observer. Ramana Maharshi, a renowned Indian sage and spiritual teacher who lived in the early to mid-twentieth century, often encouraged individuals to inquire into the nature of the 'I' or the 'self' by asking questions like, 'Who am I?' This process of self-inquiry involves looking deeply within oneself to discern the true nature of consciousness. His teachings emphasized the idea that the ultimate truth or reality is beyond the identification with the

----

[7#] Refer to the Preface

body and mind. He taught that the true self is the unchanging, eternal awareness that underlies all experiences. This concept aligns with the idea of the 'observer' as a witness to thoughts, emotions and experiences, rather than being identified with them.[8#]

Playing such a complex role requires advanced leadership capabilities that PM Modi consistently demonstrates. He is not only able to have a systems view of a given situation and appreciate the different stakeholders involved, but he is also able to move seamlessly between being an observer and then acting as the lead protagonist, mobilizing his team to act.

From the first Prime Minister of India, Jawaharlal Nehru, each subsequent PM has attempted various actions that they thought would begin to solve the Kashmir problem. They tried shifting the issue to the United Nations, tried going to war with Pakistan, buying peace with Pakistan, using trade embargoes as a weapon, cutting off all diplomatic engagement, halting sporting ties between the nations, holding elections, dismissing governments and more. Each leader attempted to implement solutions that they thought would work in the short-term. None had the willingness, the courage or the leadership to see the larger picture from a strategic perspective. It is, therefore, in this context that PM Modi's pathbreaking action of revoking Article 370 of the Indian Constitution should be seen and studied. The leadership he exercised during the months leading up to this event demonstrates his adaptiveness, resilience, strategic intent and commitment to the cause of improving the lives of the common Kashmiri despite the insurmountable challenges.

Heifetz explains that at the beginning of the adaptive process, people may not see that the new situation will be any better than the current condition and this discourages them from trying out anything experimental or bold. Most people

---

[8#] Refer to the chapter Leading with the Soul: The Intersection of Leadership and Spiritual Growth

prefer to operate within comfort zones and are not willing to risk potential disequilibrium. The elite had gotten accustomed to comfortable privileges arising out of the special status of Kashmir. Any change from this status quo meant the potential for loss. The political class and the residents of Kashmir were inclined to avoid any painful adjustments in their lives if they could postpone them. It was easier to place the burden on somebody else and call for third-party interventions. When fears and passions run high, people can become desperate looking for answers. This dynamic renders any solution inherently dangerous.[8] The political elite of Kashmir threw several dares at the Indian government and the Prime Minister, which created an environment of fear about the consequences that could emerge from the revocation of the Article 370.

It was in this situation that PM Modi had to act with sensitivity and decisiveness without losing sight of the goal of integrating Kashmir into the rest of the country and ushering in much-needed peace and prosperity. In the position of authority that he was in, there were strong internal pressures that demanded him to focus on the technical aspects of the problem by limiting solutions to holding elections, releasing special grants and ensuring a larger presence of the armed forces to provide security in Kashmir. Stepping up to the plate meant raising questions that delve into the core of people's habits and cultivated beliefs and which demand a shift in their loyalties. In the hugely factionalized ecosystem that Kashmir was in, balancing the priorities and perspectives of several stakeholders and making their losses more bearable required a kind of leadership that was at once firm but gentle, and compassionate but ready to quell violence; it required a leader who understood the prevailing environment in Kashmir and the history behind the problem without losing sight of the future that could be created. This situation required PM Modi's sustained presence, the sakshi bhava that he has cultivated, the trust he has earned from the citizens, and his ability to communicate to the common people that his actions were for their welfare now and beneficial in the long-run.

The speech he gave after the revocation demonstrates his ability to give the credit of shaping the destiny of the nation back to the people, to mobilize the people to take responsibility for the tasks needed for transformation, and his ability to take on powerful interests while staying focused on the larger purpose. Quoting a long line of stalwarts such as Sardar Vallabhbhai Patel, Shyama Prasad Mukherjee and others, who selflessly strove for the unity of the country, it was evident that PM Modi was neither interested nor intent on cornering glory. He saw the technical decisions made by several of his predecessors as opportunities that had contributed to ripening the issue, and he found his opportunity to decisively build on them. He demonstrated a great skill in leadership which is to seize the moment and initiate change when the timing is most opportune. It is also to his credit that despite the nation looking to him to solve difficult problems, he was not seduced into believing that he was the lone saviour.

While it appears natural to an observer for the Prime Minister to be willing to constantly experiment and take calculated risks, one needs to understand how the PM can embrace challenges and persist amid setbacks. In her book *Mindset*, renowned psychologist Dr Carol S. Dweck explains how one's mindset affects their attitude, behaviour and, ultimately, their success in various aspects of life. Dr Dweck proposes two main types of mindsets: the 'fixed mindset' and the 'growth mindset'. People with a fixed mindset tend to believe that their abilities, intelligence and talents are static traits that cannot be changed. They often avoid challenges because they fear failure, believing that it reflects poorly on their inherent abilities. They may also give up easily when faced with obstacles or setbacks. People with a growth mindset, on the other hand, believe that their abilities and intelligence can be developed through effort, learning and perseverance. They see challenges as opportunities for growth and view failures as a natural part of the learning process. Dr Dweck emphasizes the importance of cultivating a growth mindset to foster resilience, experience continuous learning and ultimately, achieve one's full potential. Prime Minister Modi is a perfect example of how self-awareness, effort and the power of positive thinking contribute to his growth mindset.

Hardeep Singh Puri, Modi's Cabinet colleague, believes that the PM's ability to stay focused on a specific goal is driven by the maxim of what is good for the country. He views the Prime Minister's single-minded focus on the work at hand, his ability to win the trust of the nation and his lack of desire for credit are all driven by his conviction that he is a mere instrument ushering in the change that India requires. Narendra Modi has credited his nationalistic service aspirations to the inspiration from the life and message of Swami Vivekananda. As mentioned earlier in the chapter 'Charting a Bold Course: Visionary Leadership in Action', Swami Vivekananda had proclaimed that the national ideals of India were tyaga (sacrifice) and seva (service). For him, selfless service to the masses was a way to attain eternal happiness and liberation from the mundane. While advocating for seva, he advocated for restraining the egoistic need to 'be seen' doing the seva and claiming credit for one's actions of service. Real service, as per Swami Vivekananda, was dispassionate work that one undertook in the spirit of service to the divinity one sees in another. His call for the youth of India was to see service as a means of spiritual progress to be undertaken with the conviction that they were mere instruments of the divine. He asked them to feel blessed that they were provided the opportunity to serve.

Rajnath Singh, a senior Cabinet colleague of the Prime Minister of many years, finds Narendra Modi one of the few people he knows who 'walks the talk'. Singh credits Modi's courage, creativity and decisiveness—which he uses in his professional life—for his heightened sense of self and understanding to the government ecosystem.

Similarly, BVR mentions that he could perform his role well during the difficult days of his tenure as the chief secretary of Kashmir only because of the visionary guidance, clarity of directions and the systems approach that the PM utilized in dealing with the problem. He remembers the day he reached out to the PM to understand his expectations of him in the new role. The Prime Minister was clear—he asked Subrahmanyam to focus on ensuring good governance, delivering on development, restoring the rule of law, handing the economy into the local populace's hands and preparing the ground for the restoration of the political process, as the assembly then was still in the state of suspended animation. This clarity of the work on hand inspired BVR to undertake the most challenging task of his professional career.

The ability to listen deeply and take a helicopter view of the situation enables the PM to distance himself from the immediate situation to gain a broader view of the issues at hand and make more effective decisions. The PM was aware that he would encounter resistance in his efforts and that he would need to address the loss that came with change. By acknowledging fears of the different stakeholders and managing resistance while maintaining a clear focus on the goal, he provided people like Subrahmanyam the leeway to experiment and make some hard decisions.

When Narendra Modi got into political office for the first time as the chief minister (CM) of Gujarat, he had no formal administrative experience of the government system. Though he had a long stint as an RSS pracharak and as a general secretary in the BJP, taking on the CM's role suddenly, and during a crisis, added a new aspect to his public life. While he was aware of his competencies, he needed to understand and appreciate how to negotiate a long-standing bureaucratic system. How one operates in a domain where they have not had much direct experience is a true test of leadership. It demands the humility to recognize the need to learn and the willingness to do the hard work of learning as quickly as possible. Hasmukh Adhia, a retired civil servant who worked with the Prime Minister very closely since his chief minister days, recollects how Modi spent his first forty to forty-five days as CM on a continuous

learning spree. He reviewed each of the forty-two ministries—
one a day—and spent long hours working to understand what
they did, how they did it and who were the people involved in
doing it. During those six- to eight-hour-long daily meetings,
he hardly intervened except to ask the occasional clarifying
question. Within the next couple of months, he pretty much
knew everything there was to know about governing the state.
This, coupled with his ground knowledge and citizen connect,
gave him a complete systems perspective of what existed
and what could be done in the most efficient and effective
manner possible. To this day, Modi is quick to appreciate the
importance of context, the nature of the ecosystem in which
one is operating, the different players at the table, and how
best to mobilize an entire team to function with a common end
goal in mind.

The Prime Minister's approach to addressing the Kashmir
issue serves as a clear demonstration of his commitment,
historical awareness, sensitivity, continuous learning capacity
and his ability to adopt a comprehensive perspective for
ongoing assessment and action. PM Modi gained valuable first-
hand insight into the Kashmir problem through his leadership
of the Ekta Yatra[9], where he championed national unity. He
was also well-informed about the challenges posed by Article
370, including tensions between Shia and Sunni Muslims, the
mass and forced displacement of Kashmiri Pandits and the
complexities of asymmetric federalism.

His commitment to solving the issue was a long-standing
one and had begun in 1992 itself. During the 1980s and 1990s,
the country was in a very precarious state with multiple fissure
points—such as Jammu and Kashmir, Punjab and Assam. As
a response to the unprecedented situation, the then BJP party
president, Murli Manohar Joshi, decided to embark on an Ekta
Yatra. The yatra would begin from Kanyakumari, the place
where Swami Vivekananda found the purpose of his life, and
end with the hoisting of the national flag at Lal Chowk in

Srinagar. The organizational responsibility for this yatra was given to Modi. The Ekta Yatra began on 11 December 1991, coinciding with the birth anniversary of Subramania Bharati[10] and the *Balidan Diwas* (Martyrdom Day) of Guru Tegh Bahadur.[11]

Modi was successful in this challenging endeavour and he recollected this incident in detail while serving as the CM of Gujarat:

> I had said during the public meeting in Hyderabad that those terrorists have challenged me, questioning who was daring enough to wave the Indian flag at Lal Chowk in Srinagar and return alive. I further declared at the public meeting that I would reach Lal Chowk in Srinagar on the 26th January at 11 a.m. sharp. I would not wear any bulletproof jacket nor would I board any bulletproof vehicle. I would have nothing in my hands except the Tricolour. And on 26th January at 11 a.m., it would be decided at Lal Chowk in Srinagar who is truly daring and who is the real son of his mother. Friends, I went there on time. I waved the flag and today I am here right in front of you.[12]

The ability to maintain his cool under enormous stress (being the direct target of terrorists), while still being able to make quick decisions, organize a nationwide campaign and see the task through completion requires *atmabala* (inner strength) and *vairagya* (renunciation). The symbolic elements he used, that is Swami Vivekananda's place of purpose, Balidan Diwas of Guru Tegh Bahadur and more, are not simple organizational tactics but reflect a deep connection to a hidden reservoir of Indian historical strength, which is felt by the whole of the nation.

In order to get a fresh perspective and different approach to managing the change, a new set of people had to be in charge. This was necessary to remove any prejudice in the existing leadership and to inspire confidence in the people. It was also important to communicate to the people that the spirit of *Kashmiriyat*[13] would not be compromised with. Identifying an officer who understood how to operate in a conflict situation, someone who understood the PM's thinking and problem-solving approach and someone development-oriented was needed. That is why PM Modi handpicked BVR and appointed him as the chief secretary of the state.

Within a few months of starting his tenure as the chief secretary, BVR got a sense of the people's mood. They were despondent, tired of the continued violence, helpless against the corrupt local political elite and living with a trust deficit. Most did not understand how by being an insular state with a closed economy, Jammu and Kashmir was left behind the rest of the country in development. People were hankering for peace and prosperity and were fatigued with the status quo. This was also one of the few states that had not been colonized by the British and was ruled by kings. Because of this, formal administrative mechanisms that the rest of the country was used to were absent for the people of Jammu and Kashmir. BVR took it upon himself to regularly update the Prime Minister on these realities through monthly reports, aiming to seek his guidance as well. This further validated the view the PM had, that the existence of Article 370 was the root cause of the mess that the state was in. Its revocation was critical for the erstwhile state's political, emotional, economic and social integration into the rest of the country. With the assembly being in a state of suspended animation, time was also of the essence as the decision had to be made within six months of imposing Governor's Rule.

The mood in the rest of the country was not in favour of this asymmetrical federalism and the existence of a dual situation[14] was felt unjustified. Shyama Prasad Mukherjee, the founder of the Bharatiya Jana Sangh (considered as the precursor of the Bharatiya Janata Party) had said in June 2012, '*Ek desh mein do Vidhan, do Pradhan aur do Nishan nahi chalenge* [A single country can't have two constitutions, two prime ministers, and two national emblems].' He had died during his visit to Kashmir and his death continues to be viewed with suspicion.

Taking this momentous decision of revocation meant that the Prime Minister had to be prepared for criticism, challenges and personal attacks. He had to have a strategy for dealing with the inevitable heat that comes with taking on difficult issues and leading through change. His political acumen also sensed that the rest of the country was rallying to support his efforts.

The critical role of leadership is to mobilize oneself and one's resources for societally constructive purposes amidst enormous uncertainty. The sensitivity of the decision meant the discussions were limited to a handful of people, including the Home Minister Amit Shah and the National Security Adviser Ajit Doval.

The actions that were taken included building a coalition of local people, building consensus in the larger Muslim countries and in the Muslim communities within India, keeping vested political interests in check and promoting tourism to mobilize local economies. It was also required that the government remove or amend nearly 300 obsolete laws that were impeding progress, along with a delimitation exercise.[15] Dividing the state into two entities helped contain the Kashmir issue within Jammu and Kashmir. This also allowed the government to fulfil the much-demanded aspirations of a union territory for Ladakh. To bring in freshness of thinking, a new governor was needed. A career politician, Satya Pal Malik, was brought in as Vohra's replacement.

It was Modi's intention to establish a political coalition locally by building a political process from the grassroots, upwards. Though Jammu and Kashmir had a two-tier panchayat on paper, elections were held more than a decade ago. The sarpanch (head of the panchayat) had little or no power and very little space for political growth, which ensured that the existing political elite retained their power and influence. This made it imperative that one of the early steps for the revocation had to be to amend the Panchayat Act to bring in a three-tier system with real powers given to the panchayats. Elections were held in August 2018 and a new cadre of grassroots politicians was created. Experiencing powers for local governance and development enabled panchayat leaders to appreciate the real intent of the democratization the PM had in mind. To further the impact, Gujjar Muslims and the nomadic tribes who were traditionally out of mainstream politics were also brought in. For the first time, affirmative action in reserving seats for Scheduled Tribes[16] in the Assembly was done by bringing the necessary legislation.

Furthermore, it was crucial to garner support and cooperation from the global community. In addition to ensuring that all nations were well-informed about the initiative undertaken, it was emphasized that the situation was an internal matter for India and the country would address it accordingly. Diplomats were extended invitations to visit Kashmir, providing them with an opportunity to witness the on-ground developments and observe the positive responses of the local population.

Building trust in the government meant delivering on the development promises made and eliminating corruption. Decisions had to be fair and devoid of any partisanship or petty politics. The message to the chief secretary from the Prime Minister was clear on this. Apart from asking him to stay focused on not allowing any kind of petty politics to creep in, ensuring good governance, promoting development and infrastructure growth across the state, he provided unstinted support and infused BVR with the confidence to act. He was clear about the Line of Control and kept the communication lines with him open and direct. More importantly he ensured that BVR could act with the knowledge that he had the PM's backing and that the PM was ready to take the heat and provide his sustained leadership presence throughout the process.

Ultimately, Jammu and Kashmir was brought to lasting peace through this bold move. Terror incidents have shown a 70 per cent decline compared to three decades ago, and other incidents like stone pelting and strikes have been brought down to zero. Similarly, there has been a remarkable decrease in the deaths of civilians and security personnel.[17] While there had been multiple attempts by the Opposition to rescind this step of abrogation, the Supreme Court of India put a final closure on the issue, praising the Government's intention and actions, after four years of careful deliberation.[18]

After the final closure, the PM penned his thoughts on the issue:

> . . . due to centuries of colonization, most notably economic and mental subjugation, we became a confused society of sorts. Rather than taking a clear position on basic things, we allowed duality, leading to confusion. Sadly, Jammu and Kashmir (J&K) became a victim of such a mindset . . . It was always my firm belief that what had happened in J&K was a great betrayal—of our nation and of the people living there. It was also my strong desire to do whatever I can to remove this blot, this injustice done to the people. I have always wanted to work to alleviate the suffering of the people of Jammu and Kashmir . . . while serving the people of J&K, we gave primacy to three pillars—understanding citizens' concerns, building trust through supportive actions, and prioritizing development, development, and more development . . . In its verdict on December 11, the Supreme Court has strengthened the spirit of "Ek Bharat, Shreshtha Bharat". It has reminded us that what defines us are bonds of unity and a shared commitment to good governance. Today, the dreams of the people are no longer prisoners of the past but about possibilities for the future. After all, development, democracy, and dignity have replaced disillusionment, disappointment and despondency.[19]

Leaders must find a balance between adapting to new circumstances and maintaining their core values and authenticity. These actions taken by the PM are a lesson for leaders on how to navigate such a web of tensions. PM Modi has a holistic approach to learning that has made it possible for him to adapt and thrive in complex and rapidly changing environments. Having a systems approach to his thinking, Modi is able to form a deep understanding of the interrelationships and interdependencies among various elements within an ecosystem. This approach allows him to look beyond isolated events and address the underlying structures that influence behaviours and outcomes. Apart from mapping the various stakeholders operating within a system, it also gives him an appreciation of the perspectives and the unspoken motives that each of these stakeholders bring to the table.

Mere knowledge of how systems operate may not give a person all the information they need on how best to act in the context in which they are placed. They would also need the ability, discipline and desire to engage in personal mastery. An effective leader has to be a lifelong learner who not only absorbs what they learn but who is also reflective enough to appropriately use what they learn, when the situation demands it. Modi's constant striving to achieve his full potential by developing his skills, clarifying his personal vision and aligning his actions with his values is what stands out the most. Dharmendra Pradhan, a minister in his Cabinet, puts it succinctly, ' . . . a person who speaks less but learns a lot, allows for deliberations and debate, a person with conviction in the system's approach with an eye for detail, and possesses the unusual blend of being a *rishi* and a ruler (*rajarishi*) . . . '

Peter Senge, American systems scientist who is a senior lecturer at the MIT Sloan School of Management, writes about this ability in his book, *The Fifth Discipline: The Art and Practice of the Learning Organization*. He says that 'mental models' are the assumptions, beliefs and perceptions that individuals and organizations hold. Senge highlights the need to challenge and revise these mental models to foster more effective decision-making and problem-solving. Senge emphasizes the importance of involving all members in creating and committing to a shared vision, which helps align efforts and inspire meaningful action.

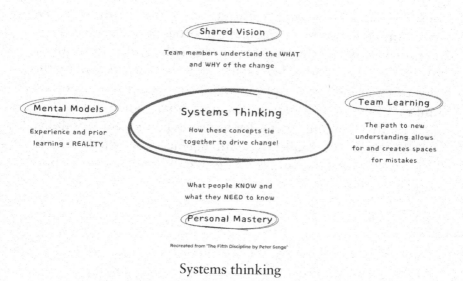

Systems thinking

(From *The Fifth Discipline* by Peter Senge)

Very few leaders around the world can seamlessly synthesize the elements of community mobilization, strategic visioning, selfless action, clarity of thought, taking ownership for the consequences of decisions and providing unstinted support to a team. By applying systems thinking, cultivating personal mastery, promoting shared vision, encouraging team learning and challenging mental models, Prime Minister Modi has pushed the limits of the governmental and societal ecosystems.

In examining Narendra Modi's leadership through the lens of adaptive leadership, one finds a compelling illustration of a leader who is unafraid to challenge conventions and drive transformation. Much like Ronald Heifetz's framework of exercising adaptive leadership, Modi has demonstrated a keen ability to understand diverse perspectives and navigate through complex sociopolitical landscapes. He mobilized a coalition with a strong domestic and international backing, raised the heat on a dormant issue to prompt action, and communicated a vision that ripened the issue for resolution in the national consciousness. His capacity to 'get on the balcony'—to rise above immediate crises and gain a broader view—has been instrumental in steering the nation through significant reforms and challenges. Modi's leadership style is a testament to the power of adaptability, emphasizing the importance of visionary thinking, and of continuous learning and course correction. In a rapidly changing world, leaders who embrace adaptability and harness the collective intelligence of their teams, communities or nations, are those that leave a lasting impact on their societies.

IV

Expanding the Leadership Horizon

सुवर्णपुष्पां पृथिवीं चिन्वन्ति पुरुषास्त्रयः ।
शूरश्च कृतविद्यश्च यश्च जानाति सेवितुम् ॥

suvarṇapuṣpāṃ pṛthivīṃ cinvanti puruṣāstrayaḥ |
śūraśca kṛtavidyaśca yaśca jānāti sevitum ||
—Vidura Neeti Shloka 64

He that is possessed of bravery, he that is possessed of learning, and
he that knows how to protect others, these three are always able to
gather flowers of gold from the earth.

~

Narendra Modi's leadership has significantly redefined India's role on the global stage, emphasizing a blend of ancient wisdom and modern pragmatism. Through initiatives like the International Solar Alliance, the Coalition for Disaster Resilient Infrastructure and the G20 Summit of 2023, Modi has showcased India as a forward-thinking and dynamic force, committed to addressing global challenges such as climate change, disaster resilience and sustainable development. His approach, rooted in the concept of *Vasudhaiva Kutumbakam* (the world is one family), has fostered a spirit of cooperation and inclusivity, enhancing India's diplomatic relations and economic partnerships. Reinforced by his personal rapport with leaders of other countries, it has served to positively influence the global consensus on many important issues. This approach, augmented by Modi's adept use of soft power and cultural diplomacy, has enhanced India's ability to build bridges across nations, fostering a shared vision for global welfare and sustainable growth. Furthermore, his leadership in navigating complex geopolitical issues and advocating for the Global South underscores India's emerging role as a key player in shaping a more equitable global order.

~

Vision Beyond Borders: Exploring the Dynamics of Global Leadership

As Europe entered its modern era, it embarked on voyages of exploration to discover new lands and peoples across the globe. This marked the onset of an era characterized by widespread interactions, ultimately shaping the current global order. Alongside technological progress, this period also witnessed the dark shadows of exploitative colonization and devastating conflicts. The resulting world order was bipolar, with superpowers assuming leadership roles and acting as global arbiters. This dynamic led to a 'with us or against us' paradigm, where alliances were formed based on self-interest and pragmatic calculations; and tactics like regime changes and debt trap diplomacy were deemed acceptable. Genuine camaraderie between nations remained elusive in that scenario.

At its core, this present understanding of the world is largely influenced by the historical experiences of the Western world, where values of individualism, realism and liberalism have been dominant shaping forces. However, delving into ancient Eastern wisdom and perspectives unveils a different lens through which the world is viewed. The Eastern viewpoint emphasizes society, considering spiritual enlightenment and collective well-being as fundamental principles that guide human interactions on the planet.[1]

According to Hindu and Jain cosmology, Mount Meru is believed to be the epicentre of all physical, metaphysical and spiritual universes. Described as a towering golden mountain, it stands as the highest point in all of existence, around which all celestial bodies orbit. Legend has it that King Bharata, from whom Bharat (India) derives its name, established himself—after numerous wars—as a *Chakravarti*, a ruler of the world. While Mount Meru is considered beyond the reach of mortal beings, it is accessible only to a Chakravarti.

After conquering all the kings in the world, King Bharata ascended Mount Meru to plant his flag and proclaim himself as the world's first Chakravarti. However, upon reaching the summit, he found countless flags of kings from bygone eras. It dawned on him that the physical conquest of the world is nothing but a fleeting achievement, and that true victory lies in conquering the self.

The Indian approach to global leadership isn't rooted in territorial conquest, but in *dharmavijaya*—a victory achieved through spiritual and cultural influence. This can only be embodied by one who believes in the concept of the entire world as a single family—Vasudhaiva Kutumbakam.

Prime Minister Modi's approach to position India as a global soft power is driven by this spirit of togetherness. Under his leadership, India's emergence as a global soft power has been a remarkable journey, propelled by a multifaceted approach that encompasses culture, diplomacy and technology. This transformation has not only bolstered India's global standing but has also made it an influential player in shaping the world's perceptions and interactions. He aligns traditional values with modern global challenges, thereby presenting India as a unique, principle-driven player on the world stage. His approach intertwines the philosophical with the practical, advocating for global peace, harmony and sustainable development, while also leveraging India's soft power to enhance trade, technology and strategic partnerships.

At the heart of India's soft power lies its rich cultural tapestry—a mosaic of traditions, languages and art forms that span millennia. Indian cuisine, renowned for its diverse flavours and aromatic spices, has found a place on tables worldwide.

The melodious strains of classical Indian music and the mesmerizing movements of dance forms like Bharatanatyam and Kathak captivate audiences internationally. Indian art, with its intricate patterns and vibrant colours, continues to inspire artists across the globe. However, perhaps the most prominent cultural export is Bollywood, the Indian film industry, which has gained a massive global following, becoming a symbol of India's cultural influence. Yoga, another jewel in India's soft-power crown, has transcended boundaries to become a global phenomenon. Millions around the world embrace yoga as a pathway to physical and mental well-being, embodying India's age-old wisdom on holistic wellness. Ayurveda, the traditional Indian system of medicine, has also made inroads into the international health and wellness arena.

India's diaspora, spread across the world, has played a pivotal role in spreading its soft power. Individuals of Indian origin have excelled in various fields, from business to politics, and have acted as cultural ambassadors, forging deep connections between India and their adopted countries. Their success stories are a testament to the opportunities and diversity that India represents. The Indian economy's impressive growth has not gone unnoticed on the global stage. As one of the world's largest and fastest-growing economies, India has become an attractive destination for trade and investment. This economic prowess has enabled India to exert influence through economic diplomacy, fostering partnerships and collaborations worldwide. In the realm of technology, India has established itself as a formidable force. The Indian IT industry, known for its software services and innovation, has contributed significantly to the global tech sector. Indian professionals and entrepreneurs have left an indelible mark on the digital landscape, demonstrating the country's technological expertise.

India's diplomatic outreach, too, has played a crucial role in enhancing its soft power. The nation actively collaborates with international organizations and in peacekeeping missions, making its presence felt on the global stage. India's contributions to addressing pressing global issues, such as climate change and sustainable development, have garnered recognition and respect. Cultural exchanges further strengthen India's soft power. The country hosts international events like the International Film Festival of India[2] and the Festival of India[3] in various countries, fostering people-to-people connections and showcasing its cultural diversity. Institutions like the Indian Council for Cultural Relations (ICCR) actively promote Indian languages, literature and art worldwide. India's ancient philosophical and spiritual heritage, which includes Hinduism, Buddhism, Jainism and various schools of thought, continues to inspire seekers of spiritual wisdom around the world. These ancient teachings resonate with those who seek a deeper understanding of life and existence. Moreover, India has taken on global challenges with a sense of responsibility. Its proactive role in addressing issues like climate change, renewable energy, and vaccine production during the Covid-19 pandemic has earned it goodwill and respect on the world stage.

This heritage and goodwill are what PM Modi leverages in his leadership, advocating for a peaceful world order that collaboratively addresses the challenges confronting humanity.

Starting with the Neighbourhood

From his early days as the chief minister of Gujarat, PM Modi has been keen on understanding the forces that drive geopolitics and the fleeting context of international relations. Whether it was organizing events like Vibrant Gujarat[4] to attract foreign investments or his travels to different countries to explore their advancements, Modi has shown an appreciation for travel since his pracharak days. Pramod Kumar Mishra, the principal secretary to the Prime Minister, mentions how he would come back brimming with ideas after each visit outside India and try to see how best to contextualize and implement them in

Gujarat. For Modi, these visits were not just about building a network or forging partnerships, they facilitated learning about the intricacies of internationalism and global politics. For a future-looking person like Modi, these visits also provided him the exposure to formulate his vision of global citizenship and an interconnected and interdependent world order.

Evidence of Modi's dedication to these goals has been demonstrated since he was elected as the Prime Minister. He knew that the Global South had to play a critical role in the emerging new world order, and that it had to start with India expressing herself as the advocating voice for this. Inviting the heads of eight neighbouring nations to his swearing-in as the Prime Minister in May 2014 was a demonstration of his desire to realize a region where peace and prosperity would be the unifying forces.

Extending an invitation to Pakistan's prime minister, Nawaz Sharif, during escalating tensions between the two nations was an extraordinary display of Prime Minister Modi's dedication to the peace process. It also underscored his resolve to position India as a pivotal player on the global stage. This gesture was widely hailed in international relations circles as a diplomatic masterstroke, showcasing India's commitment to the broader regional welfare rather than purely national interests. Subsequent gestures, including the PM's inaugural foreign visit to Bhutan[5] and his historic address to the Nepal Parliament in 2014, further bolstered the PM's intentions of goodwill. Additionally, India's utilization of the South Asia satellite[6], developed and launched by the Indian Space Research Organisation (ISRO), has greatly enhanced communication and facilitated the sharing of meteorological data throughout the Indian subcontinent.

Unfortunately, even with capable leadership and adept skill, conflicts can arise despite the best intentions. The ancient Arthashastra[7], a governance treatise spanning two millennia, outlines four steps of conflict resolution: *saama* (praise and persuasion), *daana* (monetary incentives), *bheda* (creating divisions in the enemy ranks) and *danda* (force and punishment). Throughout history, India has experienced conflicts with neighbours that can be characterized by various fluctuations within these areas over time, notably its modern challenges with Pakistan.

Arthashastra's
Four Steps of Conflict Resolution

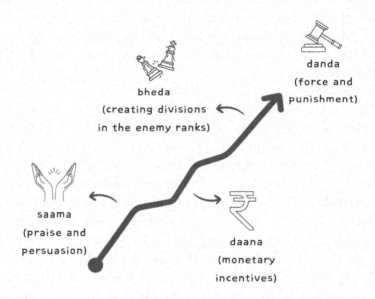

Despite multiple friendly overtures by PM Modi—including informal visits, like the one to Lahore for the wedding of the daughter of the former Pakistani PM,[8] and allowing the Pakistani military to inspect a terror strike in Pathankot[9]— terrorist activities orchestrated by Pakistani entities persisted. Following the attack on the Indian Army brigade headquarters in Uri in 2016, India pursued a two-pronged approach. This involved surgical strikes to dismantle terror infrastructure along the borders, coupled with vocal condemnation of state-sponsored terrorism on global platforms. This was complemented by strategic alliances with Gulf States, solidifying India's leadership role in the Global South. The shift in strategy—actively pursuing international isolation for Pakistan due to its involvement in sponsoring terrorism—aligns with the age-old wisdom derived from the Arthashastra, particularly the concept of *Raja–Mandala,* or the 'Circle of States'. This theory proposes that to effectively counter threats from a hostile neighbour, it is imperative to cultivate relationships with states both just outside and significantly beyond the geographical vicinity of that neighbour. This wider network serves as a strategic bulwark, reinforcing India's position in the region.

As a result of this resolute and decisive approach, Pakistan's capacity to spread terror has steadily waned. An international recognition of this resoluteness came to light when, ironically, the former PM of Pakistan, Imran Khan, lauded Indians as *khuddar quam*, meaning an extremely self-respecting people, thanks to its leadership.[10]

In addition to this decisive and strategic approach, one can witness Prime Minister Modi's compassionate diplomacy in his relations with neighbouring countries, unmistakable in his actions during the global Covid-19 pandemic in 2020. India took the initiative to convene a virtual meeting of SAARC[11] leaders on 15 March of that year, which led to the establishment of a SAARC Fund dedicated to combating the disease. India took the lead by making an initial contribution of $10 million (particularly significant as the United Nations Security Council [UNSC] was unable to convene at that time, given China's refusal to participate while holding the chair). In adherence to PM Modi's 'Neighbourhood First' policy, Bhutan and the Maldives were the first two countries to receive vaccines on 20 January 2021 (1,50,000 and 1,00,000 vaccines, respectively). Subsequently, Bangladesh and Nepal were provided doses on 21 January (two million and one million respectively) and

Myanmar, Seychelles and Mauritius on 22 January (1.5 million, 50,000 and 1,00,000 doses, respectively).[12]

This combination of soft and firm approaches, recognition of contextual role and responsibility and innovativeness in problem-solving has been the unique approach brought to Indian foreign policy by the PM.

Utilizing Foreign Policy as a Tool of Leadership

Diaspora Diplomacy

The legacy of colonization often leaves a lingering subservient mindset in the formerly colonized, even after gaining political independence. India's journey to freedom in 1947 followed nearly a millennium of continuous invasions and foreign dominions. This historical context bred a restrained approach in its foreign policies, often hesitant to assert its sovereignty even when faced with challenges.

Prime Minister Modi has consistently emphasized that the Indian populace needs to shed this subservient mentality to regain our rightful place on the global stage. Today, India's foreign policy is characterized by assertiveness, keen awareness of national interests, and a continuous reinforcement of its reliability through cultural diplomacy and outreach to the diaspora. India's external connections, particularly with its non-resident Indian community, have been galvanized to contribute to the nation's progress and take pride in its advancements. Beyond financial contributions or investments, PM Modi has also urged India's diaspora to act as brand ambassadors to bolster India's tourism potential. This was seen in action when Abu Dhabi invited PM Modi to inaugurate the first Hindu temple in its territory, in a symbolic gesture of interfaith harmony and reciprocation.[13]

India's connection with its diaspora across the world was often viewed through the narrow lens of remittances, failing to recognize the broader potential they held. Due to passive economic policies, many Indians sought opportunities abroad.

Rather than leveraging them as a conduit to establish stronger ties with advanced economies, there was a prevailing sentiment that they were ungrateful to their homeland. The PM, drawing from his experience of organizing Vibrant Gujarat summits during his tenure as the chief minister, understood and tapped into the nationalistic sentiment of the diaspora. In his inaugural address to the Indian diaspora at Madison Square Garden in the US, he declared, ' . . . I guess no politician in India would have received as much love as I have received. And I promise I will repay this loan with interest. I promise that I will build the India of your dreams'.[14] The significance of the diaspora has also been etched into the collective memory of host countries through the resounding success of these outreach events, further enhancing India's soft power. During the May 2023 diaspora event in Sydney, Australia, the Australian Prime Minister Anthony Albanese, witnessing the rockstar reception accorded to PM Modi by tens of thousands of the Indian diaspora, remarked, 'Prime Minister Modi is The Boss'.[15]

Personal Connect

Foreign policy transcends mere diplomatic formalities; it thrives on personal connections forged between leaders. Prime Minister Modi exemplifies this approach through his interactions with various heads of States, effectively leveraging these relationships to advance India's interests. His distinctive body language, characterized by warm hugs, the traditional Indian greeting of namaste, animated hand gestures, unwavering eye contact and expressive facial expressions, imparts a memorable presence on the global stage. The 'Modi Hug'[16] has evolved into a symbol of India's receptivity to warmth and collaboration in international relations, as noted by his biographer Nilanjan Mukhopadhyay. This gesture signifies camaraderie and equality, underlining Modi's intent to forge friendships.

Modi's global standing and magnetic personality are evident in the accolades he receives from world leaders. According to the Morning Consult Political Intelligence report, which tracks government leaders' approval ratings, Modi maintained his top position in global rankings with a 76 per cent approval in 2023. Italian PM Giorgia Meloni echoed this sentiment, commending him as 'the most loved one of all [leaders] around the world'.[17]

A striking illustration of this camaraderie in action occurred in 2015 when PM Modi and President Obama resolved the longstanding deadlock over the Indo-US nuclear pact. This breakthrough transpired during President Obama's visit as the Chief Guest for India's Republic Day parade, marking a pivotal moment in Indo-US relations. PM Modi astutely remarked, 'Relations between countries depend less on full stops and commas and more on the relationships between leaders . . . the chemistry between them'.[18]

On 8 March 2022 amid the Russo–Ukraine war, a humanitarian corridor was established for the evacuation of citizens from other countries, a feat initially impervious to diplomatic efforts. PM Modi personally engaged with the presidents of Ukraine and Russia, emphasizing the urgency of a ceasefire and a return to dialogue and diplomacy. This hands-on approach underscores Modi's unwavering commitment to fostering global peace and stability. In a similar time-sensitive, frictional situation, when the State of Qatar had sentenced eight Indian ex-navy personnel to death on alleged charges of espionage, the direct intervention of the PM and his meeting with the Emir of Qatar helped defuse the situation. The former navy personnel didn't just have their sentences commuted and pardoned but they were allowed safe passage back to India.[19]

Cultural Diplomacy

To effectively propagate the ethos of Vasudhaiva Kutumbakam and put it into practice, it's imperative to adopt the role of a cultural ambassador rather than that of a hegemon. Prime Minister Modi embodies this approach in every interaction with world leaders, whether it's by sharing vaccines or promoting yoga. The concept of observing International Yoga Day was initially proposed by the PM during his address at the United Nations General Assembly in September 2014. He suggested 21 June, the summer solstice, and the longest day in the Northern Hemisphere—as the date for this observance. This proposal garnered resounding support from UN member states, culminating in the adoption of a resolution on 11 December 2014, officially designating 21 June as International Yoga Day. This resolution was co-sponsored by a record 177 countries, underscoring the global acknowledgement of yoga's immense benefits and India's pivotal role in the international arena.[20]

In his address, the PM delineated his vision of development through the lens of yoga, as opposed to the consumerist approach to progress. He emphasized that achieving development, prosperity and well-being doesn't necessitate a path of reckless consumption. For India, reverence for nature is an integral facet of spiritualism. Yoga, an invaluable legacy of our ancient tradition, embodies the union of mind and body, thought and action, restraint and fulfilment, and harmony between humanity and nature. It's a holistic approach to health and well-being, transcending mere physical exercise. It fosters a sense of unity with oneself, the world and nature. By instigating lifestyle changes and raising awareness, yoga can be a potent tool in addressing climate change. The Prime Minister rallied for collective endeavours in establishing an International Day of Yoga, propelling it to become a global phenomenon and forging a mental space for all things Indian.

Ancient India was renowned for its wisdom and the temple-universities that attracted students from around the globe. This era also witnessed the construction of some of India's most magnificent structures and icons. While the pillaging of jewels from colonized nations by imperial powers is well-documented, the extent of the plundering of religio-cultural heritage often went unnoticed. Many temples, once marvels of the world, constructed during India's classical age, were pillaged, desecrated and razed during multiple iconoclastic invasions.

Additionally, priceless religious and cultural treasures in the form of idols and statues were forcibly taken and traded in the international market.

Following India's independence, insufficient efforts were made to recover these stolen legacies, which were once the spiritual heart of their communities. The historical demonstration of indifference towards India's cultural heritage bred disillusionment among large sections of the population and smuggling persisted even after India gained independence.

Under the current leadership, there's been a reinvigorated focus on restoring India's cultural pride. The Prime Minister and his administration have consistently urged their foreign counterparts to repatriate smuggled idols of deities. Before 2014, only thirteen artifacts had been recovered. However, with the change in leadership and a more resolute stance, over 200 idols have been repatriated between 2014 and 2022.

Much of the success of this endeavour is attributed to continuous cultural and diplomatic outreach through embassies and diasporas, reinforced at the highest level. Consistent reminders and assertive soft power have been the guiding principles that are now yielding tangible results.

In the eighty-sixth edition of his *Mann Ki Baat*, the PM emphasized, 'Nations where these idols were smuggled to now realize and feel India's attachment to the stolen heritage. They acknowledge the importance attached to such idols in India.'

The PM stressed that bringing these idols back to the country is a 'responsibility towards Mother India'. He said, 'Over a thousand years in our history, magnificent idols and statues were sculpted in every corner of India. Each of our idols reflects its own time. Not only were they unique examples of Indian sculpture skills, but our faiths were also tied with them. But in the past, many idols were stolen and smuggled from India to different countries. For them, the stolen objects were just idols. These idols are part of India's soul and faith'.[21]

The Prime Minister hasn't just made efforts to help retrieve these antiquities but personally accompanied them back during his official tours abroad. The recent success is a testament to continuous cultural relations with various countries worldwide and the warm personal relations that the Prime Minister shares with other heads of state. The idols aren't merely recovered; they are intended to be reinstated at their original locations, such as the idol of Annapurna Devi in the Kashi Vishwanath temple complex.[22] This kind of cultural grounding ensures that a leader maintains strong relational ties with constituents of all strata and does not get swayed by the influence of elites.

Multilateral and Strategic Partnerships

Employing the principles of seva and *aparigraha* (non-hoarding) towards the global community while prioritizing national interests and recognizing the importance of *artha* (wealth) in upholding dharma is a cornerstone of leadership for any aspiring global leader. To realize this vision, leaders must proactively explore diverse avenues, nurture relationships and forge strategic partnerships. In such partnerships, participants maintain their individual agency while sharing the benefits and risks of their joint actions. Essential to these partnerships are consistent communication, collaboration, adaptive governance and the effective use of global virtual teams.

Since assuming office, the PM has undertaken over seventy-seven foreign visits,[23] building and reinforcing ties with countries that India has had relationships with. Even amid the challenges posed by the pandemic in 2020–21, he actively participated in at least twenty-five bilateral and multilateral virtual summits.

Physical infrastructure is a key driver of economic growth, and in the global forum, an integrated economy is a resilient economy. The successful regional integration among European nations stands as a compelling model for emulation. This has prompted suggestions to replicate a similar model in the Indian subcontinent, leveraging various trade, mobility and energy networks. During the 18th SAARC summit in Kathmandu in 2014, Prime Minister Modi highlighted SAARC's underwhelming performance in terms of trade and investment. He noted that, while Indian companies were investing substantial amounts abroad, only a minute 1 per cent of these investments were directed towards the South Asian region. This led to the proposal of the SAARC Motor Vehicle Agreement for the Regulation of Passenger and Cargo Vehicular Traffic. This would have allowed member States allowing the vehicles of other Member States to ply in their territory for transportation of cargo and passengers subject to various terms and conditions in the agreement. However, the proposal was opposed by Pakistan, citing concerns about India's potential access to landlocked Afghanistan.[24]

In a move demonstrating adaptive governance, a sub-regional alliance comprising Bangladesh, Bhutan, India and Nepal (BBIN) was activated. In 2015, the signing of the BBIN Motor Vehicle Agreement (MVA) in Thimphu was hailed as a significant milestone in sub-regional unity. This agreement was crafted to facilitate a smoother cross-border movement of vehicles and goods, furthering the goal of enhanced connectivity within the region.[25]

The reorientation of India's relationship with the Arab countries is another example of strong leadership producing results-driven partnerships. Where earlier the relations of India with Arab countries were generally looked at through the prism of the Israel–Palestine issue and religion, the turnaround towards unleashing the economic potential and convergences of interest has been welcomed by both sides. The India–UAE relationship was elevated to a Comprehensive Strategic Partnership in 2017, a milestone achieved within two years of Modi's historic visit to the UAE in 2015—the first by an Indian PM in thirty-four years. This led to a series of five additional visits over the next eight years, significantly deepening bilateral ties. In 2022, further solidifying this relationship, both countries signed a Comprehensive Economic Partnership Agreement. Consequently, the UAE has emerged as India's third-largest trading partner and its second-largest export destination.[26]

In 2023, at the G20 event on the Partnership for Global Infrastructure and Investment, PM Modi announced the transcontinental India-Middle East-Europe Economic Corridor. This initiative is a part of the Partnership for Global Infrastructure and Investment (PGII) (G7 initiative), that seeks to finance infrastructure projects in underdeveloped nations through public and private contributions.

The economic corridor intends to link both continents to commercial hubs and facilitate the development and export of clean energy, lay undersea cables and link energy grids and telecommunication lines to expand reliable access to electricity, enable innovation of advanced clean energy technology and connect communities to secure and stable Internet.[27]

There is potential for India to export green hydrogen to Saudi Arabia, feeding into the proposed economic corridor to Europe via the UAE. India is targeting five-million-tonne green hydrogen capacity by 2030 and aims to become an export hub for the 'fuel of the future'. This will mark the first offshore link in the PM's 'One Sun, One World, One Grid' vision of a global grid for primarily green power.

The MoU also focuses on cooperation in the areas of petroleum reserves—a move that could lead to Saudi investment in the expansion of India's strategic oil and gas storage capacities. India currently has a strategic oil reserve of a little over five million tonnes spread across three locations and stores LPG in a cavern for commercial purposes.[28]

The PM, in his statements related to the corridor announcement, also spoke about trust enhancement globally, betterment of the Global South and transparent debt agreements. He said, 'We have implemented infrastructure projects in areas such as energy, railway, water and technology parks in several countries of the Global South as their trusted partner. In these endeavours we have laid special emphasis on a demand-driven and transparent approach, compliance with international norms, rules and laws, respect for the sovereignty and territorial integrity of all nations, promoting financial viability in place of increasing the debt burden, and following all environmental-related standards'.[29]

Access to energy is an important determinant of any country's economic health and stability. During volatile events such as wars and conflicts, the oil and gas markets fluctuate rapidly, diminishing the ability of small economies to secure their energy. There are also the moral ramifications of the war, leaving countries to choose sides, thus leaving the smaller countries to fend for themselves. At an event hosted by the Indian High Commission in London in November 2023, the Indian External Affairs Minister remarked that the domestic decision to purchase oil from Russia, amidst intense Western pressure to sanction Russia and stop purchase of its oil, helped other countries as well. Being the third-largest buyer of crude oil, India's decision to source its oil requirements from Russia helped soften the global crude oil prices and kept them in the average range of $85–95 a barrel.[30] While India did receive flak initially for not supporting Ukraine unconditionally, on the larger scale it helped it to retain its autonomy and aid other countries through the process as well.

The PM's conviction of remaining steadfast in the face of immense pressure paid off and demonstrated that if one is reasonably certain in their course of action and has the courage of conviction to follow through, success may not be that difficult to achieve.

Leadership for Global Responsibility and Responsiveness

Climate change is another front where Modi has displayed decisive leadership. India has been proactively tackling climate challenges for the sake of future generations. A departure in the approach from previous dispensations is demonstrated in the rooting of the climate agenda in India's own customs and knowledge. The PM has simultaneously built domestic support for this initiative, while at the same time, signalling that India would take the lead on this initiative instead of following the others' diktats. The Intended Nationally Determined

Contribution document that India submitted before the CoP-21 in October of 2015, began with the quote from Yajurveda, an ancient Indian scripture.[31] It states, 'India has a long history and tradition of harmonious coexistence between man and nature. Human beings have regarded fauna and flora as part of their family. This is part of our heritage and manifests in our lifestyle and traditional practices'.[32]

However, even while India is taking leadership and coaxing countries to do more, the PM has introduced a large measure of realism and frank talk with the developed countries as to what can be their ambition, and how there needs to be a 'common and differentiated responsibility' between developed and developing nations in relation to carbon emissions. For his visionary leadership in setting and working dexterously towards climate goals, the PM was conferred with the Champions of the Earth Award 2018 for Policy Leadership by UN Secretary General, Antonio Guterres.[33]

In all alliances, multi-alignment has been the approach adopted for securing India's economic and security interests. For example, India, Israel, the US and the UAE formed a quadrilateral alignment called 'I2U2' to foster joint investment in six mutually identified areas: water, energy, transportation, space, health and food security.[34]

Following the Vasudhaiva Kutumbakam model of engagement, India's outreach is not just limited to major powers or economies of the world, but the smaller countries are also given due importance. The '10x3 diplomatic outreach' model initiated by the PM showcases this. Diplomatic engagements are strategically planned with a global outlook spanning the next ten weeks, ten months and ten years. This approach results from the concerted efforts of multiple foreign visits undertaken by key figures such as the Prime Minister, the external affairs minister, the finance minister and the national security adviser. Their endeavours have significantly strengthened partnerships with countries in the Caribbean, Latin America, Africa and the far-Pacific.[35]

The various bilateral and multilateral forums have been leveraged to pursue India's strategic interests vigorously, while ensuring that it does not convert into a zero-sum game. To pursue the goal of a free and open Indo–Pacific, India is a member of the Quad grouping (India, Japan, Australia and the US). India is also a proactive member of the Shanghai Cooperation Organization (SCO), a forum which was jointly established by China and Russia in 2001. At the bilateral meeting with Russian President Vladimir Putin, on the sidelines of SCO in Samarkand, Uzbekistan, PM Modi told the Russian premier that 'today's era is not of war', referring to the Russo–Ukraine conflict. This statement was later adopted in the joint declaration of the G20 in 2022 in Bali.[36]

The G20[37] Summit of 2023 under India's leadership transformed from a traditional high-level gathering addressing economic issues and developed nations' concerns to a platform championing global responsibility and inclusivity. This shift gave prominence to voices often unheard in global dialogues, like those from the Global South and the African Union. The summit evolved beyond a meeting of world leaders, into a series of democratically engaging events, with two hundred local gatherings across the nation. This approach not only made ordinary citizens feel a part of a global conversation but also instilled a sense of national pride.

The G20 events showcased India in its full splendour—highlighting its hospitality, tourism destinations, archaeological treasures, diverse attire and culinary traditions. This celebration of India's rich cultural tapestry was set against the backdrop of a world grappling with the aftermath of Covid-19 and conflicts like the Russia–Ukraine crisis. In a world torn by social, political and economic turmoil, and polarized by diverging perspectives, the Summit stood out as a beacon of hope and healing.

India's G20 leadership echoed the Prime Minister's various slogans, engaging every Indian as a stakeholder in this prestigious global event. It marked a significant shift in mindset from individualistic views to a collective consciousness. This shift was not just symbolic; it created tangible hope for the future, fostering national unity and infusing a sense of national spirit in an event traditionally viewed as elitist.

The G20 Summit, under India's guidance, thus became a landmark event, not just in terms of global diplomacy but also in demonstrating the power of inclusivity and collective engagement in shaping a more united, hopeful world.

Rishi Sunak, the PM of Britain, who had attended the summit, remarked, 'Under India's leadership, we have demonstrated that we can come together at a time when it really matters. When you walk around in Bharat Mandapam and see the displays, we can see what PM Modi, the digital initiative and technology can do—delivering service to people in remote corners of our nations'.[38]

Against the backdrop of a fragmented world, India could successfully navigate challenges to build trust and overcome geopolitical tension. The focus was centred on addressing pressing issues, including the post-COVID, socio-economic meltdown, food scarcity, access to fuel, financial challenges, the climate crises, conflict and violence and SDG regression—all of which predominantly affect the Global South. In a symbolic gesture, the PM personally led the world leaders to the Gandhi Memorial at Rajghat, to signal the importance of non-violence and India's commitment to the same.[39] He also addressed the prevailing trust deficiency between countries at the Summit and said, 'We must remember that if we can defeat a pandemic like COVID, we can also win over the challenge of this trust deficit. Today, as the President of the G20, India calls upon the entire world to transform this global trust deficit into trust and confidence. This is the time for all of us to move together.'

Since the beginning of his prime ministership, Narendra Modi has stressed the need for developing lifestyle in accordance with the oncoming challenges humanity will face, through initiatives such as Lifestyle for Environment (LiFE). At the G20, the LiFE mission was accepted as the High-Level Principles on Lifestyles for Sustainable Development and as the call for greater climate financing, reform of multilateral institutions and a restructuring of the global debt.

The highlight of the event was the admission of the fifty-five-member-state African Union into the G20 as a permanent member. Nine months prior to the Delhi Summit, India had convened the first-ever Summit of the Global South with 125 countries participating. The inclusion of the African Union added a feather to the cap of G20 by making it more representative and, importantly, giving the bloc access to the decision-making and solution-forming process of G20, which represents most of the world's wealth. This established India as a representative voice of the Global South.

Another special highlight of the event was the mainstreaming of the concept of women-led development pioneered by PM Modi. The New Delhi Leaders Declaration had the most comprehensive and elaborate commitment to women's socio-economic empowerment. It included driving gender-responsive climate action; securing women's food security, nutrition and well-being; and ending violence and bias.[40] This kind of local yet global outlook and long-term vision is a prerequisite for any leader in today's day and age.

Humanitarian Diplomacy

The ability to demonstrate theory in practice is the litmus test of leadership. The 'One Earth, One Family, One Future' mandate espoused by the PM is reflected in India's approach towards the global good, as perceived in her actions.

On the 6 February 2023, Türkiye and Syria were struck by a 7.8-Richter magnitude earthquake which led to the loss of over 50,000 lives combined, in both countries. India was one of the first responders, sending her disaster management teams and aid material to Türkiye. Under Operation Dost[41], India sent search and rescue teams from the National Disaster Response Force (NDRF) to Türkiye and Syria, as well as a field hospital, materials, medicines and equipment. There was criticism from some domestic quarters as Türkiye isn't known to be friendly towards India, especially in its stance towards the status of Kashmir, but India has never been reticent in providing aid to countries in need.

In a similar vein, India had also provided Taliban-ruled Afghanistan with aid in the form of food supplies and other essentials, even though it had not officially recognized the Taliban regime in Kabul.[42] These acts are all in line with the traditional Indian value of 'sarve bhavantu sukhinah, sarve santu niramayah [may all be happy, may all be well].' The Indian government does not let strategic calculations at a Nation-State level come in the way of helping people in need.

India's disaster diplomacy was also witnessed during the 2015 Nepal earthquake. In a swift response, India had become the first responder in that crisis too and organized various search and rescue teams and medical aid. This had also helped in thawing the previously held bilateral ties, while also establishing India as a major dependable responder to disasters.[43]

The biggest test of living up to India's core values came in the form of the Covid-19 pandemic, where nearly all major countries had isolated themselves, and the developing world was left to fend for itself, with no supply of vaccines. Speaking on the UN's seventy-fifth anniversary in September 2020, PM Modi pointed out that the world body faced a 'crisis of confidence', as it operated on outdated structures. On the same occasion, Modi affirmed that India's vaccine production capacity would be used to help humanity fight the virus and was the origin of the Indian Government's Vaccine Maitri initiative. Following the vision of 'One Earth, One Health', India started sharing its vaccines with the outside world within four days of the commencement of its own vaccination drive.

Apart from countries in India's immediate and extended neighbourhood, Brazil and Morocco, close strategic partners, also received two million doses each on 22 January 2021. Brazilian President Jair Bolsonaro thanked PM Modi for sending the vaccine supplies and equated the gesture with that of Lord Hanuman bringing the holy Sanjeevani to an injured Lakshmana in the Ramayana.[44, 45]

India had to temporarily curtail these supplies when the second wave of the virus struck India in April 2021, but they were resumed as soon as the situation and supplies normalized. This initiative significantly enhanced the influence and image of the country. The fact that India has been able to develop, manufacture and use several vaccines domestically has significantly enhanced its status as a rising scientific and technological power.[46]

Another aspect of humanitarian diplomacy has been the proactiveness and seamlessness of the multiple evacuation drives facilitated by the government during crises around the world. During the coronavirus pandemic, the Indian government conducted the world's largest civilian repatriation exercise in the form of Vande Bharat[47] missions. Despite the proactive national lockdown from 24 March 2020, when calls for repatriation from foreign countries intensified, the government started the Vande Bharat mission on 7 May 2020, to facilitate return of stranded Indian nationals abroad in a phased manner.[48]

Transit during world lockdown was not easy, especially given the scale of the exercise. However, beyond the movement itself was the intricate planning and execution of organizing, gathering, testing and logistics.[49] Demonstrating excellent coordination capabilities between the ministries of external affairs, home affairs, civil aviation and the various States, the government had operated more than 2,17,000 flights and brought back 18.3 million stranded passengers by 31 October 2021.[50]

When the Russo–Ukraine conflict erupted on 24 February 2022, India found itself responsible for the safety of over 18,000 of its citizens in Ukraine, predominantly students.

This situation led to the initiation of Operation Ganga, aptly named after the revered mother and protector, River Ganga. With remarkable swiftness and strategic finesse, India mobilized all available resources and diplomatic expertise to ensure the safe return of its citizens.[51]

The diplomatic channels were cranked at their highest levels so that the PM could directly communicate with the Russian President to secure a ceasefire during the evacuation period and obtain designated routes for the evacuation.

Not only Indians, but people from other nationalities, including Pakistan, had been evacuated during the war from the especially hot conflict zone of Sumy City, after the PM's talks with the Russian and Ukrainian Presidents—leading to a brief ceasefire for operating humanitarian corridors from Kyiv, Sumy, Kharkiv and Mariupol.[52] The value of the tricolour was also demonstrated when students of India as well as some other nationalities used the Indian tricolour to pass through checkpoints freely within Ukraine.[53]

Referring to these exercises of trust, the PM remarked: 'In the heart of every Indian, there rests a profound faith: No matter the challenge, no matter how daunting the circumstance, they know their government stands with them and will bring them back home safely. This isn't merely policy—it is our testament of humanity. This is a bond we have seen strengthen time and again, reflecting the indomitable spirit of our Nation.'[54]

Economic and Digital Diplomacy

In 2014, when Narendra Modi came to power as Prime Minister, India was categorized as part of the 'fragile five'—as classified by Morgan Stanley in a 2013 report[55]—a grouping of countries that faced economic vulnerability due to over-reliance on foreign investment. In the nearly ten years of Narendra Modi's prime ministership, the Indian economy has charted a turnaround from being the tenth-largest economy to being the fifth-largest economy in the world.[56] This has been, in part, due to the continuous confidence-building measures taken and the projection of India as a favourable global investment destination.

Over the past nine years, in nearly all his visits abroad and to the dignitaries visiting India, Modi has pitched the idea of Make in India, Make for the World.[57] To spur foreign investment, the PM deployed multiple tactics like reducing compliances, streamlining laws, decriminalizing minor economic offences and more.[58] He has also consistently sought suggestions from investors and industry leaders as to the measures needed to unlock investment potential in the country.

During his state visit to the US in June 2023, the PM met various delegates and industry leaders and pitched them to invest in India. The CEO of SpaceX, Elon Musk, said that he is a fan of Modi's. 'I can say he really wants to do the right thing for India. He wants to be open; he wants to be supportive of new companies, obviously, but at the same time, make sure it accrues to India's advantage'.[59]

Various other politically risky reforms have also been undertaken by the government, in the larger interest of the nation, such as reforms in Foreign Direct Investment (FDI) through automatic route, coal mining, contract manufacturing, civil aviation, defence, insurance and telecom. A special preference has been shown to technologies of the future, such as manufacturing of electric vehicles (EVs), defence equipment and semiconductors. On semiconductors, the government offered up to 50 per cent financial incentive to firms that set up units to manufacture them in India. Terming the investments as the seed of the fourth industrial revolution, the PM states, 'Today the world is becoming witness to Industry 4.0. Whenever the world has passed through any such industrial revolution, its base has been the aspirations of the people of a particular region. The same relation was seen between the first industrial revolution and the American Dream. Today I see the same relation between the fourth industrial revolution and Indian aspirations'.[60]

It is not just that investments have been sought in the newest technologies, but the PM has utilized his outreach to promote Indian exports such as traditional medicine and millets. In April 2022, the PM laid the foundation for the World Health Organization Global Centre for Traditional Medicine (GCTM) in Jamnagar, Gujarat. The establishment of this global knowledge centre, backed by a substantial investment of $250 million from the Government of India, aims to leverage the potential of traditional medicine worldwide by combining it with modern science and technology to improve global health outcomes. Similarly, the year 2023 was declared by the United Nations as the International Year of Millets, as proposed by India. The Government of India implemented a multi-stakeholder approach and the action plan for celebrating IYM focused on strategies to enhance production, productivity, consumption and export; to strengthen value chains; to raise awareness of health benefits; and more.[61]

India is no longer a mere recipient of technology from outside but is becoming an exporter as well. During the pandemic, India convened the Global CoWin Conclave to share its indigenously developed CoWIN platform to the world at the virtual global meet of representatives from 142 countries. The CoWIN platform was used in India for effective and easy vaccination drives throughout the country. Similarly, Unified Payments Interface (UPI)—India's homegrown digital payments platform—has been adopted by multiple countries such as Singapore, the UAE, France and others; and the PM pitched for UPI network uptake in his address at the 15th BRICS summit as well.[62]

The Prime Minister has not solely relied on a reformist agenda but has also engaged in tough bargaining when it aligns with national interests. A notable example was the country's decision to withdraw from the Regional Comprehensive Economic Partnership (RCEP), a move driven by the assessment that the potential disadvantages for the nation outweighed the benefits. Furthermore, the country has adopted what is known as the Distributive Strategy. This approach involves mobilizing coalitions of developing nations and promoting a narrative that underscores their economic vulnerabilities and the power imbalances they face, aiming to protect its interests at the World Trade Organization. This strategy has played a crucial role in discussions on key sectors such as agriculture, e-commerce and fisheries subsidies.[63]

US Secretary of Commerce Gina Raimondo has hailed Prime Minister Narendra Modi as 'unbelievable' and 'a visionary'. Raimondo was in India in March 2023 and held a meeting with the PM. Later, while recounting her experience at an event hosted by the Indian embassy in the US, she shared: 'I had an incredible opportunity to spend more than an hour and a half with PM Modi. He is the most popular world leader for a reason. He is unbelievable, a visionary and his level of commitment to the people of India is just indescribable—deep, passionate, real and authentic. And his desire to lift people out of poverty and move India forward as a global power is real, and it is happening'.[64]

Many have echoed thoughts similar to Raimondo and in the realm of global leadership, Narendra Modi's tenure has been nothing short of transformative. Nationalist poet Dinkar's[65] poignant questions resound: 'Who is it that becomes the leader of the world? Who wins the entire Earth? Who is endowed with incomparable fame and who brings forth a new world order?' Then he characteristically answers: 'The one who has never rested, and who works tirelessly amidst adversities.' Modi embodies this ethos as his strategic initiatives and proactive diplomacy propel India on to the world stage as a dynamic force for positive change. From championing environmental sustainability through initiatives like the International Solar Alliance, to promoting disaster resilience with the Coalition for Disaster Resilient Infrastructure, he has demonstrated a visionary approach to global challenges.

His adept handling of complex geopolitical issues and pragmatic stance on economic and security matters have earned him widespread respect. The recent G20 Summit of 2023 stands as a testament to India's growing influence and Modi's ability to navigate the complexities of international relations. Through platforms like SAARC and BIMSTEC[66], Modi has shown a dedication to fostering stability and prosperity in the Global South, exemplifying the spirit of Vasudhaiva Kutumbakam. Through mutual respect, shared interests and collaborative problem-solving, Modi's leadership has elevated India's global standing, contributing to a more connected and more inclusive global community.

Epilogue

A Legacy of Transformation

काममय एवायं पुरुष इति ।
स यथाकामो भवति तत्क्रतुर्भवति ।
यत्क्रतुर्भवति तत्कर्म कुरुते ।
यत्कर्म कुरुते तदभिसंपद्यते ॥

kāmamaya evāyaṃ puruṣa iti |
sa yathākāmo bhavati tatkraturbhavati |
yatkraturbhavati tatkarma kurute |
yatkarma kurute tadabhisaṃpadyate ||
—Brihadaranyaka Upanishad
Chapter 4, Section 4, Verse 5

You are what your deep, driving desire is. As your desire is, so is your will.
As your will is, so is your deed. As your deed is, so is your destiny.

~

Amidst the global turmoil and the dichotomy of the sovereign individual versus the surveillance state, Modi emphasizes a harmonious blend of planet, people, peace and prosperity, underpinned by the principle of dharma as a guiding force. Learning from the finest in the world and combining it with the civilizational knowledge of India provides a path for ensuring sustainability in the future. This not only serves well for the world but also opens the avenue for self-actualization. Modi's approach, focusing on self-restraint, service and the pursuit of universal joy through righteous action, offers a compelling blueprint for future leadership amidst the complexities of the twenty-first-century world order, advocating for a leadership style that is rooted in cultural wisdom while embracing innovation and global interconnectedness.

~

Dharma of Legacy and the Legacy of Dharma

We are often reminded that we are part of a global civilization. But where is this civilization headed?

American political scientist Francis Fukuyama's proclamation of the 'End of History'[1] might have been premature, but it encapsulated a prevalent intellectual zeitgeist. The ideals of Democracy, Free Markets, Globalization and Human Rights were heralded as the cornerstones for a unified global order. The ultimate playbook for a united Global Future.

As we stand today at the cusp of a protracted chaos, each of the elements that held this compact are under stress. The many crises we face today are related to energy and the environment, disruptions in the global order, ageing societies grappling with cultural assimilation and aggressive ideologies engaged in State capture.

The mega-political institutions are breaking down and the world is being pulled into two opposite directions—the Sovereign Individual and the Surveillance State.

The Sovereign Individual is the liberty-seeking, 'technological somnambulist' of a radically networked global village. The ideas of nationalism, local bonds and constraints do not register in this conscience. This has put the Nation-State structure under tremendous strain. Digital rights, privacy, artificial intelligence and singularity are the campfire that the global collection of sovereign individuals meets at.

On the other hand, the State's response is to protect and entrench itself, aiming to harness the unprecedented power and predictive capabilities provided by technology to discipline society into a specific order. This approach is 'Seeing like a State'[2] on steroids. Social credits, digital IDs and surveillance technology have become the deities of this new paradigm.

This represents uncharted territory for the world, as existing models of leadership are ill-equipped to address this vertical split. The last significant shift of this magnitude occurred during the European Renaissance in the fifteenth and sixteenth centuries. During that era, the dominant mega-political institutions of the church and nobility succumbed to the pressures of Enlightenment thinking, which paved the way for the emergence of the 'nation state' paradigm.[3]

Political scientists today are analysing the emerging contours of this phenomenon. We hear of the 'civilizational state', the 'global state' and even the 'networked state'. We cannot predict where the chips will land but the stress on 'nation state' and the prevailing liberal democratic consensus is visible.

It is against this backdrop that we should understand what Narendra Damodardas Modi stands for as a leader. As a representative of nearly one-sixth of humanity and the country with the largest youth population, his idea of four 'p's—planet, people, peace and prosperity combined with State innovation—is the paradigm of the future.

This framework demands urgent attention from the global community as it shapes our collective future. It uniquely marries individual autonomy with state resilience, redefining the traditional power dynamics by acknowledging the inherent goodness in humans.

Public policy is rooted in institutional design, which, in turn, is informed by political and social philosophy. This philosophical foundation draws from the metaphysics of the 'self', a concept deeply intertwined with our understanding of the State and polity.

For the past 500 years, English philosopher Thomas Hobbes' depiction of life as 'solitary, poor, nasty, and brutish' in his Leviathan model[4] has influenced the construction of governance, states and institutions, framing human nature as a battle against both nature and society. In stark contrast, Modi's leadership shifts the narrative from the Leviathan's bleak outlook to one of '*sat–chit–ananda*'—truth, consciousness, bliss.

This shift embodies the belief in the divine potential of humans, positing the State as a facilitator in individuals' journey towards realizing their true essence and purpose. This vision of governance, where the State supports the personal growth and fulfilment of its citizens, represents a sustainable model for the future.

As we've tried to highlight through this book, it is not an accident that this paradigm, this epoch of dharma leadership is coming from the ancient land of India that Modi embodies.

The Indian model of leadership was never beholden to extremes. Dharma is the thermostat, the harmonizing principle. Millennia ago, Chanakya captured this in his seminal treatise, the Arthashastra, which combines statecraft, economic theory and, most critically, public leadership.

His core vision and formulation of Rajadharma is captured in the following sutra from the Arthashastra:

sukhasya moolam dharmaha dharmasya moolam arthaha
arthasya moolam rajyam rajyasya moolam indriya jayah
indriyajayasya moolam vinayaha vinayasya
moolam vrddhopaseva

It translates as:

The basis of *sukha* or all true pleasantness is dharma.
The basis of all dharma is artha, or wealth. The basis
of all artha is rajya or the State. The basis for the
stability of the State lies in control over the *indriya* or
sense faculties providing pleasure.

This can be represented as a hierarchy beginning with the 'indriya vijaya' of the leader and culminating in sukha of the entire population.

In one magnetic sweep, Kautilya captures the entire essence of nation-building, when he clarifies the inextricable link between a leader's integrity and the values enshrined in society. He exhorts that the State (or king) should draw legitimacy only from the pursuit of Yogakshema of its people, and only a leadership that has gained control over its senses, termed by Kautilya as indriya vijayi, can afford to stake a claim to power.

The pinnacle of human aspiration is *sukham*, or joy, achievable only through dharma—righteous actions aligned with the cosmic order. However, dharma thrives on the foundation of artha, economic prosperity. This prosperity, in turn, depends on the effective functioning of the 'country', which is contingent upon leadership that has achieved mastery over the senses.

In the West, the philosophical discourse has often oscillated between deontology and consequentialism, focusing on the moral integrity of actions versus their outcomes. From an Indian civilizational world view, we can trace the roots of this predicament to a fundamental rupture between the material and the sacred. The object and the subject. The central idea of dharma combines the universal, the contextual and, most critically, the 'consciousness' of the actor. It is through yoking oneself with this sacred core, that the ability to bridge divergences and forge commonality emerges.

Modi's leadership brings this ability to fuse the binaries, eschew the extremes and harmonize divergence. As we collectively face a convergence of destinies yet a divergence of intentions, this is a paradigm for our times and for the future of an integrated world. He has, in fact, given the clue in how he thinks about these poles—his idea of four 'p's: planet, people, peace and prosperity.

Whereas the previous paradigm promoted wanton exploitation of resources for an anthropocentric world, nature has sobered those aggressive instincts. With the real challenge of climate change upon the world, the reorientation of the leadership instinct from local to global, from nation to planet, all while upholding sovereignty, has been a positive impact ushered in by Modi. The initiatives such as Voice of Global South Summit, financing climate resilient infrastructure through multilateral development banks and more have been testament to that.

Similarly, the LiFE (Lifestyle for Environment) approach promotes a people-centric development that is different from the anthropocentric 'development surplus' of previous waves of industrialization. The consistent advocacy of Modi, from promoting yoga to millets to traditional medicine, advances a traditional approach to a healthy lifestyle, which is the need of the hour.

We see in the Indian episteme, the concept of *purusharthas*, or pursuits, that must be undertaken to lead a harmonious life. The four pursuits as mentioned before are: dharma, artha, kama and moksha. The premise of Vasudhaiva Kutumbakam functions on dharma *vijaya*. It is only people guided by dharma who can guide others correctly in turn, and combined with dharma vijaya, it explains how the two 'p's of people and planet are envisaged in the Indian leadership paradigm.

Furthermore, the principles of artha and kama—'means for attainment' and 'desire'—when tethered to the axis of dharma, explain the idea of the global prosperity involved in the four 'p's. It is not a prosperity extracted at the cost of nature or future generations, but one that takes all stakeholders into consideration, both human and non-human inhabitants of the planet.

Finally, all of this is ensconced in the philosophy of moksha, that state of liberation which is sat-chit-ananda. When moksha is the end goal, the inevitable result of the remaining pursuits automatically generates a surplus of peace.

Peace is imperative, irrespective of the era. However, it is correctly identified that as resources become scarce, peace too will be short in supply. From calling out terrorism at every forum to pursuing ever better utilization of energy resources, all of those measures guide the path as to how future leadership should appear and function for attainment of these ideals and also prosperity. Soft yet firm, conservative yet innovative.

How then should we understand the impact and project the legacy of Prime Minister Narendra Modi? We have journeyed through his trials and tribulations, through his ideas and actions, his strengths and his drive for continuous learning.

We began like good adventurers at the base camp—with the process. The craft, character and conviction. Through the first two sections of this book, we tried to get a glimpse of the conditions that forged the extraordinary and a glimpse of the personal make-up. The subsequent two sections were a study of the impact—his beginnings from a humble background, using his experience to craft people-centric policies and programmes and straddling the global stage in a world of great complexity and uncertainty.

Narendra Modi is likely to be amongst the most studied and analysed leaders of history—there are leaders who row, there are leaders who steer, and then there are those rare leaders, who change the frame of analysis itself. They bring the destination towards us and within us.

History provides us with examples of influential leaders even in modern times. Let's briefly examine three such personalities whose leadership has had a lasting impact in the contexts in which they operated. While these individuals demonstrated paradigm-shifting leadership, the challenges of the twenty-first century, especially those facing India with its population of 1.4 billion, require a broader scope of operation. For this reason, while drawing parallels can be insightful, a complete understanding involves considering what Narendra Modi's leadership means for a shared global future.

Abraham Lincoln

Abraham Lincoln, the 16th President of the United States, is celebrated for his leadership during one of the nation's most turbulent times—the Civil War. He skilfully navigated the country through the conflict between the Unionists, who sought to abolish slavery, and the Confederates, who wished to maintain it. Lincoln rose up to the responsibility of presidentship and steered his country through a civil war, preventing partition and paving the way for slave emancipation. The success of America as a democratic, human rights-endorsing country inspired many others to imbibe the same values in their countries.

Lincoln was known for his emotional intelligence, ability to learn from mistakes and his unique approach to leadership, exemplified by his Team of Rivals[5] strategy. This approach involved including capable, outspoken individuals in his Cabinet, fostering a culture of diverse opinions and consensus-building. Despite some setbacks, like the initial misjudgement in the appointment of General George McClellan, Lincoln's dedication to self-education and focus on key issues was remarkable.

What set Lincoln apart from other leaders, apart from his empathy and sense of humour, was his discernment in identifying the main issues at hand (work at the centre) and in focusing all his energies on solving them. The ability to let go of peripheral concerns through delegation and other means and focus on the main mission is the hallmark of a great leader. For Lincoln, he chose to focus his energy into fighting the practice of slavery in his country and was successful to a large degree in bringing the whole nation to his side. Thus, he created a legacy of a leader who could stick to his principles, take hard decisions and through persistence and deftness, emerge victorious.

Lee Kuan Yew

Lee Kuan Yew, the first Prime Minister of Singapore, is renowned for his exceptional leadership in transforming the country from a poor nation with a lot of internal strife into a prosperous global hub. Narrowly escaping execution during the Japanese occupation of Singapore, he became an ardent advocate for Singapore's independence and competitiveness. His 'Follow the Rainbow'[6] principle inspired a spirit of adventure and excellence in his people, emphasizing the use of human capital to compensate for Singapore's lack of natural resources.

Yew's leadership was direct and uncompromising, often favouring unpleasant truths over political correctness. This approach, while sometimes criticized as autocratic, was underpinned by his personal integrity and the trust he garnered from the people. His strong leadership ensured internal stability, with even strikes and protests ending cordially.

Crucially, when Singapore's federation with Malaysia failed in 1965, Yew's leadership helped to steer the country towards becoming a global financial and manufacturing powerhouse. He focused on investing in human capital and nurturing a new generation of leaders. He famously emphasized the need for resilience in governance, stating, 'Whoever governs Singapore must have iron in them or give it up. This is not a game of cards; this is your life and mine'.[7]

Yew's innovative approach extended to diversifying Singapore's economy, reforming the bureaucracy and judiciary, adopting a business-like approach to State management that prioritized efficiency and attracted top talent into government service.

His most enduring legacy, however, lies in his focus on political stability and social harmony. Singapore, being a melting pot of Malay, Chinese and Indian ethnicities, faced potential inter-ethnic strife. Yew's leadership ensured equal rights and State language recognition for all communities. While not a strong proponent of a welfare state, he concentrated on developing efficient housing and medical infrastructure, which significantly reduced homelessness and disease, contributing to the success and drive of the Singaporean populace.

Deng Xiaoping

Deng Xiaoping served as the paramount leader of the People's Republic of China from 1978 to 1989. He was responsible in many ways for the turnaround of the Chinese economy from a thoroughly communist model to a capitalist model with a communist state apparatus. This catapulted China from being a non-industrialized country to being the manufacturing capital of the world.

Deng's ability lay in ushering in radical change while not divorcing the past and providing absolute steadiness of leadership. To prepare for modernization, Deng began cultivating closer ties with Western countries and Japan, presumed to be traditional enemies of communism. His philosophy for choosing policies was efficiency, in his own words: 'It doesn't matter whether it is a white cat or black, I think a cat that catches mice is a good cat'.[8]

He was instrumental in decentralizing the decision-making in the Chinese government and promoting a 'hands off' approach, that is formulating economic policies and then delegating authority to others to carry out his plans. He undertook agriculture reforms, industrial reforms and opened the economy to Special Economic Zones. Unlike the previous glorification of poverty in socialism, Deng's motto resonated differently: 'Socialism is not poverty, and poverty is not socialism'.[9]

Deng was immensely successful economically in bringing China out of the scarcity mindset and preparing the next generation of leaders to carry forward the reforms. He did this while following an alternate governance model to democracy.

Each of these leaders left behind a legacy. Abraham Lincoln upheld liberty, Lee Kuan Yew instilled excellence and Deng Xiaoping adopted pragmatism. They were all responsible for a turnaround in their national destinies by facilitating deep cultural and mindset changes in their countries and societies, thus exercising century-shaping leadership.

A product of their times, the leadership of these three individuals was based on the requirements and exigencies of their countries. Advertently or inadvertently, their influential actions often accentuated prevailing materialistic tendencies. Without a solid grounding in Indic concepts such as indriya nigraha (control of the senses), and ideals like moksha (liberation), seva (service) and *nishkama karma* (selfless action without attachment to results), their efforts may not have the desired impact on finding solutions to current global challenges.

The leadership that the world demands today, however, needs to extend beyond boundaries and perch on the universals that are the common heritage of humanity. Without the guiding principles of selflessness and a deeper spiritual perspective, the pursuit of personal pleasures can lead the human mind to recklessly exploit and deplete the environment. This shortsighted approach has played a role in exacerbating various crises that have become increasingly prominent in contemporary times, including crisis of trust, crisis of ethics, crisis of knowledge and crisis of the self.

To be able to navigate them requires a strong sense of duty, a recognition of the value of life and the inevitability of death. Modi's life of service, particularly to those incapacitated by circumstances or age, has highlighted this realization. Thus, he uses the instrument of politics as a moral force. Politics becomes a means of using the democratic character (Janbhagidaari) to innovatively solve the wicked problems facing the world and usher in peace and prosperity.

Modi, like all other great leaders, is a keen student of history and historical personalities. Astute observers of the political economy with knowledge of Indian history, mass politics and democratic impulses would see how Modi draws from all of them. It would be difficult to box him into the conservative–liberal binary, for his understanding of artha draws from wealth as a universal force for good. He has produced a rare alchemy of civilizational knowledge combined with the human zeal of innovation. So, inertia is countered by gati shakti (power of momentum) and maladministration is countered by karma yoga (selfless service).

The freedom struggle of India from British colonization produced two streams of thought: the traditional streak eschewing modernity and the modern streak blindly copying Western extravagance. Modi combines the mass, folksy genius of Mahatma Gandhi with the integrity and courage of Sardar Vallabhbhai Patel along with the modernist, progressive, global stage play of Atal Bihari Vajpayee. This is an achievement of enormous proportion, with perhaps no precedent in modern history.

In all the above leaders, it is a top-down approach, a single brilliant flash of light that sustains for some decades and then fades. Modi inverts that. His legacy can be considered large-scale Janbhagidaari or people's participation in governance. While the idea of democracy might seem to be automatically one of participative governance, in actual practice it rarely manifests as that. The present-day democratic set-up has become a playground for interest groups, lobbyists, Big Tech and bureaucrats, with people's participation being relegated as an exercise of voting once every few years. Correspondingly, the gulf between the ruler and the ruled has widened. The exhortation of the PM when he assumed office, that he is the *Pradhan Sevak* (Prime Servant) as opposed to the Prime Minister, was a glimpse into the attitude needed to effect a change of power back to the people.

This attitude is especially important to restore confidence in people who had been subjected to devastating foreign rules for nearly a millennium. While promoting the concept of service, there has been a consistent thrust against servility and elite capture in Modi's leadership. Swami Vivekananda once remarked on Indian education: 'The child is taken to school, and the first thing he learns is that his father is a fool, the second thing that his grandfather is a lunatic, the third thing that all his teachers are hypocrites, the fourth that all the sacred books are lies! By the time he is sixteen he is a mass of negation, lifeless and boneless'.[10] When people see that the global leadership which Modi embodies is based on their own cultural wisdom, it builds a resonance of confidence and an atmabala (inner strength) is developed. This is the strength which the leader can then harness and through it change the fate of the world.

We read in the previous chapters that *seva bhav* is required to exercise consistent leadership without fatigue. The initiatives taken by the PM to reach the last mile, either through schemes under Antyodaya, or through myriad communication channels reflect a deep commitment that is required to cultivate *ekatvam,* or oneness, between himself and others. His communication model, combining deep listening with experiential wisdom, serves as the framework for application of Sadharanikaran. The use of traditional symbols and the integration of development into the cultural matrix of the country, ensuring seamless continuity, are examples of statesmanship worthy of emulation.

His constant motivation to cultivate self-reliance while integrating further with the world, building modern symbols of new India, promoting indigenous culture nationally and internationally and encouragement to re-include Indian knowledge systems in education has restored a national self-confidence.

The world is moving towards a period of uncertainty, with many black swan events such as pandemics, wars and the rise of multi-polar world order. While the ideal of the nation state was built upon parameters of commonality at a national level, the homogenization through digital networking leads to erosion of culture and replacement with a common global culture. This will inevitably generate significant debates around sovereignty and leadership. In this state of flux, future leaders need to be nimble and adaptive. This will require the meta-ability of learning and relearning, while having the North Star fixed on dharma.

Over 130 years ago, Swami Vivekananda spoke of a life characterized by seva and tyaga, and the spiritual potency of such a life devoted to the selfless service of others—*atmano mokshartham jagat hitaya cha*. Among today's public figures, Modi's life and actions most closely embody the practical application of this principle.

Indian civilization has since its dawn emphasized transformation as opposed to changing of belief systems. It recognized that there are two forces that act on a man, one which draws him higher to the *sukshma* (subtle) world, and one which draws him lower to the *sthula* (material) world. While pursuit of the lower makes the life *jada* (inert) and *dukha* (depressing), the higher pursuit provides an everlasting abode of sukha (joy) in *sat* (truth).

The more one practices *pratyahara* (restraining of senses) and purification of *manasa*, *vacha* and *karmana* (thoughts, speech and actions), the more they develop the dharma *drishti* (vision) and plug into the higher consciousness. Modi's life has been replete with these practices, which thus explain his empathy, equanimity and impact. It is inevitable that individuals on such paths develop extraordinary skill, for the mind has been cultured to such a high degree that it manifests what it wills. This is the power of *shuddha sankalpa* (pure will), which has been attested by the sages of all times and not just in India. That is the legacy of dharma.

The next challenge of leadership will be to identify the human universals and harness it for the four 'p's. As witnessed throughout the book, the universals are discovered through the light of sadhana. The example of Modi's life elucidates how it is possible to stay culturally rooted, contextually relevant, technologically abreast and compassionately generative. It is made possible through the ideals and timeless wisdom of ages past, and it is this author's opinion that leaders who follow these principles of sadhana through *nisvartha seva* (selfless service) will be able to exercise Enlightened Leadership driven by the power from within.

Notes and Bibliography

Preface

1 The Puranas are a genre of ancient Indian texts that form an integral part of Hindu literature and tradition. Puranas are defined as, '*Pura api nava* [old yet new].' These works have therefore been held by the Indian civilization as texts documenting past events and values that are relevant for the present too.

2 R. Balasubramaniam, *Leadership Lessons for Daily Living*, (1st ed.), Grassroots Research and Advocacy Movement (GRAAM) and India Leaders for Social Sector (ILSS), 2020.

3 Advaita is a central philosophical concept in Hinduism, particularly in the Vedanta school of thought. The word 'Advaita' is Sanskrit and means 'not two' or 'non-dual'. It emphasizes the fundamental oneness or non-duality of reality. According to Advaita Vedanta, the ultimate reality (Brahman) is devoid of any differentiation or multiplicity. It asserts that the individual self (Atman) and Brahman are ultimately identical. This means that the true nature of the self is not different from the ultimate reality. The perceived differences in the world are considered to be the result of ignorance (avidya).

4 *Mann Ki Baat* is a popular radio programme in India hosted by the Prime Minister of India, Narendra Modi. The term 'Mann Ki Baat' translates to 'Talks from the Heart' in English. It is a monthly radio address where the Prime Minister shares his thoughts, ideas and experiences with the citizens of India.

5 The Capacity Building Commission (CBC) is an independent body of the Government of India with executive powers, created to facilitate and oversee Mission Karmayogi, https://cbc.gov.in/about_cbc.

6 Mission Karmayogi is a government initiative in India aimed at building a future-ready, efficient and accountable civil service. It is a scheme that exhorts the civil servant to maintain a very high standard of conduct and behaviour to earn the trust of the people and be emulated by peers and subordinates.

Introduction: The Leadership We Need

1 'Wicked problems' is a term coined in 1973 by design theorists Horst Rittel and Melvin Webber and is used to describe problems so complex that standard methods for identifying solutions often prove insufficient.

2 The 'Self' is a complex and multidimensional concept that encompasses a person's individuality, identity and consciousness. It represents the totality of one's thoughts, feelings, experiences, beliefs and perceptions, all of which contribute to a sense of individual existence and uniqueness. 'Self' in Indian philosophy, often referred to as 'Atman' or 'Brahman', varies across different philosophical schools. According to Advaita Vedanta, the ultimate reality is Brahman, an infinite, unchanging and indivisible consciousness. Atman, the individual Self, is considered identical to Brahman. The realization of this identity is the goal of life, and it leads to liberation (moksha) from the cycle of birth and death (samsara).

3 R. Balasubramaniam, *Leadership Lessons for Daily Living*, (1st ed.), Grassroots Research and Advocacy Movement (GRAAM) and India Leaders for Social Sector (ILSS), 2020.

4 W.G. Bennis, *On Becoming a Leader*, revised and updated, New York, Basic Books, 2009.

5 The Mahabharata is the ancient Indian epic depicting the life and stories of two clans of cousins, and the final war

between them, which shaped the destiny of the Indian civilization. It is one of only two itihasas (narrative account of history), the other being the Ramayana. Bhishma is the preceptor of both clans of cousins and is known as pitamaha (paternal grandfather) and Yudhisthira is the king from the Pandava clan of cousins, the eldest among five brothers.

6 T. Carlyle, A.R. Marble, eds., *On Heroes, Hero-Worship and the Heroic in History*, New York, London, Macmillan Company, 1897, pdf, retrieved from the Library of Congress, https://www.loc.gov/item/12031527/.

7 Proposed by Paul Hersey and Ken Blanchard, the situational leadership theory posits that leaders should not follow a one-size-fits-all approach but adjust their style of leadership depending on the performance maturity of their teams. Based on the competence-commitment quotient of their followers, leaders should either tell, sell, participate or delegate.

8 The contingency theory of leadership states that leadership is dependent on many contingencies such as economy, labour, skill, organization culture, etc. and that the main factors which contribute to effective leadership are: attributes of the leader and the degree to which the situation gives the leader power, control and influence.

9 The transactional leadership model is based on the premise that followers will cater to their own self-interests, and thus the leader needs to motivate and direct the followers to ensure compliance and accountability. The power of transactional leaders comes from their formal authority and position in the organization.

10 Douglas McGregor was an American management professor at the MIT Sloan School of Management. He proposed that the attitude of the manager has an impact on employee motivation, which can be categorized by two theories: Theory X and Theory Y. Theory X assumes employee motivation to be primarily monetary and security-based, whereas Theory Y assumes employee motivation to be a factor of self-fulfilment.

11 S.P. Huntington, *The Clash of Civilizations and the Remaking of World Order*, Simon & Schuster, New York, 2011.

Charting a Bold Course: Visionary Leadership in Action

1 Dr Keshav Baliram Hedgewar, the founder of the Rashtriya Swayamsevak Sangh (RSS), was a prominent figure in Indian history, renowned for his strong nationalist views. Born on 1 April 1889, in Nagpur, he pursued a medical degree before devoting himself to social and political activities. Dr Hedgewar established the RSS in 1925, envisioning it as a volunteer organization aimed at promoting Hindu culture and values. His leadership and ideology significantly influenced the shaping of modern Indian socio-political landscapes.

2 Archive, M., [@modiarchive], *An important milestone in Modi's evolution [Tweet]*, https://twitter.com/modiarchive/status/1571034095643426825, 17 September 2022.

3 Ramakrishna Math and Ramakrishna Mission are worldwide, non-political, non-sectarian spiritual organizations which have been engaged in various forms of humanitarian, social service activities for more than a century. Founded by Swami Vivekananda on 1 May 1897, the aim of the organization is personal spiritual unfoldment through selfless service.

4 The Advaita Ashram was established by Swami Vivekananda in March 1899 for the study, teaching and spreading of the Advaita philosophy. Advaita, often termed Advaita Vedanta, is a school of Hindu philosophy and spiritual practice.

5 Vadnagar is a UNESCO World Heritage Site and is one of the oldest continually inhabited cities of the world. It has had a rich culture of Hindu Buddhist heritage in the past, and finds mention in the writings of Chinese traveller Hiuen Tsang.

6   S. Vivekananda, *The Complete Works of Swami Vivekananda* (Vol. 6), Advaita Ashrama, 2016.

7   Laxmanrao Inamdar, widely known as Vakil Saheb, was an influential figure in the Indian cooperative movement. His work was marked by a strong belief in self-reliance and community-driven initiatives. He helped to foster the growth of cooperatives as a means of socio-economic development, especially among rural communities.

8   A. Marino, *Narendra Modi: A Political Biography*, Gurugram, Harper Collins India, 2014.

9   R. Balasubramaniam, *Leadership Lessons for Daily Living*, (1st ed.), Grassroots Research and Advocacy Movement (GRAAM) and India Leaders for Social Sector (ILSS), 2020

10   Ibid.

11   J. Kouzes, B. Posner, *The Leadership Challenge: How to Make Extraordinary Things Happen in Organizations.* John Wiley and Sons, San Francisco, 2012.

12   DNA Web Team, 'How a spiritual journey changed the "undecided, unguided and unclear" life of teenager Narendra Modi', *DNA*, 10 January 2019, https://www. dnaindia.com/india/photo-gallery-how-a-spiritual-journey-changed-the-undecided-unguided-and-unclear-life-of-teenager-narendra-modi-2706363/i-returned-home-with-clarity-and-a-guiding-force-to-lead-the-way-2706373.

13   Goods and Services Tax (GST) is a nationwide taxation law which came into force from 1 July 2017. Post many resolutions and amendments, GST was finally implemented in 2017, subsuming seventeen large taxes and thirteen cesses and turning India into one single market. Syncing with the PM's whole of society approach, GST lowered the tax rates gradually, increased the tax base and significantly improved India's Ease of Doing Business Rankings. One of the biggest triumphs associated with GST is the spirit and display of cooperative federalism, with almost all decisions

on GST being taken with consensus among members of the GST Council.

14 'Narendra Modi's first Independence Day speech: Full text', *India Today*, 15 August 2014, https://www.indiatoday.in/india/story/narendra-modi-independence-day-speech-full-text-red-fort-204216-2014-08-15.

15 The Rig Veda is one of the oldest and most significant texts in Indian history and Hindu tradition. It is an ancient Indian collection of Vedic Sanskrit hymns. Part of the four Vedas, which are the foundational scriptures of Hinduism, the Rig Veda stands as the oldest among them, both in language and content.

16 B. George, *True North: Discover Your Authentic Leadership*, Jossey-Bass, San Francisco, 2007.

17 J. Kouzes, B. Posner, *The Leadership Challenge: How to Make Extraordinary Things Happen in Organizations*, John Wiley and Sons, San Francisco, 2012.

18 Antyodaya: Rise of the last person. This is part of the Bharatiya Janata Party's (party to which Modi belongs) guiding principle, formulated by twentieth-century thinker Deen Dayal Upadhyaya. The principle is expressed as: 'The measurement of economic plans and economic growth cannot be done with those who have risen above on the economic ladder but of those who are at the bottom.'

19 Swachh Bharat: Clean India. Beginning on 2 October 2014, this is the most ambitious project of the Government of India to eliminate open defecation and improve solid waste management. The ongoing mission has clocked considerable success with the declaration of 4234 cities and 6,00,000 villages as Open Defecation Free, and the rate of solid waste management in urban areas reaching 65 per cent.

20 Broadly, as a construct, decoloniality posits that despite legal and physical decolonization of former colonies, overt and subconscious coloniality: (a) persists in the State institutions inherited by post-colonial States; (b) affects

thinking at the societal level; and (c) manifests itself even at the level of an individual. J.S. Deepak, 'The Nation State, Decoloniality and the Non-Nation State', *Daily Guardian*, 20 May 2014, https://thedailyguardian.com/the-nation-state-decoloniality-and-the-non-nation-state/.

21 In his address to the nation on Indian Independence Day 2022, the PM asked the citizens to take five pledges (Panch Pran), for successful fulfilment of turning India into a developed country by 2047. The five pledges are: Building a developed India, Freedom from every concept of slavery, Being proud of India's heritage, Unity and solidarity and Civic duty.

22 The India Vision 2047 is the vision for the country with developed infrastructure, self-reliance and Vishwaguru (World Teacher) status, as expressed by Prime Minister Modi. The twenty-five-year run-up to 2047 (from 2022) has been described as the Amrit Kaal (Golden Age), which will be a technology-driven and knowledge-based era where India will ensure economic growth, social justice and fulfil all its humanitarian obligations.

23 Janaka was a legendary king mentioned in ancient Indian scriptures like the Ramayana and various Upanishads, particularly the Brihadaranyaka Upanishad. He was the king of Mithila, a kingdom in ancient India, and is often depicted as an ideal ruler, embodying the traits of a philosopher-king. He was the father of Sita, the main female character in the Ramayana, who married Rama, the epic's protagonist.

24 Chanakya, also known as Kautilya or Vishnugupta, was a teacher, philosopher, economist, jurist and royal adviser in ancient India. He is traditionally identified as the author of the Arthashastra, a treatise on economics, politics, military strategy and statecraft, and is considered a pioneer in the field of political science and economics in India. His works predate Machiavelli's by about 1800 years, marking him as one of the earliest political realists.

25 *Chanakya Neeti* is a collection of aphorisms, said to be selected by Chanakya from various shastras (Hindu scriptures, code books). This work focuses on practical aspects of life: how to understand people, how to choose reliable friends, how to be aware of the real intentions of others and how to lead life in a righteous way. It is known for its pragmatic approach to governance and daily life, emphasizing ethical behaviour and smart strategies.

26 *Chanakya Neeti: Verses of Wisdom*, New Delhi, Rupa Publications, 2022.

Artful Mastery: Communicating to Lead and Nurturing Human Connections

1 Modistory.in, 'Modi: A warm and patient listener', Modi Story, n.d., https://modistory.in/short/61f923c1dc0ecc086858a893, retrieved on 29 February 2024.

2 The Ujwal DISCOM Assurance Yojana (UDAY) was launched by the Government of India in November 2015 with the primary aim of finding a permanent solution to the financial mess that the power distribution companies (DISCOMs) in India were in. It was designed to ensure a sustainable operational, financial and technical turnaround of DISCOMs, which are crucial for the health of the Indian power sector.

3 W. Bennis, B. Nanus, *Leaders: Strategies for Taking Charge*, Gurugram, Harper Business, 2004.

4 Navaratri or 'Nine Nights' is the festival spanning nine nights celebrating the nine forms of the Goddess Durga. It is celebrated as a time of victory of dharma (good) over adharma (evil) and is considered an auspicious time for spiritual practice and transformation.

5 P. Deora, '"Mann ki Baat" used for Development Communication', Academia, 2017, https://www.academia.

edu/40772932/Mann_ki_Baat_used_for_Development_
Communication.

6   PIB, 'Ahead of 100th episode, IIM Survey finds Mann
    Ki Baat has reached 100 crore listeners', Pib.gov.
    in., 2023, https://pib.gov.in/PressReleaseIframePage.
    aspx?PRID=1919261#:~:text=Nearly%20ninety%20
    six%20percent%20of,the%20programme%20at%20
    least%20once.

7   G.K. Reddy, 'Mann ki Baat@100: A program for the people',
    Indian Express, 30 April 2023, https://indianexpress.com/
    article/opinion/columns/mann-ki-baat100-a-programme-
    for-the-people-8584270/.

8   S. Singh, 'Clean India to New India—Modi's Mann Ki Baat
    weren't just messages. They became movements', ThePrint,
    29 April 2023, https://theprint.in/opinion/clean-india-to-
    new-india-modis-mann-ki-baat-werent-just-messages-
    they-became-movements/1546093/.

9   Narendramodi.in., 'Mann Ki Baat Live - PM Shri Narendra
    Modi Radio Program Today', www.narendramodi.in, 11
    May 2015, https://www.narendramodi.in/mann-ki-baat.

10 S. Bhasin, 'Mann Ki Baat: Democracy dialogue', Pioneer, 24
    April 2023. https://www.dailypioneer.com/2023/columnists/
    mann-ki-baat--democracy-dialogue.html.

11 The Shannon Weaver model was developed by Warren
    Weaver and Claude Shannon in 1948. It is a linear
    mathematical communication theory to describe how
    communication occurs between a sender and a receiver.

12 Theresa and Gaby's communication model uses similar
    elements of communication as the Shannon Weaver
    model, but unlike the linear, unidimensional approach, it is
    multidimensional and multidirectional.

13 Proposed by German political scientist Elisabeth Noelle-
    Neumann in 1974, the spiral of silence model discusses
    two reasons for the tendencies of people to remain silent

when their views are in opposition to the majority: fear of isolation and fear of reprisal.

14 Abhinavagupta (924–1020 CE), was a great spiritual master and literary critic from Kashmir who was a proponent of Kashmiri Shaivism. He is known for writing *Abhinavabharati*, a commentary on Bharata Muni's *Natya Shastra* with explanation on chapters for Rasa and Bhava. He is thus known for explaining the rasa theory i.e. Rasasvada, similar to the experience of Highest Bliss. The rasa theory had a great impact on the whole of Sanskrit poetics.

15 Bharata Muni's *Natya Shastra* is a compendium of performing arts, drama, music, dance and fine arts with a special emphasis on rasa (essence) of the art.

16 In communication theory, 'noise' refers to any unwanted or disruptive interference or distortion that can affect the transmission or reception of a message between a sender and a receiver. It can degrade the quality of communication and make it more challenging for the intended message to be accurately understood.

17 Developed by John Fiske, the process school of communication understands communication as transmission of messages, with the effect of producing the intended outcome in the receiver. Any deviance in outcome is understood as a communication failure, and the process is re-examined for inaccuracies.

18 Developed by John Fiske, the semiotics school of communication understands communication as the production and exchange of meanings, and it is concerned with the role of culture in communication.

19 Interactional research is a qualitative methodology that examines human interactions and communication patterns within social and cultural contexts. Researchers observe and analyse how people convey meaning, negotiate social realities and construct shared understandings.

20 Pranava is known as the word of power in Hindu philosophy as it is thought to be the primordial sound from which the universe originated. It is the most sacred of all mantras and syllables because it causes all prana to unite with the Divine. Om can be thought of as the sound of God. 'Pranava', Yogapedia, 8 April 2016, https://www.yogapedia.com/definition/5588/pranava.

21 Robert T. Oliver was an American author, professor, specialist in Asian rhetoric and communication, and adviser to South Korean President Syngman Rhee.

22 R.T. Oliver, Communication and Culture in Ancient India and China, Syracuse University Press, 1971.

23 Ibid.

24 Ninya Vachamsi means 'secret words (of guidance) that speak out their sense to the seer'. Glossary of terms in Sri Aurobindo's writings. https://auromaa.org/sri-aurobindo-ru/terms/01709_e.htm.

25 'Kavyani Kavaye Nivacana' means words that 'utter their inner meaning to the seer'. [cf. ṚV 4.3.16] The Incarnate Word, incarnateword.in, 2023, https://incarnateword.in/dict/sans/kavyani-kavaye-nivacana.

26 'Cetanti Sumatinam' means 'one who awakens the sense of righteousness'.

27 Ramachandra Roddam is a trustee of Ekathara Kalari, a non-profit organization promoting Indian spiritual traditions.

28 In the Sundara Kanda, after his wife has been kidnapped by the Lankan king Ravana, Rama wanders the forest along with his brother Lakshmana seeking alliances for the upcoming war. During this search, he chanced upon the ousted king of Kishkinda, Sugriva, who first sent his minister Hanuman to identify the motive of the two princes.

29 The Kishkindha Kanda is one of the seven kandas (sections) of the ancient Indian epic, the Ramayana, which is one of the two major ancient epics of India, the other being the

Mahabharata. It is the fourth kanda in the Ramayana's narrative sequence and is named after the city of Kishkindha, which plays a central role in this section of the epic.

Essential Traits: The Mosaic of Integrity, Tenacity, Resilience and Commitment

1 Bhishma Pitamaha is a pivotal and grand figure in the epic the Mahabharata. 'Pitamaha' means grandfather, and it is an epithet used for Bhishma to indicate his status as the grand patriarch of the Kuru dynasty.
2 Madhav Sadashiv Golwalkar, commonly known as M.S. Golwalkar, was an Indian thinker and the second *Sarsanghchalak* (Supreme Chief) of the Rashtriya Swayamsevak Sangh (RSS). Golwalkar served as the head of the RSS from 1940 to 1973, and he is often referred to by his followers as Guruji.
3 This mantra is a modified version of the Yajurveda mantra, '*Idam Na Mama*' meaning 'this is not mine'. This mantra has been popularized in the teachings and sayings of M.S. Golwalkar, the second sarsanghchalak (head of the organization) of the RSS.
4 The Kailash Mansarovar Yatra is a significant pilgrimage journey for Hindus, Buddhists, Jains and followers of the Bon religion. It involves circumambulating Mount Kailash and visiting Lake Mansarovar, both of which are in Tibet, an autonomous region of China. This yatra (journey) is considered one of the most sacred and challenging pilgrimages in the world due to its remote and high-altitude location.
5 Ram Swarup (1920–1998), was a Hindu thinker and a prolific writer known for his works on comparative religion, human spirituality and civilizational analysis.
6 R. Swarup, *Meditations: Yogas, Gods, Religions*, Aditya Prakashan, New Delhi, 2000.

7 M. Nilanjan, *Narendra Modi: The Man, The Times*, Tranquebar Press, India, 2013.

8 The Statue of Equality, located in Hyderabad, India, is a monumental tribute to the eleventh-century Hindu philosopher and saint, Shri Ramanujacharya. Inaugurated in 2022, this impressive statue stands at 216 feet, symbolizing the 216 years of Ramanujacharya's life on earth. It is made of 'panchaloha', a combination of five metals, and is one of the tallest metallic statues in a sitting position in the world.

9 Shri Ramanujacharya was a revolutionary thinker and theologian within the Sri Vaishnavism tradition of Hinduism. He promoted the idea of equality in spiritual access, regardless of caste or class, and his teachings have had a lasting impact on Hindu philosophy and religious practices.

10 PIB, 'English rendering of PM's address at inauguration of "Statue of Equality" commemorating Bhakti Saint Shri Ramanujacharya in Hyderabad', Pib.gov.in, 2022, https://pib.gov.in/PressReleasePage.aspx?PRID=1795838.

11 The Ramayana, one of the two historical epics of India, primarily narrates the life story of Sri Rama, an avatar of Vishnu, one among the Trinity in the pantheon of Hindu divinities. The epic encompasses a wide range of themes, including duty (dharma), righteousness, morality and the eternal battle between good and evil.

12 PIB, 'English rendering of PM's address on the occasion of the launch of "Main Nahin Hum" Portal & App, and interaction with IT professionals on Self4Society', Pib.gov.in, 2018, https://pib.gov.in/PressReleasePage.aspx?PRID=1550680.

13 S. Das, 'PM Modi felicitates 11 workers who built new Parliament building, gifts shawls', *Hindustan Times*, 28 May 2023, https://www.hindustantimes.com/india-news/pm-modi-felicitates-workers-involved-in-new-parliament-building-construction-development-101685299301432.html.

14   Modistory.in, 'Narendra Modi's compassion for every life', https://www.modistory.in, 29 February 2024, https://modistory.in/long/6402f45432770d1cc7025ed4.

15   https://youtu.be/qj0VrWyiYoE?si=W3i0HzGdEm_hNR5q

16   PIB, 'English rendering of PM's address in Rajya Sabha during farewell of four members', Pib.gov.in, 2021, https://pib.gov.in/PressReleasePage.aspx?PRID=1696445

17   NITI Aayog, which stands for the National Institution for Transforming India, is a policy think tank of the Government of India, established with the aim of achieving sustainable development goals through cooperative federalism and fostering the involvement of state governments of India in the economic policy-making process using a bottom-up approach.

18   Pradhan Mantri Vishwakarma scheme is a scheme of the Government of India under the Ministry of Micro, Small and Medium Enterprises, which envisages providing end-to-end holistic support to traditional artisans and craftspeople in scaling up their conventional products and services.

19   Narendramodi.in., 'Who is an ideal Karyakarta? Narendra Modi explains', www.narendramodi.in, 10 July 2022, https://www.narendramodi.in/who-is-an-ideal-karyakarta-narendra-modi-explains-biography-563258.

20   Bharat Mandapam is the International Exhibition-cum-Convention Centre (IECC) complex at Pragati Maidan in New Delhi, which was dedicated to the nation on 26 July 2023 by PM Modi.

21   For hosting world-class exhibitions-cum-conferences, phase 1 of the India International Convention and Expo Centre (IICC), called Yashobhoomi (land of fame), was dedicated to the nation on 15 September 2023 by PM Modi.

22   Modistory.in., 'Modi's conviction in the strength of NRIs', https://www.modistory.in, 25 February 2024, https://modistory.in/long/untold-stories/modi-s-conviction-in-the-strength-of-nris-6312087b13180c774056e754.

23 The Vana Parva, also known as the 'Book of the Forest', is the third of the eighteen parvas (books or sections) of the Indian epic Mahabharata. It takes place during an unjust exile of the Pandavas into the forest.

24 Bali was a benevolent asura king, known for his generosity. According to sacred texts, Lord Vishnu banished Bali, who was in possession of the immortal elixir, to the netherworld. However, he was allowed to return to his subjects once a year. This homecoming is celebrated as Onam in Kerala.

25 Prahalad was a devotee of Vishnu whose devotion resulted in the incarnation of Vishnu as Narasimha, i.e Man-Lion. Prahalad's story symbolizes unwavering faith and resilience.

26 A. Agarwal, 'Forgive Now and Fight Later?', swarajyamag. com, February 2016, https://swarajyamag.com/columns/forgive-now-and-fight-later

27 The Doklam crisis was a seventy-three-day military standoff between India and China in 2017 over a disputed border area near the Bhutan-China-India trijunction, highlighting territorial tensions and geopolitical rivalries in the region.

28 The Indian surgical strike on Pakistan in September 2016 was a secretive military operation aimed at neutralizing terrorist threats and disrupting launch pads following a deadly attack on an Indian Army base in Uri.

29 Swami Sarvapriyananda is a distinguished monk of the Ramakrishna Order and has garnered international acclaim for his profound teachings on Vedanta, a major school of Hindu philosophy.

30 Ramakrishna Math and Ramakrishna Mission are worldwide, non-political, non-sectarian spiritual organizations which have been engaged in various forms of humanitarian, social service activities for more than a century. Founded by Swami Vivekananda on 1 May 1897, the aim of the organization is personal spiritual unfoldment through selfless service.

31   '60 Years Ago: President Kennedy Proposes Moon Landing
     Goal in Speech to Congress', NASA, 25 May 2021, https://
     www.nasa.gov/history/60-years-ago-president-kennedy-
     proposes-moon-landing-goal-in-speech-to-congress/.
32   PTI, '10 punch lines from Narendra Modi's speech at SRCC',
     Economic Times, 6 February 2013, https://economictimes.
     indiatimes.com/people/10-punch-lines-from-narendra-
     modis-speech-at-srcc/slideshow/18370143.cms.
33   Intentional Change Theory (ICT) is a psychological
     framework developed by Boyatzis which focuses on how
     individuals can achieve sustainable change in their lives
     through personal development. It is a five-step process
     consisting of Discovering the Ideal Self, Exploring the
     Real Self, Experimenting and Practising New Behaviours,
     Thoughts and Feelings, creating a Learning Agenda and
     Developing Supportive and Trusting Relationships.
34   Resonant Leadership is a concept grounded in the idea
     that effective leadership is not just about making strategic
     decisions or possessing technical expertise; it's also about
     the ability to create emotional resonance with others—that
     is, to connect with them on an emotional level in a way that
     inspires and motivates.
35   Kaizen is a Japanese concept which means continuous
     incremental change for the better. It is a part of Japanese
     business philosophy pertaining to improving employee
     engagement and making the job more fulfilling and
     less tiring.
36   The Upanishads are a collection of ancient Indian texts
     that form the philosophical and spiritual foundation
     of Hinduism. There are 108 Upanishads, with many
     notable ones such as Isha, Taittiriya, Mundaka, Maha,
     Brihadaranyaka and others.
37   The Brihadaranyaka Upanishad is a part of the Yajurveda
     (one of the four vedas) and is known for its profound
     philosophical teachings and discussions on the nature of
     reality, the Self (Atman), and the ultimate reality (Brahman).

38 Adi Shankaracharya, or the first Shankaracharya, is the most prominent proponent and elucidator of the Advaita (non-dual) concept of reality. Born in 507 BCE, he was a sage of extraordinary calibre who propounded Advaita, composed numerous hymns and works, established mathas (religious organizations) for the spread of the doctrine and nearly single-handedly rejuvenated the Upanishadic (accompanying corpus of Vedas) knowledge throughout the length and breadth of Bharat.

39 Shlokam, *Bhaja Govindam- Verse 11 - Bhaja Govindam - 11-mā kuru dhanajana - By Adi Sankaracharya - In Sanskrit with English Transliteration, Word-by-word meaning and Translation*, Shlokam, 19 October 2020, https://shlokam. org/texts/bhaja-govindam-11/.

Leading with the Soul: The Intersection of Leadership and Spiritual Growth

1 Chandrayaan–2 was India's second lunar exploration mission, developed by the Indian Space Research Organisation (ISRO), and launched on 22 July 2019. Following the success of Chandrayaan–1, this mission represented a more advanced and ambitious attempt to study the Moon, particularly its south pole region, which had not been explored extensively before. It unintendedly crash-landed on the moon, thus failing to deploy its lander and rover.

2 PIB, 'PM addresses Team ISRO on success of Chandrayaan-3', Pib.gov.in, 2023, https://pib.gov.in/ PressReleaseIframePage.aspx?PRID=1952360.

3 R. Balasubramaniam, *Leadership Lessons for Daily Living*, Grassroots Research and Advocacy Movement (GRAAM) and India Leaders for Social Sector (ILSS), 2020.

4 PIB, 'English rendering of PM's address to the nation from ISRO Control Centre', pib.gov.in, 2019, https://pib.gov.in/ PressReleasePage.aspx?PRID=1584418.

5 The Bhagavad Gita is a 700-verse Hindu scripture that is part of the Indian epic, the Mahabharata. It is a sacred text of great significance in Hindu philosophy and spirituality. The Bhagavad Gita is essentially a conversation between Prince Arjuna and Lord Krishna, who serves as his charioteer and spiritual guide. This conversation takes place on the battlefield just before the Kurukshetra War, where Arjuna is filled with doubt and moral dilemma about fighting in the war.

6 Krishna is one of the most widely revered and popular of all Indian divinities, worshipped as the eighth incarnation of the Hindu God Vishnu, and also as a supreme God in his own right. He is a cousin of the Kuru and Pandava clans in the epic of Mahabharata and is a close friend of Arjuna, to whom he imparts the Bhagavad Gita during his moral dilemma at the time of the war.

7 Ramana Maharshi, also known as Bhagavan Sri Ramana Maharshi, was a renowned Indian sage and spiritual teacher who lived in the early to mid-twentieth century. Ramana Maharshi's teachings were primarily centred on the practice of self-inquiry (Atma Vichara) as a means to attain self-realization and spiritual enlightenment.

8 Ravishankar, popular known as Sri Sri Ravishankar, is a globally recognized spiritual leader and humanitarian known for his work in promoting peace and human values. Born on 13 May 1956, in Tamil Nadu, India, he is the founder of the Art of Living Foundation, an international non-profit organization aimed at relieving individual stress, societal problems and violence.

9 Hindu cremation is a significant and sacred ritual that is performed after the death of a Hindu individual. It is based on the belief in Samsara, the cycle of life, death and rebirth, and the idea that the physical body is temporary while the soul (Atman) is eternal. Cremation is seen as a way to release the soul from its physical form and allow it to continue its journey.

10 The Hindu concept of Trimurti/Trinity, represents the three fundamental aspects of the Supreme Reality or Brahman, manifested in three distinct forms: Brahma, Vishnu and Shiva. This concept is central to Hindu cosmology and philosophy, signifying the cyclical nature of the universe in creation, preservation and destruction.

11 NDTV, '"In Maa, I've Always Felt . . . ": PM Modi's Moving Tribute to His Mother, NDTV.com, 30 December 2020, https://www.ndtv.com/india-news/pm-narendra-modis-mother-heeraben-mother-dies-in-maa-ive-always-felt-pm-modis-tribute-to-his-mother-3649585.

12 Karma Yoga, a concept in Hindu philosophy, is the path of unselfish action. It is one of the four spiritual paths in Hinduism, the others being Jñāna Yoga (the path of knowledge), Bhakti Yoga (the path of devotion) and Rāja Yoga (the path of meditation). The term 'Karma Yoga' comes from the Sanskrit 'Karma', meaning 'action' or 'deed', and 'Yog', which means 'union'. Therefore, Karma Yoga literally translates to the 'path of union through action'.

13 The Vyadha Gita, also known as the 'Butcher's Gita', is a lesser-known spiritual text within Hinduism, forming a part of the Mahabharata. It is a conversation between a learned Brahmin, named Kaushika, and a butcher, identified as Vyadha (meaning 'butcher' in Sanskrit). This dialogue occurs in the 'Vana Parva' or 'Aranyaka-parva' (The Book of the Forest) section of the Mahabharata.

14 Project Gutenberg, *The Project Gutenberg eBook of The Mahabharata, Vana Parva, Part II*, Gutenberg.org, 13 May 2004, https://www.gutenberg.org/files/12333/12333-h/12333-h.htm.

15 Eknath Easwaran (1910–1999) is a spiritual teacher and the author of more than thirty books on spiritual living. Easwaran is a recognized authority on the Indian spiritual classics. His translations of the Bhagavad Gita, the Upanishads, and the Dhammapada are the best-selling editions in the US, and over 1.5 million copies of his books are in print.

16 E. Easwaran, *Conquest of Mind: Take Charge of Your Thoughts and Reshape Your Life through Meditation*, Nilgiri Press, Tomales, California, 2010.

17 M. Csikszentmihalyi, *FLOW: The Psychology of Optimal Experience*, Harper Perennial Modern Classics, 2008.

18 Project Gutenberg, *The Mahabharata, Vana Parva, Part I*, gutenberg.org, 3 April 2004, https://www.gutenberg.org/files/11894/11894-h/11894-h.htm.

19 Aurobindo Ghose was a renowned Indian philosopher, poet, yogi and spiritual teacher. He is best known for his integral yoga philosophy and his significant contributions to Indian spirituality and the broader world of philosophy and literature.

20 A. Ghose, *Letters on Yoga-IV*, Sri Aurobindo Ashram, 2014.

21 O.L. Carter, D.E. Presti, C. Callistemon, Y. Ungerer, G.B. Liu, and J.D. Pettigrew, 'Meditation alters perceptual rivalry in Tibetan Buddhist monks', *Current Biology*, 15(11), 2005, R412–R413, https://doi.org/10.1016/j.cub.2005.05.043.

22 Teresa de Cepeda y Ahumada, commonly known as Saint Teresa of Ávila, was a prominent Spanish mystic, writer and reformer in the Catholic Church. She lived during the sixteenth century and is considered one of the most significant figures in the history of Christian mysticism. In her writings, she explored the stages of the spiritual journey and provided practical guidance for those seeking a deeper relationship with God.

23 Minimum Support Price is an important agricultural policy in India aimed at ensuring that farmers receive a fair and stable price for their crops. The MSP is announced by the Indian government, and it serves as a kind of price floor at which the government promises to purchase the farmers' produce if market prices fall below the specified MSP.

24 The mandi system, also known as Agricultural Produce Market Committees (APMCs), is a network of regulated wholesale markets or mandis across India. These

mandis serve as intermediaries between farmers and buyers (including traders, wholesalers and processors) and provide a platform for the sale and purchase of agricultural produce.

25 PIB, 'English rendering of PM's address in the 18th Episode of "Mann Ki Baat 2.0" on 29.11.2020', pib.gov.in, 2020, https://pib.gov.in/PressReleasePage.aspx?PRID=1676933.

26 The Guru Nanak Prakash Parv, or Guru Nanak Jayanti, is a special celebration in Sikhism that commemorates the birth anniversary of Guru Nanak Dev Ji, the founder of Sikhism.

27 PIB, 'English rendering of the PM's address to the Nation', pib.gov.in, 2021, https://pib.gov.in/PressRelease Page.aspx?PRID=1773162.

28 E. Easwaran, *Conquest of Mind: Take Charge of Your Thoughts and Reshape Your Life through Meditation*, Nilgiri Press, Tomales, California, 2010.

From the Podium to the People: Decoding the Essence of Public Leadership

1 J. Hartley, 'Ten propositions about public leadership', *International Journal of Public Leadership*, Vol. 14, No. 4, 2018, pp. 202–17, Emerald Publishing Limited, 2056–4929, DOI 10.1108/IJPL-09-2018-0048.

2 J. Habermas, *Structural Transformation of the Public Sphere: An Inquiry into a Category of Bourgeois Society*, Polity Press, Cambridge, UK, 1992.

3 De Jure: This term means 'by law' or 'according to law' in Latin. It refers to something that exists because of legal measures or is mandated by law

4 De Facto: This term means 'in fact' or 'in practice' in Latin. It is used to describe situations that exist in reality, even if not legally recognized or formalized.

5 The cabinet secretary is the topmost executive official and seniormost civil servant of the Government of India. The cabinet secretary is the ex-officio head of the Civil Services

Board, the Cabinet Secretariat, the Indian Administrative Service (IAS) and all civil services under the rules of business of the government.

6   PM CARES, short for Prime Minister's Citizen Assistance and Relief in Emergency Situations Fund, is a public charitable trust in India. It was created in March 2020, in the wake of the COVID-19 pandemic, to provide relief to those affected by the pandemic and other similar emergencies. https://pmcares.gov.in/en/web/page/about_us.

7   Following the massive earthquake that struck Türkiye and Syria on 6 February 2023, Operation Dost ('friend' in Hindi) was launched to provide necessary search and rescue (SAR) support and medical assistance. India sent more than 250 personnel, specialized equipment and other relief material (amounting to more than 135 tons) to Türkiye on 5 C-17 IAF aircrafts.

8   Vidura is a prominent character in the ancient Indian epic, the Mahabharata, known for his wisdom, impartiality and moral integrity. His most significant contribution was his repeated counsel to the king to stop the Mahabharata war from happening and for his teachings on morality and ethics, which are compiled in the section known as Vidura Neeti, or The Counsels of Vidura.

9   Buddhi is a Sanskrit term derived from the root, *budh*, which means 'to know' or 'to be awake'. Therefore, buddhi refers to intellect, wisdom and the power of the mind to understand, analyse, discriminate and decide.

10 The Arthashastra is an ancient Indian treatise on statecraft, political science, economic policy and military strategy. Kautilya, also identified as Vishnugupta and Chanakya, is traditionally credited as the author of the text.

11 The Sanskrit phrase 'sarvabhūtahite ratāḥ' can be translated as 'those who are devoted to the welfare of all beings'.

12 D. Bell, *The Cultural Contradictions of Capitalism,* Basic Books, New York, 1976.

13 Dani Rodrik is currently the Ford Foundation Professor of International Political Economy at Harvard University's John F. Kennedy School of Government. He is also the president of the International Economic Association and co-director of the Economics for Inclusive Prosperity (EfIP) network. Rodrik's research focuses on globalization, economic growth and development, and political economy.

14 *'Yathā piṇḍe tathā brahmāṇḍe'* translates to 'as is the microcosm, so is the macrocosm'.

15 The Give It Up campaign refers to a specific initiative launched in India that encouraged citizens to voluntarily give up their subsidies on cooking gas (LPG) cylinders. This campaign was introduced by the Government of India as part of its efforts to target subsidies more efficiently and ensure that they reach those who need them most.

16 'Janbhagidaari' translates to 'people's partnership' or 'public involvement' in English. This concept is a cornerstone in many democratic and developmental processes, emphasizing the active engagement and contribution of the general public in governance, decision-making and implementation of various policies and programmes.

17 'Revdi Culture' is a term used in India to describe the practice of political parties promising freebies to voters in order to win elections. The term 'revdi' refers to a type of sweet dish that is often given as a gift or bribe. In post-independent India, many political parties have gained power promising freebies but have ruined the state's finances in the process.

18 MyGov is a platform launched by the Government of India to promote active citizen engagement in governance and policymaking. It was established in July 2014 as a part of the Digital India initiative. https://www.mygov.in/.

19 The period of twenty-five years from 15 August 2022 (seventy-fifth year of Indian independence) to 15 August 2047 was dubbed as Amrit Kaal (auspicious period) by the PM, for the attainment of Vision 2047.

20 Green leadership refers to a style of leadership that prioritizes and integrates environmental sustainability into decision-making processes and organizational practices.

21 The Conference of the Parties (COP) is a crucial component of international environmental agreements, particularly the United Nations Framework Convention on Climate Change (UNFCCC). COP is an annual gathering of representatives from countries that are signatories to the relevant international agreements. The primary purpose of COP meetings is to assess progress, negotiate further actions and make decisions related to the implementation of these agreements.

22 Green jobs, also known as environmentally friendly or sustainable jobs, are positions in various industries that contribute to environmental preservation, sustainability and the reduction of negative impacts on the environment.

23 The National Green Hydrogen Mission is a Government of India initiative to make India the largest producer of green hydrogen, thus reducing its dependence on fossil fuels and helping keep the environment clean.

24 LiFE or Lifestyle for Environment is a lifestyle model proposed by Modi to replace the prevalent 'use-and-dispose' economy with a circular economy, which would be defined by mindful and deliberate utilization. Economies operating on this principle are herein referred to as LiFE economy.

25 The Yajurveda is an ancient collection of Sanskrit mantras and verses, used in Hindu worship and rituals. It is one of the four primary scriptures of Hinduism. This text describes the way in which religious rituals and sacred ceremonies should be performed.

26 The term 'short-termism' refers to an excessive focus on short-term results at the expense of long-term interests. This concept is commonly used in the context of a political economy, where there can be a tendency to prioritize immediate electoral gains over long-term sustainability and growth of the country.

27 Sengol is the word used by the Tamil Chola kings for the sceptre which serves as a sacred symbol of just and Dharmic rule in Indic tradition. Sceptres or Raja Dhanda as they are also called, were held by the kings in Bharat as a constant reminder to tread the path of Dharma in their rule. They were used during coronations of kings to depict transfer of power from one ruler to another. On India becoming free from the British, a sceptre, modelled after a sengol used by the Tamil Chola kings and the Vijayanagar Empire, was specially made and used by a free India to symbolically receive the rule back from the British on the eve of Independence. It was presented to the first PM of India, Jawaharlal Nehru, and has subsequently been shifted from his museum and installed in the newly built Parliament building.

28 Ayushman Bharat Pradhan Mantri Jan Arogya Yojana (PM-JAY), commonly known as Ayushman Bharat, is a government health insurance scheme in India. Launched on 23 September 2018, Ayushman Bharat is the world's largest government-funded healthcare programme aimed at providing financial protection to over 100 million vulnerable families.

29 Civilian award given to people who had done meritorious work in different domains.

Inspiring Change, Igniting Hope: Public Leadership as a Catalyst for Transformation

1 A charge sheet is a formal document of accusation prepared by law enforcement agencies or, in the context of employment, by an organization's disciplinary authority. It lists the charges or allegations against an individual, usually because of an investigation. In the workplace, especially within government sectors, a charge sheet is issued to an employee who is alleged to have committed misconduct or a violation of rules and policies.

2   Chintan Shivir is a Hindi term which means 'Introspection Camp'. Started by Modi in 2003 when he was the CM of Gujarat, it was an attempt to bring together bureaucrats, ministers and district officers to brainstorm together and chart the road map for vision accomplishment.

3   The transition from a rule-based to a role-based HR management system empowers officials to develop the skills, knowledge and attitudes that they require for fulfilling their roles within the government at all points in their careers, rather than providing them training resources based on one-size-fits-all rules.

4   Coined by Jamais Cascio, an American futurist and author, BANI provides a lens to view the complexities and uncertainties of the twenty-first-century world. It helps in acknowledging the challenges faced in decision-making, planning and forecasting in a rapidly evolving global environment.

5   Speaking in reference to the earlier involvement of the government in running businesses, the PM had said: 'I believe the government has no business to do business. The focus should be on Minimum Government but Maximum Governance.'

6   Aadhaar is a twelve-digit unique identity number issued by the Unique Identification Authority of India (UIDAI), serving as a proof of identity and residence for Indian citizens. It is the world's largest biometric ID system, linking biometric and demographic data of individuals to a unique number.

7   Direct Benefit Transfer is a government programme in India that transfers subsidies and financial benefits directly to citizens' bank accounts, eliminating intermediaries and reducing fraud.

8   DigiLocker is a digital platform initiated by the Government of India for citizens to securely store and access electronic versions of their official documents and certificates.

9   Centralized Public Grievance Redress and Monitoring System (CPGRAMS) is an online platform by the Government of India for citizens to submit and track their complaints and grievances regarding government services.

10 MyGov is a digital platform initiated by the Government of India, aimed at fostering citizen participation in governance. It acts as a medium where citizens can suggest ideas, participate in discussions and contribute to policymaking. The platform serves as a public feedback mechanism, and hosts campaigns, contests and innovation challenges to engage the populace. It is also used for disseminating information on government schemes and services.

11 Before India gained independence from British colonial rule in 1947, the Indian subcontinent comprised provinces and numerous princely states. These princely states were semi-sovereign entities under the indirect rule of the British Crown. At the time of independence, there were around 562 princely states in India. Integrating these princely states into the newly formed Republic of India was a complex and challenging process which was carried out by Sardar Vallabhbhai Patel, the first Deputy Prime Minister and Home Minister of India, and his able team.

12 R. Sagar, *The Progressive Maharaja: Sir Madhava Rao's Hints on the Art and Science of Government*, Gurugram, HarperCollins India, 2022.

13 Nirmal Bharat Abhiyan, formerly known as the Total Sanitation Campaign, was a comprehensive programme by the Government of India aimed at eradicating open defecation and promoting toilet use in rural areas for improved sanitation.

14 Vision India@2047 is the aspiration of India by 2047 for attaining new heights of prosperity; making best facilities available both in villages and cities; eliminating unnecessary interference by the Government in the lives of citizens; and building the world's most modern infrastructure.

15 PIB, *Factsheet Details,* pib.gov.in, 16 November 2021, https://pib.gov.in/FactsheetDetails.aspx?Id=148579

16 P.L. Kaul, 'Swachh Bharat Mission achievements and milestones', Jammu Kashmir Latest News | Tourism | Breaking News J&K, 28 November 2022, https://www.dailyexcelsior.com/swachh-bharat-mission-achievements-and-milestones/.

17 Daksha Smriti is a traditional text attributed to the sage Daksha, focusing on Dharma (moral and ethical conduct), covering aspects of civil and social law, and guiding individual and societal conduct.

18 Jal Jeevan Mission, 2023, Jaljeevanmission.gov.in.

19 A. Marino, *Modi: A Political Biography,* HarperCollins, Gurugram, 2022.

20 PMJDY is a National Mission on Financial Inclusion encompassing an integrated approach to bring about comprehensive financial inclusion of all the households in the country. The plan envisages universal access to banking facilities with at least one basic banking account for every household, financial literacy, access to credit, insurance and pension facility.

21 *COVID-19 Boosted the Adoption of Digital Financial Services,* World Bank Group, 21 July 2022. https://www.worldbank.org/en/news/feature/2022/07/21/covid-19-boosted-the-adoption-of-digital-financial-services#:~:text=Globally%2C%20some%201.4%20billion%20adults,go%2C%20much%20more%20is%20needed.

22 The aim of the Aadhaar unique identity is targeted welfare distribution. Through linking of the user's bank account with their Aadhaar ID, welfare benefits could be more efficiently delivered to the end user, replacing the middlemen.

23 The JAM Trinity refers to the Indian Government's integrated use of Jan Dhan bank accounts, Aadhaar identification and Mobile telephony to enhance the

efficiency of public welfare programmes through direct benefit transfers and financial inclusion.

24 Pradhan Mantri Jan-Dhan Yojana | Department of Financial Services | Ministry of Finance, pmjdy.gov.in, 2023, https://pmjdy.gov.in/account.

25 The informal/grey economy comprises activities that have market value and would add to tax revenue and GDP if they were recorded. According to the International Labour Organization, about two billion workers, or 60 per cent of the world's employed population aged fifteen and older, spend at least part of their time in the informal sector.

26 The Panchayat system in India is a traditional form of rural local governance, where the village is loosely governed by five people (Panch). Its newer avatar under the Indian state, the Panchayati Raj system, structured in a three-tier format—village (Gram Panchayat), block (Panchayat Samiti) and district (Zilla Parishad) levels—empowers elected representatives to administer local development tasks and ensures people's participation in decision-making processes.

27 NPCI, *Unified Payments Interface (UPI) Product Statistics | NPCI*, npci.org.in, 2018, https://www.npci.org.in/what-we-do/upi/product-statistics.

28 The Insolvency and Bankruptcy Code (IBC) is a comprehensive legislation enacted in India in 2016 to address insolvency and bankruptcy issues in a time-bound manner. The primary objective of the IBC is to promote entrepreneurship, availability of credit and balance the interests of all stakeholders, including creditors and debtors.

29 A unicorn is a privately held start-up company valued at over US$1 billion.

30 Hurun Research Institute. *HURUN GLOBAL UNICORN INDEX 2023 – Hurun India*, hurunindia.com, 2023, https://hurunindia.com/blog/hurun-global-unicorn-index-2023/

31 https://www.india.gov.in/spotlight/pm-gati-shakti-national-master-plan-multi-modal-connectivity

32   Azadi Ka Amrit Mahotsav is an initiative of the Government of India to celebrate and commemorate 75 years of independence and the glorious history of its people, culture and achievements.

33   PIB, 'English rendering of PM's address at the launch of PM Gati Shakti, National Master Plan for Multi-Modal Connectivity', pib.gov.in, 13 October 2021, https://pib.gov.in/PressReleasePage.aspx?PRID=1763594.

34   PIB, 'Government committed to promote a gender just society and increased representation of women in various domains', pib.gov.in, 15 December 2023, https://pib.gov.in/PressReleaseIframePage.aspx?PRID=1986793.

Navigating Change: The Journey of Adaptive Leadership

1   A union territory (UT) is a political and administrative division of the country that is directly governed by the central Government of India. Unlike states, which have their own governments and more extensive powers, union territories have less autonomy and are primarily administered by officials appointed by the President of India.

2   PIB, 'English rendering of the PM's address to the Nation', pib.gov.in, 2019, https://pib.gov.in/PressReleasePage.aspx?PRID=1581598.

3   Princely states, also known as native states or Indian states, were semi-autonomous territories in the Indian subcontinent during the British colonial period and prior to India's independence in 1947. These states were ruled by local monarchs or princes, often with their own governments and administrative systems, and they enjoyed a degree of sovereignty within their territories.

4   President's Rule is a term used in the context of the governance of certain regions or states within a federal system of government. It primarily refers to a situation where the elected government of a state or region is

temporarily suspended, and the administration of the state is handed over to the governor or a representative appointed by the central Government.

5   Ronald Heifetz is an American leadership and public leadership expert, educator and author known for his work on adaptive leadership and leadership in the context of complex and challenging situations. Heifetz is a faculty at the Harvard Kennedy School and the founder of the Center for Public Leadership.

6   Ronald A. Heifetz and Marty Linsky, *Leadership on the Line: Staying Alive through the Dangers of Change*. Harvard Business Review Press, Cambridge, MA, 2017.

7   R. Balasubramaniam, *Leadership Lessons for Daily Living (1st ed.)*, Grassroots Research and Advocacy Movement (GRAAM) and India Leaders for Social Sector (ILSS), 2020.

8   Ronald A. Heifetz and Marty Linsky, *Leadership on the Line: Staying Alive through the Dangers of Change*, Harpers Business Review Press, 2017.

9   Ekta Yatra, which translates to 'Unity March' or 'Unity Journey' in English, was a political march organized by the Bharatiya Janata Party (BJP) in India in 1992. The primary goal of the Ekta Yatra was to promote national unity and solidarity in the face of various fissiparous tendencies in the nation.

10   Subramania Bharati, also known as Mahakavi (Great Poet) Bharati, was a pioneering figure in Tamil literature and Indian nationalism. He was born on 11 December 1882, in Ettayapuram in the then Madras Presidency of British India and passed away on 11 September 1921. Bharati was a poet, freedom fighter and a social reformer. He is considered one of the greatest Tamil literary figures of all time. He wrote on various themes, including patriotism, devotion and love.

11   Balidan Diwas, also known as the Martyrdom Day of Guru Tegh Bahadur, is a day of great significance in Sikhism. It commemorates the sacrifice of Guru Tegh Bahadur, the ninth Sikh Guru, who was executed in 1675 on the orders

of the Mughal Emperor Aurangzeb. Guru Tegh Bahadur is revered for his deep spirituality and his commitment to protecting religious freedom.

12 G. Tiwari, 'Read what Modi said 30 years ago while unfurling India's tricolour at Lal Chowk in Srinagar', OpIndia, 26 January 2022, https://www.opindia.com/2022/01/pm-modi-unfurled-indian-tricolour-at-lal-chowk-srinagar-1992-at-bjp-ekta-march/.

13 Kashmiriyat, a phrase coined by former PM Atal Bihari Vajpayee, means the way of life and distinct identity of the people of Kashmir.

14 Through Article 370 of the Indian Constitution, the state of Jammu and Kashmir was able to have a separate constitution, flag and emblem of its own. Many of the laws and their protections passed by the Indian Legislative Assemblies could not be implemented in Kashmir due to this dual situation.

15 Delimitation is the process of defining or redefining the boundaries of electoral constituencies or administrative units within a country. The primary objective of delimitation is to ensure equal representation for all citizens in the political system by creating electoral districts or constituencies that have roughly equal populations.

16 The Indian government recognizes and provides special protections and affirmative actions for certain tribal communities in order to facilitate their seamless integration into mainstream society.

17 PIB, 'Union Home Minister and Minister of Cooperation, Shri Amit Shah replied to the discussion on Jammu and Kashmir Reservation (Amendment) Bill, 2023 and Jammu and Kashmir Reorganization (Amendment) Bill, 2023 in the Lok Sabha today, later these bills were passed in Lok Sabha', pib.gov.in, 2023, https://pib.gov.in/PressReleaseIframePage.aspx?PRID=1983311.

18 P. Sharma, 'Article 370 A Temporary Provision: Supreme Court Upholds Abrogation of Special Status of Jammu and Kashmir', Live Law, 11 December 2023, https://www.livelaw.in/top-stories/article-370-supreme-court-abrogation-of-special-status-of-jammu-and-kashmir-244198.

19 N. Modi, 'Narendra Modi writes on Article 370 verdict: Today, a clean canvas for every child in J&K', the *Indian Express*, 12 December 2023, https://indianexpress.com/article/opinion/columns/pm-narendra-modi-article-370-verdict-jammu-and-kashmir-9064035/.

Vision Beyond Borders: Exploring the Dynamics of Global Leadership

1   A. Pandya, 'Vasudhaiva Kutumbakam: A new theoretical framework to make sense of the world order. Usanas Foundation', 14 July 2023, https://usanasfoundation.com/vasudhaiva-kutumbakam-a-new-theoretical-framework-to-make-sense-of-the-world-order.

2   The International Film Festival of India (IFFI) is one of the most prestigious and oldest film festivals in Asia, organized by the Government of India since 1952. IFFI aims to showcase and celebrate the art of cinema by bringing together filmmakers, artists and cinema enthusiasts from around the world.

3   Festival of India is a celebration organized by Indian Missions abroad, to promote Indian culture and soft diplomacy among the people of the host country.

4   Vibrant Gujarat is a biennial investors' summit held by the government of Gujarat in Gujarat, India. It was initiated in 2003 by Narendra Modi, who was then the Chief Minister of the state. The event is aimed at bringing together business leaders, investors, corporations, thought leaders, policy and opinion makers for networking, promoting investment

opportunities in the state and fostering economic and social development.

5   Bhutan is the smallest country in the Indian subcontinent, which had not been prioritized previously due to its limited diplomatic heft.

6   The South Asia Satellite, officially known as GSAT-9, is a geostationary communications satellite launched to provide various communication services like telecommunication, television, direct-to-home (DTH), VSAT and tele-education to countries in the South Asian region.

7   The Arthashastra is an ancient Indian text attributed to the scholar Kautilya, also known as Chanakya. It is a comprehensive treatise on statecraft, economic policy, military strategy and political philosophy. The text is written in Sanskrit and is a key work in the field of classical Indian political thought.

8   In December 2015, Indian Prime Minister Narendra Modi made a historic and unexpected visit to Pakistan. Modi made a stop in Lahore, Pakistan, on his way back to India from Afghanistan, where he met with then-Pakistani Prime Minister Nawaz Sharif. It was seen as a goodwill gesture and an effort to resume high-level talks between the two countries.

9   The Pathankot terror attack occurred in January 2016 when terrorists from the Pakistan-based Jaish-e-Mohammed (JeM) group infiltrated the Pathankot Air Force Station in India's Punjab state.

10   S. Mukhopadhyay, 'Imran Khan hails India's Prime Minister Narendra Modi again, this time on corruption', *Mint*, 22 September 2022, https://www.livemint.com/news/world/imran-khan-hails-india-s-prime-minister-narendra-modi-again-this-time-for-on-corruption-11663803959505.html.

11   The South Asian Association for Regional Cooperation (SAARC) is a grouping of eight countries: India, Nepal, Bhutan, Bangladesh, Sri Lanka, the Maldives, Pakistan

and Afghanistan, which was formed in 1985 to promote economic cooperation, cultural development and strengthen collective self-reliance between the countries of South Asia.

12 A. Sajjanhar, 'India Emerges as a Global Actor during the Pandemic Crisis', *Khmer Times*, 25 January 2022, https://www.khmertimeskh.com/501013433/india-emerges-as-a-global-actor-during-the-pandemic-crisis/.

13 BAPS Swaminarayan Sanstha, *Consecration Ceremony | Inauguration of BAPS Hindu Mandir*, BAPS, 14 February 2024, https://www.baps.org/News/2024/Consecration-Ceremony--Inauguration-of-BAPS-Hindu-Mandir-25369.aspx.

14 S. Jiwrajka, 'Live Narendra Modi Madison Square Garden speech updates: Narendra Modi concludes his speech as crowd shouts "Modi Modi"', India.com, 28 September 2014, https://www.india.com/news/india/live-narendra-modi-madison-square-garden-speech-updates-160449/.

15 NDTV, 'PM Modi Is "The Boss": Australian PM's Bruce Springsteen Comparison', NDTV.com, 23 May 2023, https://www.ndtv.com/india-news/australian-pm-anthony-albanese-says-prime-minister-narendra-modi-is-the-boss-at-big-sydney-event-4058610/.

16 Modi's approach to hugging world leaders has become a characteristic feature of his interactions on the global stage and has generated both praise and criticism. One of the most widely recognized instances of the 'Modi Hug' occurred during his tenure when he warmly hugged former US President Barack Obama during President Obama's visit to India in 2015. This gesture garnered significant media attention and was seen as a symbol of the growing friendship and strategic partnership between India and the US.

17 A. Dhar, 'PM Modi remains most popular global leader with 76% rating: Rishi Sunak at . . .', *Hindustan Times*, 15 September 2023, https://www.hindustantimes.com/india-news/pm-modi-remains-most-popular-global-leader-with-76-rating-rishi-sunak-at-survey-101694785952120.html.

18 J. Cartillier, 'US-India relations renewed as Obama and Modi break nuclear deadlock', *Sydney Morning Herald*, 25 January 2015, https://www.smh.com.au/world/usindia-relations-renewed-as-obama-and-modi-break-nuclear-deadlock-20150126-12xy4q.html.

19 P. Chakraborty, 'Qatar releases 8 Indian Navy veterans jailed on espionage charges, 7 back in India', *India Today*, 11 February 2024, https://www.indiatoday.in/india/story/qatar-indian-navy-veterans-freed-espionage-charges-india-mea-diplomatic-breakthrough-2500512-2024-02-12?utm_source=directhp&utm_medium=clicktopstories&utm_campaign=hptopstories.

20 United Nations General Assembly, *Resolution adopted by the General Assembly on 11 December 2014, 69/131,* International Day of Yoga, (A/RES/69/131), https://www.un.org/en/observances/yoga-day#:~:text=Recognizing%20its%20universal%20appeal%2C%20on,many%20benefits%20of%20practicing%20yoga.

21 PIB, English rendering of PM's address in the 86th Episode of 'Mann Ki Baat' on 27 February 2022, pib.gov.in, https://pib.gov.in/PressReleasePage.aspx?PRID=1801550.

22 PIB, The recently retrieved idol of Goddess Annapurna to begin its journey on November 11 for its rightful place at Kashi Vishwanath temple, Varanasi: Shri G. Kishan Reddy, 2021, pib.gov.in. https://pib.gov.in/PressReleasePage.aspx?PRID=1768992.

23 https://www.mea.gov.in/prime-minister-visits.htm.

24 ICWA, 'Sub-regional Cooperation under BBIN Framework: An Analysis - Indian Council of World Affairs (Government of India)', icwa.in, 2019, https://www.icwa.in/show_content.php?lang=1&level=3&ls_id=4817&lid=2833

25 S. Haidar, 'Bangladesh, India, Nepal move ahead on motor vehicle agreement project', *The Hindu*, 8 March 2022, https://www.thehindu.com/news/national/bangladesh-india-nepal-move-ahead-on-motor-vehicle-agreement-project/article65205145.ece.

26 PIB. 'India-UAE Joint Statement during the visit of Prime Minister, Shri Narendra Modi to UAE', pib.gov.in., 15 June 2023, https://pib.gov.in/PressReleaseIframePage. aspx?PRID=1939795#:~:text=India%20is%20the%20 UAE%27s%20second,CEPA%20on%201%20May%20 2022.

27 The White House, 'FACT SHEET: World Leaders Launch a Landmark India-Middle East-Europe Economic Corridor', The White House, 9 September 2023, https:// www.whitehouse.gov/briefing-room/statements-releases/2023/09/09/fact-sheet-world-leaders-launch-a-landmark-india-middle-east-europe-economic-corridor/.

28 S. Dutta, 'India, Saudi Arabia look to marry power grids with undersea cable', the *Times of India*, 11 September 2023, https://timesofindia.indiatimes.com/business/india-business/ india-saudi-arabia-look-to-marry-power-grids-with-undersea-cable/articleshow/103586545.cms?from=mdr.

29 M. Pant, 'G20 Summit: PM Modi announces India-Middle East-Europe Economic Corridor to counter Beijing's OBOR', *Business Today*, 9 September 2023, https://www. businesstoday.in/g20-summit/story/g20-summit-pm-modi-announces-india-middle-east-europe-economic-corridor-to-counter-beijings-obor-397688-2023-09-09.

30 BS Web Team, '"Waiting for the thank you": S Jaishankar on India softening oil markets', *Business Standard*, 16 November 2023, https://www.business-standard.com/india-news/waiting-for-the-thank-you-s-jaishankar-on-india-softening-oil-markets-123111600489_1.html.

31 The Yajur Veda is an ancient collection of Sanskrit mantras and verses, used in Hindu worship and rituals. It is one of the four primary scriptures of Hinduism. This text describes the way in which religious rituals and sacred ceremonies should be performed.

32 A. Narlikar, 'India's role in global governance: A Modification?', *International Affairs*, Volume 93, Issue

1, 1 January 2017, pp. 93–111, https://doi.org/10.1093/ia/iiw005.

33 PIB, 'Prime Minister conferred Champions of Earth Award 2018 for Policy Leadership', pib.gov.in, 2017, https://pib.gov.in/PressReleasePage.aspx?PRID=1548376.

34 V. Anand, 'Modi's multilateral approach influenced by his personality & changes in context, the *Times of India* blog, 28 August 2022, https://timesofindia.indiatimes.com/readersblog/the-daily-dialogue/modis-multilateral-approach-influenced-by-his-personality-changes-in-context-44530/.

35 S. Gupta, 'What is the 10X3 diplomatic outreach model of Modi government?' *Hindustan Times*, 15 October 2022, https://www.hindustantimes.com/india-news/what-is-the-10x3-diplomatic-outreach-model-of-modi-government-101665805630451.html.

36 'G-20 Bali Declaration Adopts PM Modi's Message on Ukraine, says "Today's Era Must Not Be of War",' *Outlook India*, 16 November 2022, https://www.outlookindia.com/national/g20-bali-declaration-adopts-pm-modi-message-on-ukraine-says-today-era-must-not-be-of-war-news-237793, on 16 November 2022.

37 The G20, or Group of Twenty, is an international forum for governments and central bank governors from nineteen countries, the European Union and the African Union. It was established in 1999 to promote international financial stability and cooperation among major economies. The G20 countries represent a mix of both advanced and emerging economies.

38 'World leaders praise PM Modi's "decisive leadership" as the G20 Summit concludes', *India Today*, 10 September 2023, https://www.indiatoday.in/india/story/g20-world-leaders-hail-pm-modi-joint-declaration-global-south-2433807-2023-09-10.

39 A. Divya, 'G20 at Rajghat: United in voice for peace, tributes to the Mahatma', the *Indian Express*, 10 September

2023, https://indianexpress.com/article/cities/delhi/rajghat-pm-modi-welcomes-g20-leaders-pay-tributes-mahatma-gandhi-8932970/.

40 L. Puri, 'Bharat's G20 presidency: Shaping global governance for development', Firstpost, 18 September 2023, https://www.firstpost.com/opinion/bharats-g20-presidency-shaping-global-governance-for-development-13136012.html.

41 Operation Dost was a Search and Rescue (SAR) cum medical assistance mission sent by India to Türkiye in the aftermath of the 6 February 2023 earthquake. Through quick decision-making and intergovernmental coordination, the mission was able to effectively deliver relief and rescue. Dost is the Urdu word for friend.

42 S. Sibal, 'In a first since Taliban takeover, India to deliver aid to Afghanistan via Chabahar port', WION, 7 March 2023, https://www.wionews.com/india-news/in-a-first-since-taliban-takeover-india-to-deliver-aid-to-afghanistan-via-chabahar-port-569704.

43 S. Mattoo, 'How India's "disaster diplomacy" became a potent tool of statecraft', Mint, 19 February 2023, https://www.livemint.com/news/world/how-india-s-disaster-diplomacy-became-a-potent-tool-of-statecraft-11676830705933.html.

44 During the war between Ravana and Rama in the epic, the Ramayana, when Rama's brother Lakshmana was wounded by a poisoned arrow, it required a rare native herb of the Himalayan mountains to revive him: Sanjeevani. Hanuman, Ram's emissary, was tasked with bringing this herb quickly. However, upon reaching the mountain, when he was unable to identify the herb, he carried the whole Dronagiri mountain back with him from the Himalayas to Lanka.

45 A. Sajjanhar, 'India's "Vaccine Maitri" Initiative | Manohar Parrikar Institute for Defence Studies and Analyses', idsa.in, 2016, https://idsa.in/idsacomments/indias-vaccine-maitri-initiative-asajjanhar-290121.

46 Ibid.

47   The Vande Bharat Mission was an initiative launched by the Indian government to repatriate Indian citizens who were stranded abroad due to the COVID-19 pandemic and travel restrictions imposed globally. The mission was named Vande Bharat as a gesture of national unity and solidarity, with 'Vande Bharat' meaning 'Salute to India' in Sanskrit.

48   S.I. Rajan and H. Arokkiaraj, 'Unprecedented repatriation programme: India's Vande Bharat Mission in 2020', eth. mpg.de, 2020, https://www.eth.mpg.de/molab-inventory/ mobility-events/unprecedented-repatriation-programme-indias-vande-bharat-mission-in-2020.

49   DH Web Desk, '"Vande Bharat Mission" is the largest evacuation exercise in human history: EAM', *Deccan Herald*, 24 March 2022, https://www.deccanherald.com/ india/vande-bharat-mission-is-largest-evacuation-exercise-in-human-history-eam-1094323.html.

50   PIB, 'More than 2,17,000 flights operated under Vande Bharat Mission', pib.gov.in., 2021, https://pib.gov.in/ Pressreleaseshare.aspx?PRID=1776091.

51   ANI, 'A year on, here's why PM Modi called Ukraine rescue as "Operation Ganga"', *Mint*, 22 February 2023, https://www.livemint.com/news/india/a-year-on-here-s-why-pm-modi-called-ukraine-rescue-as-operation-ganga-11677102266783.html.

52   A. Singh, 'Ukraine crisis: Not just Indians, Pakistan, Bangladesh & Nepal students rescued too', the *Times of India*, 9 March 2022, https://timesofindia.indiatimes.com/ india/ukraine-crisis-not-just-indians-pakistan-bangladesh-nepal-students-rescued-too/articleshow/90110254.cms.

53   TN Digital, 'Operation Ganga: When India flag helped Pakistani, Turkish students to escape from war-ravaged Ukraine', TimesNow, 8 April 2022, https://www. timesnownews.com/world/when-india-flag-helped-pakistani-turkish-students-to-escape-from-ukraine-article-89939370.

54 HT Entertainment Desk, 'The Evacuation: Operation Ganga: History TV18 brings India's rescue mission', *Hindustan Times*, 16 June 2023, https://www.hindustantimes. com/entertainment/tv/the-evacuation-operation-ganga-on-history-tv18-101686901392865.html.

55 Linda Yueh, 'The Fragile Five', BBC News, 26 September 2013, https://www.bbc.com/news/business-24280172.

56 Forbes India, 'The Top 10 Largest Economies in the World In 2024', *Forbes India*, 7 February 2024, https:// www.forbesindia.com/article/explainers/top-10-largest-economies-in-the-world/86159/1.

57 'Govt moving ahead with idea of "Make in India, Make for World", says PM Modi at WEF', 17 January 2022, the *Times of India*, https://timesofindia.indiatimes.com/ business/india-business/govt-moving-ahead-with-idea-of-make-in-india-make-for-world-said-pm-modi-at-wef/ articleshow/88957982.cms.

58 H. Kashyap, 'Economic Survey 2022-23: India Reduced 39,000+ Compliances for Ease of Doing Business', Inc42 Media, 31 January 2023, https://inc42.com/buzz/economic-survey-2022-23-india-reduced-39000-compliances-ease-of-doing-business/.

59 'Elon Musk on meeting PM Modi, future India visit and bringing Starlink to the country', 21 June 2023, the *Times of India*, https://timesofindia.indiatimes.com/gadgets-news/elon-musk-says-he-is-a-fan-of-pm-modi-and-why-he-is-excited-about-india/articleshow/101148010.cms.

60 NDTV, 'PM Modi's Mega '50% Offer' for Firms to Set Up Semiconductor Manufacturing', NDTV.com, 28 July 2023, https://www.ndtv.com/india-news/pm-narendra-modis-mega-50-offer-for-firms-to-set-up-semiconductor-manufacturing-4248177.

61 PIB, 'Promoting Millets Consumption', pib.gov.in, 2023, https://pib.gov.in/PressReleasePage.aspx?PRID=1906894.

62 A. Rao, 'UPI goes global: The past, present & future of India's payments platform', WION, 30 August 2023,

https://www.wionews.com/business-economy/upi-goes-global-the-past-present-future-of-indias-payments-platform-630396.

63 A. Narlikar, 'India's foreign economic policy under Modi: negotiations and narratives in the WTO and beyond', *Int Polit 59*, 148–166 (2022), https://doi.org/10.1057/s41311-020-00275-z.

64 PTI. '"Unbelievable, visionary": U.S. Commerce Secretary Raimondo recounts her meeting with Prime Minister Narendra Modi', The Hindu, 16 April 2023, https://www.thehindu.com/news/national/unbelievable-visionary-us-commerce-secretary-raimondo-recounts-her-meeting-with-prime-minister-narendra-modi/article66743460.ece.

65 Ramdhari Singh, also known by his pen name Dinkar, was a nationalist poet, essayist, freedom fighter, patriot and academic, proficient in both Hindi and Maithili languages.

66 BIMSTEC, or the Bay of Bengal Initiative for Multi-Sectoral Technical and Economic Cooperation, is a regional organization comprising seven Member States lying in the littoral and adjacent areas of the Bay of Bengal. Comprising Bangladesh, Bhutan, India, Myanmar, Nepal, Sri Lanka, and Thailand.

Dharma of Legacy and the Legacy of Dharma

1 Fukuyama's thesis of 'End of History' revolves around the idea that liberal democracy may constitute the endpoint of mankind's ideological evolution and the final form of government.

2 *Seeing like a State: How Certain Schemes to Improve the Human Condition Have Failed* is a book written by political scientist James C. Scott, which explores the idea that certain government and planning initiatives aimed at improving society often fail because they oversimplify complex social and natural systems.

3   The Enlightenment, a philosophical and intellectual movement in seventeenth and eighteenth century Europe, ushered in significant changes. It championed reason, empiricism and scientific progress. Enlightenment led to the secularization of society and had a profound impact on events like the American and French Revolutions, shaping modern European thought and society.

4   Thomas Hobbes' *Leviathan* is a philosophical and political work written in 1651. In this work, Hobbes presents his social contract theory and his conception of the ideal government, which he calls the Leviathan. Hobbes' Leviathan model is a metaphorical representation of his vision of a strong and centralized government.

5   D. Coutu, 'Leadership Lessons from Abraham Lincoln', *Harvard Business Review*, April 2009, https://hbr.org/2009/04/leadership-lessons-from-abraham-lincoln.

6   M. Haynes, 'Lee Kuan Yew: Singapore's Leadership & Global Powerhouse Transformation', *Business & Leadership*, 10 September 2023, https://www.businessandleadership.com/leadership/item/lee-kuan-yew-leadership-transformed-singapore/.

7   Ibid.

8   W.R. Gruver and H.T. Zhu, 'Deng Xiaoping: A Leadership Case Study', ResearchGate, 2016, https://www.researchgate.net/publication/304996613_Deng_Xiaoping_A_Leadership_Case_Study.

9   A.K. Biswas and C. Tortajada, 'How China eradicated absolute poverty', *Chinadaily*, 2021, https://global.chinadaily.com.cn/a/202104/12/WS60738cc0a31024ad0bab4c0c.html#:~:text=And%20that%20is%20exactly%20what,and%20poverty%20is%20not%20socialism.%22.

10 *The Complete Works of Swami Vivekananda*, Volume 3, Lectures from Colombo to Almora, The Future of India.

Glossary of Indic Terms
with Explanations

This glossary presents Indic terms with their popular and associated meanings, along with their simplified grammatical composition made of prepositions, verb roots and their shades of senses as well as their definitions wherever relevant.

A

abhaya (n) –
a+bhaya – [a (absence) + bhī (to fear)]
absence of fear, removal of fear, freedom from fear, safety, security

abhivyañjanā (n) –
abhi+vi+añj
abhi+vyañjana – [abhi (towards) + vi (bringing forth) + añj (to speak/to talk)]
making manifest, speaking forth, expression

abhīhi (v) –
a+bhīhi – [a (absence) + bhī (to fear)]
fear not, be fearless, don't be afraid

abhijāta-bala (n/adj)

abhi+jan – [abhi (superior) + jan (to be born) + bala (power/ strength)]

power of noble descent

abhyāsa (n) –

abhi+āsa – [abhi (upon) + āsa (to sit)]

practice

(defined as the firm psychological state [dṛḍhabhūmiḥ] which is long term [dīrghakāla], continuous [nairantarya], full of goodwill [satkārāsevita] – Yogasūtra, 1.14)

advaita (n/adj) –

a+dvaita – [a (absence) + dvita (duality)]

non-duality, monism

ahiṃsā (n) –

a+hiṃsā – [a (absence) + hiṃs (to kill/destroy/give pain)]

non-violence, non-injury, non-aggression

āmātya-bala –

āmātya+bala – [āmātya (minister) + bala (power/strength)]

power of good counsel

amṛta (n/adj) –

a+mṛta – [a (absence) + mṛ (to die)]

literally – immortal, elixir for immortality

aparigraha (n) –

a+pari+graha – [a (absence) + pari (from around) + gṛh (to seize /take/accept)]

non-seizing from around, non-accumulation, non-possessiveness

āpta + vākya (n) –

āpta-vākya – [āpta -> āp (to get/obtain) -> āpta (apt) + vākya -> vac (to speak) -> vākya (speech)]

apt speech; authoritative, authentic statements, trustworthy words, sentences

artha (n) –

artha – [arth (to beg, to request)]

meaning, wealth, one of the four goals of life (puruṣārthas) as envisaged in Bhārata which implies financial security

āsana (n) –

āsana – [ās (to sit)]

posture

in Patañjali's aṣṭāṅgayoga, this is the third limb

asaṅgatva (n) –

a+saṅgatva – [a (absence) + sam (together) + gam (to go)]

without company, aloneness, solitude

aśrama (n) –

ā+śrama – [ā (from beginning till the end) + śram (to put effort)]

literally – application of effort from the beginning till the end;

hermitage, place of continuous effort for self-development, a place of spiritual shelter and support often

ātma-bala (n) –

ātma+bala – [ātma (Self/self) + bala (power/strength)]

power of the Self, spiritual strength

B

bāhu-bala (n) –
bāhu+bala – [bāhu (arms) + bala (power/strength)]
power of valour

bāla-svayaṁsevaka (n) –
bāla+svayam+sevaka – [bāla (young) + svayam (self/volunteer)
+ sevaka (servitor)]
youth-volunteer, child volunteer

bhārata –
belonging to Bharata, a king of ancient India
bhārata is the indigenous name of India and used synonymously
as such in the Preamble of the Constitution
some say it is a combination of bhā (light) + rata (immersed in)
– implying a land that is immersed in light (knowledge)

bhāratīya –
pertaining to India; an Indian

bhāva (n) –
bhāva – [bhū (to be)] feelings, emotions

bheda (n) –
bheda – [bhid (to cut, to break, to divide)]
division

brahma-vihāra –
brahma+vihāra – [brahma (bṛh – to grow, to prosper) + vi +hāra
-> hṛ (temple/abode)]
abodes of brahma

C

cakravartī –

an emperor, universal monarch, sovereign of the world

citta-vṛtti-nirodhaḥ –

[citta (consciousness/mind) + vṛtti -> vṛt (circular patterns/ movements) + nirodhaḥ -> ni (in a special manner) + rudh (to obstruct, to stop)]

restraining of the fluctuations and activities of the mind

This is the second aphorism/ sutra of the Yogasūtra text and the definition of Yoga

D

dāna –

dāna – [dā (to give)]

offering, donation

daṇḍa –

daṇḍa – [daṇḍ (to punish, to fine)]

punishment, literally means stick

darśana –

darśana – [dṛś (to see)]

seeing, a philosophical path, view, sight, vision

dhairya –

dhairya – quality of dhīra – [dhi (to hold, to possess, to become)]

forbearance

dhana-bala –
dhana+bala – [dhan (to bear fruit, to produce crops) +
bala (power/strength)]

dhāraṇā –
dhāraṇā – (dhr – to hold, to support)
holding, bearing, supporting; to contemplate

dharma – [dharma (dhṛ – to hold, to support, to possess)]
inherent quality; that which upholds, righteousness;
universal law

dharma-dṛṣṭi –
dharma+dṛṣṭi – [dharma (dhṛ – to hold, to support) + dṛṣṭi -> dṛś
(to see, to look)]
perception of righteousness/sustainable perspective

dharma-vijaya –
dharma+vijaya – [dharma (dhṛ - to hold, to support) + vi (in a
special manner) + jaya (to win, to conquer)]
victory of righteousness

dhārmika –
dhārmika – [quality of dharma -> dhṛ (to hold, to support)]
righteous; virtuous

dhyāna –
dhyāna – [dhyai (to think, to meditate, to recollect, to
concentrate upon)]
meditation; thinking with concentration

divyāṅga –
divya+aṅga – [divya (div – divine) + aṅga (limb)]
specially abled, limbs granted by the divine

doṣa –

doṣa – [duṣ (to soil, to cause pain, to hurt, to make impure, to sin)]

disorder, defect, wrong; negative trait

duḥkha –

duḥ+kha – [duḥ (bad) + kha (space)]

sorrow, literally bad space (interesting questions to be asked are which space is bad when one has sorrow and what are the factors that cause those 'bad spaces')

E

ekatva –

ekatva – quality of oneness

oneness

G

gati-śakti –

gati+śakti – [gati (gam – to go) + śakti (śak – to be able, to be possible, to be powerful)]

power/force of movement, power of momentum

I

icchā-śakti –

icchā+śakti – [icchā (iṣ – to wish, to desire, to want) + śakti (śak – to be able, to be possible, to be powerful)]

power/force of desire/will, willpower, power of desire

(According to the Tantra texts, there are said to be three main Forces/Śaktis of creation that make it function and are the basis of all our actions: icchā-śakti – Force of Will, jñāna-śakti – Force of Knowledge and kriyā-śakti – Force of Action)

indriyas –

indriya [ind (to be powerful, to be gifted, to have divine powers
-> also senses)]

sense organs

indriya-nigraha –

indriya+nigraha – [indriya (ind – to be powerful, to be gifted, to
have divine powers -> also senses) + ni (special) + graha -> gṛh
(to take, to seize, to accept)]

seizing/controlling of the senses, restraining of senseorgans

(The Bhagavad Gītā highlights the importance of this practice for
one's well-being when it says '[. . .] one who has utterly restrained
the excitement of the senses by their objects, his intelligence sits
firmly founded in calm self-knowledge' – Ch.2.68)

indriya-vijaya –

indriya+vijaya – [indriya (ind – to be powerful, to be gifted, to
have divine powers -> also senses) + vi (in a special manner) +
jaya (ji – to win, to conquer)]

victory/conquest over the sense organs

itihāsa –

iti+ha+āsa – [iti (thus) + ha (it) + āsa (as – to be -> was)]

corpus of Indian epics the Rāmāyaṇa, Mahābhārata and Purāṇas

(Definition of itihāsa as given in the bhārata texts –

dharmārtha-kāma-mokṣāṇām-upadeśa-samanvitam,

pūrva-vṛtta-kathā-yuktam-itihāsaṃ pracakṣate.)

meaning – itihāsa refers (pracakṣate) to those stories (kathā-
yuktam) that have happened in the past (pūrva-vṛtta) that
contain advice (upadeśa-samanvitam) on dharma, artha, kāma
and mokṣa (dharmārtha-kāma-mokṣāṇām)]

J

jaḍa –

jaḍa – (jal – to cover, to hide)

lifeless, inert

jagad-guru –

jagat+guru – [jagat (gam – to go -> that which moves is jagat -> universe) + guru -> gṝ (to eat, to swallow) – swallows ignorance (girati ajñānam) and gṝ – (to sound, to talk – instructs about dharma – gṛṇāti upadishati dharmam)]

universal spiritual preceptor, universal guru

jana-āndolana –

jana+āndolana – [jana (jan – to be born, to come into existence -> jana – people) + āndolana (āṅ – for good) + (dul – to shake, to move, to swing, to uproot, to remove)]

people's movements for a greater cause, people's agitation for a greater cause

jana-śakti –

jana+śakti – [jana (jan – to be born, to come into existence -> jana – people) + śakti (śak – to be able, to be possible, to be powerful)]

power of the people

jholā –

a cloth sling bag

jñāna-śakti –

jñāna+śakti – [jñāna (knowledge from jñā – to know, to realize, to understand) + śakti (power from śak – to be able, to be possible, to be powerful)] power/force of knowledge

(According to the Tantra texts, there are said to be three main Forces/Śaktis of creation that make it function and are the basis of all our actions: icchā-śakti – Force of Will, jñāna-śakti – Force of Knowledge and kriyā-śakti – Force of Action)

power of knowledge

K

kāma –

kāma – [kam (to love, to desire, to long for, to have intercourse with)]

wish, desire, lust

kāma-chanda –

kāma+chanda – [kam (to love, to desire, to long for, to have intercourse with) + chanda – often rhythm from chand (to cover)]

endless cycle of desires, pursuit of desires, sensual desire

karma –

karma – (kṛ – to do, to act, to make)

action; fruit of action

(The cycle of karma includes action 1 [karma 1] which generates impression 1 [saṃskāra 1] leading to tendency 1 [vāsanā 1] resulting in action 2 [karma 2] which is often the outcome of action 1 and therefore its fruit)

karmacārī –

karma+cārī – [karma (kṛ – to do, to act, to make) + cārī (goer/ practitioner from (car – to go, to walk)]

an employee, personnel, staff or worker

kārmanā –

(instrumental case of the word karma from the root word karman)
by actions, with actions

karma-yoga –

karma+yoga – [karma – action from (kṛ – to do, to act, to make)
+ yoga from yuj – to restrain, to control, to bind)]

Action performed in the spirit of yoga, i.e. doing one's best
in every context and leaving the result to the divine wisdom,
detached performance of actions, offering of all actions to a
higher power

karma-yogī –

karma+yogī – [karma (action from kṛ – to do, to act, to make)
+ yogī meaning one who is in yoga from yuj – to restrain, to
control, to bind)]

One who performs actions by being established in yoga, one
who performs actions as perfectly as possible as an instrument
of the divine and thereby is not affected by the results, a
detached performer of actions; one who offers all actions to a
higher power

kartavya –

kartavya – [action to be done from kṛ (to do, to act, to make)]
duty; responsibility

karuṇā –

compassion

(Defined as *iṣṭa-nāśāt-aniṣṭāpte karauṇākhyo raso bhavet* meaning
when something desirable is destroyed/lost [iṣṭa-nāśāt] and
something undesirable happens [aniṣṭa-āpte] then the feeling
known as karuṇā should arise)

kārya-kartā –

kārya+kartā literally work-doer [kārya (or work from kṛ – to do, to act, to make) + kartā (doer from kṛ – to do, to act, to make)]

a doer; working personnel

kleśas –

kleśas – (kliś – to torment, to distress, to hurt, to suffer and to misbehave)

impurities

(Patañjali's Yogasūtras identifies five main kleśas that obstruct human mental processes. They are misperceptions/ignorance [avidyā], ego [asmitā], attachment [raga], aversion [dveṣa] and fear of death [abhiniveśa]).

kriyā-śakti –

kriyā+śakti – [kriyā (action from kṛ – to do, to act, to make) + śakti (or power from śak – to be able, to be possible, to be powerful)]

power/force of action

(According to the Tantra texts, there are said to be three main Forces/Śaktis of creation that make it function and are the basis of all our actions: icchā-śakti – Force of Will, jñāna-śakti – Force of Knowledge and kriyā-śakti – Force of Action)

kṣamā –

kṣamā – [kṣam (to endure, to suffer, to tolerate, to forgive)]

patience, forbearance, pardon, forgiveness

(Defined as: *bāhye bādhyātmike caiva duḥkhe cotpātike kvacit na kupyati na vā hanti sā kṣamā parikīrtitā*)

Meaning, when being hindered from the outside (bāhye bādhyātmike) and being instigated to be sorrowful (duḥkhe cotpātike) in certain circumstances (kvacit), (the person) does not get angry (na kupyati), neither destroys/kills (na hanti) that is known recognized as kṣamā.

L

lobha –

lobha (lubh – to long for, to wish, to be greedy, to desire)
covetousness; greed

loka-saṅgraha –

loka+saṅgraha – [loka meaning world from ruc (to shine, to glow, to please, to like, to enjoy) + saṅgraha meaning (saṃ (from all sides) + grah (to take, to accept, to obtain)]
welfare of the gathering of people/world

M

mānasā –

(instrumental case of manas meaning mind which is defined as *saṅkalpa-vikalpātmaka-vṛttimad-antaḥkaraṇe* translated as – those thought processes (vṛttimad) in the internal instruments of consciousness (antaḥkaraṇe) that determines the actions to be undertaken (saṅkalpa) and the alternative ones (vikalpātmaka) by the mind

mantra –

mantra (defined as *mananāt trāyate iti mantraḥ* meaning the contemplation of which protects the chanter)
metrical hymns from Vedas

mantra-śakti –

mantra+śati – [mantra (defined as *mananāt trāyate iti mantraḥ* meaning the contemplation of which protects the chanter) + śakti (or power from śak – to be able, to be possible, to be powerful)]
power of Vedic hymns

mātṛ-bhūmi –

mātṛ+bhūmi – [mātṛ (mother) + bhūmi (land)]

motherland

māyā –

māyā – [mā (to measure, to weigh, to limit, to compare in size)]

that which arises out of limited perception; an illusion

mettā –

mettā – a Pāli term for the Saṃskṛt word maitrī meaning friendship (mid – to soften, to melt, to love)

friendship; kindness towards others

mokṣa –

mokṣa – [muc (to free, to liberate, to leave, to release, to loosen, to abandon)]

state of being liberated from the worldly bindings that obscure realization of true knowledge, existence

mudita –

mudita – [mud (to be glad, to be happy)]

joyful

N

namaste –

namaḥ+te meaning salutation (namaḥ) to you (te)

reverential salutation to the divinity in the concerned person

naraka –

naraka – [nṝ (to carry) to hell]

a temporary state of torment experienced by the subtle body post life

netā –

netā – [nī (to obtain, to carry, to take)]
leader, one who takes his/her followers to a specific destination

niṣkāma-karma –

niṣkāma+karma – [niḥ (without) + kāma (desire) + karma (action)]
selfless action

niḥsvārtha-sevā –

niḥsvārtha+sevā – [niḥ (without) + svārtha (self) + sevā (service)]
selfless service

niyama –

ni+yama – [ni (in a special manner) + yama (yam – to keep under control, to nourish, to nurture, to serve food)]
observance
according to Patañjali's Yogasūtra, the second of the eight rungs is the five Niyamas (2.32), which have to do with your relationship within yourself. They involve the following: purifying your body and mind (śauca) (2.40-2.41); cultivating an attitude of contentment (santoṣa) (2.42); training one's senses (tapa) (2.43); inner exploration (svādhyāya) (2.44); letting go into your spiritual source (īśvara-praṇidhāna) (2.45).

P

pagḍi; pagaḍi –
headdress or turban worn by men

pañca-mahā-bhūta –

pañca+mahā+bhūta – [pañca (five) + mahā (great) + bhūta (elements)]
the five primordial elements of earth, water, fire, wind and space

prabhāva-śakti –

prabhāva-śakti – [prabhāva meaning influence from pra (more) + bhāva (feelings/emotions) + śakti or power from śak – to be able, to be possible, to be powerful)]

power of influence

pracāraka –

pracāraka – [pra (forth) + cāraka (means one who makes news) promoter, publicizer, preacher]

pradhāna-sevaka –

pradhāna+sevaka – [pradhāna (pra – more) + dhāna (dhā - to obey, to bear, to support, to nourish, to protect) + sevaka (sev – to serve, to devote oneself, practise)]

chief servant

prajñā –

prajñā – [prajñā (pra – more) + jñā (to know, to realize, to understand)]

spiritual wisdom; highest intelligence and understanding

prajñā-bala –

prajñā+bala – [pra (pra – more) + jñā (to know, to realize, to understand) + bala -> bal (to have power, to gain power, to explain)]

power of wisdom

prāṇāyāma –

prāṇa+āyāma – [prāṇa (life energy) + āyāma (stretching, extending)]

regulation of life breath

prāpaka –

prāpaka – [pra (forth) + āpaka (makes something reach)]

bringer, conveyer

prati-kriyā –

prati+kriyā – [prati (returned towards) + kriyā meaning action (kṛ – to do, to act, to make)]

reaction, response

pratyāhāra –

prati+āhāra [prati (towards) + ā (inwards) + hāra -> hṛ (to take away, to carry)]

withdrawal of senses

this is the fifth limb of Patañjali's aṣṭāṅgayoga practices

preṣaka –

preṣaka – one who sends

sender

preyas –

preyas – (pr – to satisfy, to please)

that which might seem fleetingly pleasing but is deleterious in the long term

puṇya-bhūmi –

puṇya+bhūmi – [puṇya meaning sacred (pun – to be pure, to be virtuous, to do holy work) + bhūmi (earth, land)]

sacred-land

puruṣārtha –

puruṣa+artha – [puruṣa (person) + artha (meaning or goal)]

aspirations of all humans which were four – righteousness (dharma), wealth (artha), desire (kāma) and liberation (mokṣa) of which the last was considered to be the most important lasting goal for human life.

R

rāja-maṇḍala –

raja+maṇḍala

refers to the enemy and friendly states surrounding a particular king's state

rājadharma –

rāja+dharma – [rājā (rāj – to reign, to be lustrous) + dharma (dhṛ – to hold, to support, to possess)]

a king's duty; code of conduct for rulers

rājarṣi –

rājā+rṣi [rājā (rāj – to reign, to be lustrous) ->king + rṣi (seer)]

a king who has the qualities of both a statesman and a sage

rasa –

rasa – [rasa (ras – to taste, to love, to have affection)]

juice; essence

rasāsvāda –

rasa+āsvāda – [rasa (juice or essence) + āsvāda (taste)]

tasting, appreciating, relishing of flavour

ṛṇa –

ṛṇa – [ṝ (to go)]

spiritual debt; an obligation

in Bhārata, every individual is said to fulfil five ṛṇas or debts. They are:

a debt to the gods (deva-ṛṇa); a debt to teachers and sages (ṛṣi-ṛṇa); a debt to ancestors (pitṛ-ṛṇa) starting with parents and going back three generations on each side; a debt to society (manuṣya-ṛṇa); a debt to the environment (bhūta-ṛṇa)

ṛṣi –

ṛṣi – *(ṛṣati prāpnoti sarvān mantrān jñānena paśyati saṃsārapāraṃ vā iti –*

one who receives all the Vedic mantras and sees beyond the boundaries of the world with knowledge)
seers of the Vedic hymns

ṛta –

ṛta – [ṛ (to go, to obtain, to reach)]
cosmic order in movement to help obtain/reach cosmic goals

S

sāfā –

a headscarf or long cloth used to form a turban for men in parts of India

sāma –

conciliation; bringing into alignment

sādhaka –

sādhaka – [(sādh – to accomplish, to attain, to fulfil, to achieve)]
one who is engaged in spiritual advancement to attain self-realization

sādhanā –

sādhanā – [sādh – (to accomplish, to attain, to fulfill, to achieve)] spiritual practice or discipline of worship including contemplation and asceticism to help an individual attain self-realization

sādhāraṇī-karaṇa –

sādhāraṇī+karaṇa – [sādhāraṇī – simplification + karaṇa – doing/making]

a Hindu theory of communication through simplification

sahṛdaya –

sa+hṛdaya (with heart)

empathy; one who is compassionate

sākṣī-bhāva –

sākṣī+bhāva – [(sākṣi (witness) + bhāva (consciousness/feeling)]

attitude of remaining as a witness, a witness consciousness

samādhi –

samādhi – [sam (from all sides equally) + ā (from the beginning till the end) + dhā (to bear, to support, to nourish, to protect)]

a state of intense concentration achieved through meditation leading to merger, union of subject (meditator) and object (of meditation).

it is defined as: *samādhīyate'smin mano janairiti*

meaning: people (janaiḥ) make their minds (mano) calm (samādhīyate) asmin (in this).

samatā –

samatā – (sam – to be calm, to be cool-headed)

equanimity, equality, sameness, fairness

samatvam –

samatvam – (sam – to be calm, to be cool-headed) being equipoised, undisturbed in distress or happiness,

sameness, equanimity, evenness of mind

saṃmohana –

saṃ+mohana [saṃ (from all sides) + mohana (muh – to lose senses, to faint, to be foolish, to err)]

delusion, fascination, allure

sandarbha –

sandarbha – [saṃ (from all sides) + dṛbh (to relate, to give reference)]

context

sandeśa –

sandeśa – [saṃ (from all sides) + diś (to give, to grant)]

message

saṅgacchhadhvaṃ –

saṅgacchhadhvaṃ – [saṃ (from all sides) + gam (to go)]

may you move together in harmony

sannyāsī –

sannyāsī – [saṃ (from all sides) + ni + as (to place in a special manner) – one who has done so]

renunciate

sannyāsaḥ is defined as:

kāmyakarmāṇāṃ nyāsa meaning putting away (nyāsa) of all desired/prescribed actions/works (kāmyakarmāṇāṃ).

one who has put away all desired/prescribed actions and works is a sannyāsī

sāraṇī –

sāraṇī – [sṛ – (to go, to move, to approach, to slip)]

medium, conduit, pipe

sarva-bhūta-hite-rata –

sarva+bhūta+hite+rata – [sarva (all) + bhūta (beings) + hite (welfare) – rata (immersed in)]

one who wishes for the welfare of all beings

saccidānanda –

sat+cit+ānanda – [sat (Truth) + cit (Consciousness) + ānanda (Bliss)

truth-consciousness-absolute joy – bliss are the three qualities of the underlying Consciousness of creation.

sat –

sat – [sat literally means being (as – to be, to exist)

Absolute Truth

sevā –

sevā – [sev – (to serve, to devote oneself, to practise)]

service

sevaka –

sevaka – (one who does sevā)

servant; attendant

śabdabrahman –

śabda+brahman – (sound/vibrations of the Brahman or universal consciousness)

spiritual knowledge consisting of words, Veda

śākhā –

śākhā – [śākh (to pervade, to spread, to penetrate, to occupy)]

branch

śaktis –

śakti – [śak (to be able, to be possible, to be powerful)]

powers, capacities

śauca –

śauca – (śuc – to be wet, to be clean, to be purified)

internal and external cleanliness

this is one of the niyamas in Patañjali's Yogasūtras

śaurya –

śaurya – (śūr – to be powerful, to be courageous, to be brave, to have victory)

valiant

śraddhā –

śraddhā – [śrath (to make effort, to try) + dhā (to bear, to support, to nourish, to protect)]

belief pending understanding

śreyas –

śreyas –

That which is beneficial in the long term

śuddha-saṅkalpa –

śuddha+saṅkalpa – [(śudh – to become pure) + saṃ (from all sides) + kṛp (to be able, to be capable)]

pure intentional thought

smṛti –

smṛti – [smṛ (to remember, to recollect, to think upon, to recite mentally, to memorize)]

memory

sthita-prajña –

sthita+prajña – [sthita (established) + prajña -> pra (more) + jñā (to know, to realize, to understand)]

a wise person who is free from all delusion and is content; a spiritually evolved person

sthūla –

sthūla – (sthal – to stand firm, to stand, to be stunned)

gross

sukha –

su+kha – [su (excellent) + kha (spaces, limbs)]

literally excellent spaces, joy, pleasure, excellent experience

sūkṣma –

sūkṣma – (sūc – to indicate, to do a favour, to explain, to point out mistakes)

subtle

svabhāva –

sva+bhāva – [(sva (self) + bhava -> bhū (to exist, to become, to be, to happen) -> feeling]

intrinsic nature of a person, personal disposition

svādhyāya –

sva+adhyāya – [sva (self) + adhyāya -> dhyai (to think, to meditate, to recollect, to concentrate upon)]

self-study; spiritual introspection, study of scriptures

this is one of the practices under the niyamas of Patañjali's aṣṭāṅgayoga

svāmī –

svāmī from sva – oneself, one who is one's own boss

a title used for renunciates to indicate they are their own masters and not subject to desires.

svayam-sevakas –

svayam+sevakas – [svayam (self) + sevaka -> sev (to serve, to devote oneself, to practise)] volunteers; those who serve other people selflessly on a voluntary basis

T

tapasyā –

tapasyā – [tap (to perform penance, to heat)]

spiritual austerity

there are three types of tapas or austerities:

tapas of Body which includes cleanliness, non-violence and sexual fidelity;

tapas of Speech which includes truthfulness, compassion and beneficial words;

tapas of Mind which includes silence, self-restraint and gentleness

teja –

tejas – [tij (to sharpen, to whet, to endure, to tolerate, to bear, to forgive)]

heat; radiance, brilliance

tyāga –

tyāga – [tyaj (to renounce, to let go, to quit, to abandon, to leave)]

sacrifice

U

upekṣā –

upekṣā – [upa (above) + ikṣ (to see, to perceive)]

equanimity; non-attachment, indifference

utsāha-śakti –

utsāha+śakti – [ut (a lot) + sah (to bear, to tolerate, to be powerful, to be satisfied) + śakti (power)]

power of enthusiasm

V

vācā –

[instrumental case of vac (to speak, to tell, to talk)]

by speech

vairāgya –

vairagya – [vi (away from) + rañj (to colour, to be involved, to be attracted to (rāga)] non-attachment, detachment, dispassion

vāk –

vāk – (vac – to speak, to tell, to talk)

speech

There are four levels of speech – parā (the highest form of sound/potential speech), paśyantī (seeing speech/revelation), madhyamā (middle/thought-forms held in our mind and vaikharī (articulated speech)

vasudhaiva kuṭumbakam –

The world indeed is one family

The original verse from the Mahopaniṣad 6.71–72:

ayaṃ bandhurayaṃ neti kalanā laghucetasām |

udāra-caritānāṃ tu vasudhaivakuṭumbakam ||

'This is my kin, this is not' thus is the calculation of the narrow-minded.

But for the generous – the earth (vasudhā) indeed (eva) (is) a small family (kuṭumbakam).

vīrya –

vīrya – [vīra (valiant)]

vigour; virility

vikāsa –

vi+kāsa/vikāśa – [vi (in a special manner) +kāsa/kāśa (kaś – to shine, to glow)]

development, growth, progress

viveka –

viveka – [vi (in a special manner) + vic (to distinguish, to divide, to separate, to remove from)]

(*yāthārthyena vastu-svarūpāvadhāraṇe* – beholding the real nature of objects/situations as they really are/ *sadasadvibhedakarī buddhiḥ* – discretionary intelligence that can distinguish between what is true and what is false)

discernment

(https://ashtadhyayi.com/upasargarthachandrika/99, No.225)

vyādha –

hunter

Y

yajña –

yajña – [yaj (to sacrifice, to offer to a deity, to worship, to get associated with, to give)]

sacrificial rite; any offering of oblation

There are five mahā-yajñas that are prescribed for every individual in Bhārata that complement the concept of five ṛṇas or debts. They are:

the study of Vedic scriptures, meditating and practising yoga (brahma-yajña); daily ritualistic worship, including feeding fire with ghee and purifying herbs while reciting mantras from the Vedas, it also involves cultivating devotion and expressing gratitude for all that is given (deva-yajña); serving learned teachers, scholars, parents, old people, great yogis and holy persons. It is divided into two parts, śhraddhā and tarpaṇa (pitṛ-yajña); helping other human beings (manuṣya-ṛṇa) and putting aside a small amount of food on the ground for animals and vagrants before beginning a meal, this is to atone for the death of creatures that may be losing their lives while washing clothes, taking a bath, or sweeping the house (bhūta-yajña).

yama –

yama – [yam (to keep under control, to nourish, to nurture, to serve food)]

moral discipline, self-restraint

There are five yamas prescribed as the first step of the aṣṭāṅgayoga of Patañjali (Yogasūtra – 2.30). They are:

non-injury or non-harming (ahiṃsa), truthfulness (satya), abstention from stealing (asteya), walking in awareness of the highest reality (brahmacharya), and non-possessiveness or non-grasping with the senses (aparigraha), these are the five yamas, or codes of self-regulation or restraint, and are the first of the eight steps of Yoga.

yoga-kṣema –

yoga+kṣema – [yoga (yuj – to restrain, to control, to bind) + kṣema (giving rest or ease or security)]

(anāgata-ānayana-āgata-rakṣaṇe (Manu) – to bring that which has not yet come and to protect that which has come)

possession as well as security of possession; welfare and well-being

yogī –

yogī – [yuj (to concentrate, to focus, to abstain from senses, to meditate)]

one who is established in yoga

(one who practises any spiritual exercise towards union with the higher power/state)

Acknowledgements

As I reflect on the journey of writing this book, my heart fills with profound gratitude for those who have been instrumental in its creation.

Foremost, I pay homage to the late Swami Sureshanandaji, whose inspiration kindled the flame of this endeavour. His wisdom and guidance have been the North Star, guiding me through this exploration of leadership.

I must acknowledge, with deep respect, Prime Minister Narendra Modi himself. Without his distinctive leadership and the unique path that he has carved in the political landscape of India, this book would not have found its subject. His life and work have been the wellspring of inspiration for this narrative.

This book owes much to the valuable contributions of those I had the honour of interviewing, including Prime Minister Modi and some of his Cabinet colleagues, bureaucrats and many who have known him for decades. Their first-hand experiences and observations have been the backbone of this narrative.

My deepest appreciation extends to my wife, Bindu, and my son, Aniruddh. Their unwavering support and belief in me were the pillars upon which this work rested. Their patience and encouragement were my constant companions during the most challenging times. A special note of gratitude goes to the diligent Brhat research team: Anshuman Panda, Kavita Krishna Meegama, Raghava Krishna and Akshay Jha. Their commitment and thoroughness have been indispensable. I must particularly highlight the extraordinary efforts of Anshuman Panda, whose dedication and expertise have significantly shaped this work.

I also thank Simran Parmar for her creative translation of concepts into meaningful graphics.

I am also deeply grateful to Jamila Daniels for her editorial support. Her sharp attention to detail and professional expertise have significantly improved the quality of this manuscript. I extend my heartfelt thanks to Amit Chandra, Govind Iyer, C.R. Hanumanth, Arun Karpur, Adil Zainulbhai, D.K. Hari and Hema Hari for dedicating their time and effort to review the manuscript and offer invaluable suggestions. My thanks to Anuradha Choudry for her contributions in enriching the glossary with appropriate explanations. The youth of today are looking for a role model and several young people helped shape this book to make it relatable to them. While they want to remain anonymous, it is my responsibility to thank them for all that they have done.

I am deeply thankful to Nitin Nohria for his gracious contribution of the foreword to the book on leadership, his wisdom and support have truly elevated its essence. Additionally, I express my sincere appreciation to all those who have penned insightful blurbs endorsing the book; your encouragement and endorsement mean the world to me.

For a manuscript to evolve into a book that one can hold and appreciate, it needs a publisher who not only agrees to publish the book but believes in what the author has set out to write. I thank Penguin Random House India for agreeing to publish this book and ensuring that all the deadlines set were met. Without the constant guidance and professional support of the Penguin Random House India team of Milee Ashwarya, Premanka Goswami, Gunjan Ahlawat and Yash Daiv, this book would not be what it is. I extend my gratitude to Ralph Rebello for proofing the book and Rajath Kumar at MAP Systems for typesetting.

Writing this book has been a journey of discovery, and it would not have been possible without the collective support and encouragement of each individual mentioned and the many unnamed who have contributed to this project. To all, I extend my heartfelt thanks.

Contributors

Apart from several conversations with Prime Minister Modi, inputs based on the discussions with the following people are used in the book. No separate citations are given for them.

1	Ajay Sood
2	Ajit Doval
3	Amit Shah
4	Anurag Thakur
5	B.V.R Subhramanyam
6	Bibek Debroy
7	Dharmendra Pradhan
8	Mansukh Mandaviya
9	Hardeep Singh Puri
10	Hardik Shah
11	Hasmukh Adhia
12	Jitendra Singh
13	Kuniyal Kailashnathan
14	Nirmala Sitharaman
15	Pramod Kumar Mishra
16	Rajiv Gauba
17	Rajnath Singh
18	Smriti Irani
19	Sri Sri Ravi Shankar
20	T.V. Somanathan

Index

Scan QR code to access the
Penguin Random House India website